Lightning From Heaven

~ Luke 10:18 ~

Our Christian Cosmology

BOOK ONE
The Celestial Hierarchy

BY
Luke Aaron

Disclaimer: To preserve and honor the sanctity of Sacred Scripture all Biblical texts in this Contemplation have been meticulously translated from the original Latin Vulgate with scholarly comparison to the Douay-Rheims, NABRE, and RSVCE Translations.

All images are Public Domain, the majority of which are by Gustave Doré from his Dante, Paradise Lost and Bible collections, with the exception of: Page 23, The Throne of Grace by Glass Roundel; Page 27, Angel and the Book by Unknown Artist; Page 30, God the Father and the Lamb of God by Stradanus; Page 33, Angels Trumpets by Julius Schnorr von Karolsfeld; Page 39, Our Lady of Guadalupe on tilma of Juan Diego; Page 45, The Marriage of the Lamb by Schnorr von Karolsfeld; Page 107, Coronation of Mary Mother of God by Unknown Artist; Page 148, The Whore of Babylon by Henry John Stock; Page 154, God the Father by Julius Schnorr von Karolsfeld; Page 268, Vision of Ezekiel by Grafissimo; Page 278, Isaiah's Vision by Frank Marsden Lea; Page 283, Seraphim by Unknown Artist; Page 292, Seven Archangels by Hieronymus Wierix; Page 304, The Annunciation by Sandro Botticelli; Page 312, The Virgin with Angels by William Adolphe Bouguereau; and Page 336, Prince of the Heavenly Host by Luke Aaron

Front/Back Cover & Book Design by Paraclete Press
Special Thanks to: Sr. Anna-Hope Mitchell, Sr. Brigid Minor, Br. Christopher, and Grace Chasuk for painstakingly editing the book.

IN MEMORIAM DR. LAURENCE L. SHIELDS

He was a man who could captivate a room with his enigmatic wisdom and recondite cough. He pondered the Holy Scriptures in a patient, persistent, and collegial manner and became a theologian both humble and profound. This book and its author owe him a direct debt, as it would not have come about without his simple yet penetrating inquiries. —Eternal rest grant unto him, O Lord and let perpetual light shine upon him. May his soul and all the souls of the faithful departed rest in peace. Amen.

First Printing Edition 2024

ISBN: 979-8-218-97218-9
Library of Congress Control Number to come

TABLE OF CONTENTS

The Celestial Hierarchy

THE FALL

DIVINE MERCY

THE CELESTIAL LADDER

EXILE

APPENDIX

—ANGELIC APOLOGETICS—

—ANGELIC PRAYERS—

—MARIAN PRAYERS—

DEDICATION

I dedicate this work to our Illustrious Prince, St. Michael the Archangel, who through so many musings from the Holy Scriptures has inspired and manifested such a tender love and devotion in me to Mary, Daughter, Spouse, & Mother of God. Along with my Guardian Angel, St. Michael has fought valiantly to protect my meager soul during these many years of writing and prayer; now, through their vigilance, I have this work to offer to Holy Mother Church for the praise and glory of God the Father. May this work likewise inspire in all those who pray it such a tender love and devotion to Mary that she becomes their mother, and through her, Christ becomes their brother.

ACKNOWLEDGMENTS

First and foremost, I could not have even attempted such an undertaking if not for the inspiration of St. Ignatius, who so many years prior had set out the framework for 'contemplation', instructing future generations on how to immerse oneself into Scripture to experience the Ever-living God.

Secondly, I must thank John Parker Wilmeth who through many nights of discussion, translation, prayer, and editing has helped me to produce a gift worth giving to the Church. You have undoubtedly worked off much time in Purgatory helping me. Thank you, my friend.

Thirdly, I must give a special thanks to my most loving mother, Ruby, who for more than twenty long years has borne a 'thorn in the flesh' for the outpouring of grace into my soul. All good fruit that I bear is the result of your sufferings united with Christ on the Cross. No one could ask for a better mother.

Finally, to Lea, flesh of my flesh and bone of my bone, and Aurelia & Athena, the completion of our love—thank you for having such patience, allotting me the late nights and solitary time to finish my book. I know it was not easy. With all my heart afire, I love you.

PREFACE

We were not created to pray as the angels do, God specifically crafted us from the clay of the Earth, forming us body and soul, in the Image and Likeness of His own Triune Self. This St. Ignatius understood when he set to contemplate the Scriptures, for he did not examine the pages of Holy Writ scouring each line for peculiar grammar or investigate the historical credentials of its authors, rather trusting in the true Author, he thrust himself headlong into the hands of the Holy Spirit, where he through the precious gift of the Imagination entered body and soul into the Living Word. In subjugating his senses to the Holy Spirit he experienced Wisdom, the ever-living Christ: seeing into His eyes; listening to His Word; smelling the aroma of His wine; tasting the body of His bread; and even touching His sacred wounds. This is the power of Ignatian Contemplation to truly encounter through the Imagination and guidance of the Holy Spirit the reality of Scripture, the Eternal Word, Second Person of the Trinity.

Such contemplation is usually personal revelation utilizing the powers of the Imagination in conjunction with the Holy Spirit to produce a true, although be it personal, encounter with the Living Christ as the Word. However, for the purposes of teaching and to ensure a dogmatic and trustworthy interpretation, this Ignatian Contemplation on our *Christian Cosmology: The preternatural state of Man and Angel*, utilizes Scripture itself as a supplement to the Scriptural narrative of the *Book of Genesis*. Thus, I have gathered together the many visions of the Prophets, songs of the Psalter, and revelations of the New Testament, which reveal crucial truths about the genesis and fall of man and angel, in order to produce an all-encompassing contemplation of our Christian Cosmology, the *Epic of Eden*. Thus, this book ought to be read in the prescribed manner of St. Ignatius not as description or fantasy but as Prayer and encounter, offering the contemplative soul a way into the eternal reality of Scripture.

Finally, St. Ignatius in his construction of *The Spiritual Exercises* supplied *points* as well as *preludes* to center the reader on the most fruitful aspect of each subject of contemplation. Likewise, notes have been supplied to guide the reader in their contemplation of our Christian Cosmology. In keeping with Ignatian Contemplation, begin each reading with the *Preparatory Prayer* and conclude with the *Colloquy Prayer*, conveying the many experiences of your contemplation to Jesus, allowing yourself to speak with Him heart to heart.

PREPARATORY PRAYER

"O God our Lord, I beg for the grace, under the direction of our careful guide St. Ignatius, that all my intentions, actions and operations may be ordered purely for the praise and glory of Your Divine Majesty. I beseech you, Lord, immerse me in Scripture today, swathe me body and soul in Your Holy Word, that in the Holy Spirit I may live and so encounter the ever-living Christ in true contemplation, heart to heart in conversation."

COLLOQUY PRAYER

"Having then experienced the Word of God in both body and soul I turn to Christ our Lord, who Himself entered into the flesh and became man, conversing heart to heart the many experiences imparted to me through the Holy Spirit." *Our Father & Glory Be…*

IGNATIAN CONTEMPLATION
WITH QUOTES FROM THE SPIRITUAL EXERCISES

THE PREPARATORY PRAYER
"In this preparatory prayer I will beg God our Lord for grace that all my intentions, actions, and operations may be directed purely to the praise and service of His Divine Majesty."

IGNATIAN CONTEMPLATION
Is the complete immersion of oneself, body and soul, into the Scriptures, transported in the Spirit, to so live and encounter the reality of the Eternal Word.

FIRST PRELUDE
"A mental representation of the place"

- "When the contemplation is on something visible, the representation will consist in seeing in imagination the material place where the object is that we wish to contemplate."

SECOND PRELUDE
"The petition must be according to the subject matter."

- "Thus in a contemplation on the Resurrection I will ask for joy with Christ in joy. In one on the Passion, I will ask for sorrow, tears, and anguish with Christ in anguish."

FIRST POINT
Salvation History

- "This will consist in calling to mind the history of the subject I have to contemplate."
- Recall then the Scriptures, the great Story of Salvation, and bring to mind where this passage takes place in Salvation History.

SECOND POINT
The Persons Present

- "This consists in seeing in imagination the persons, and in contemplating and meditating in detail the circumstances in which they are, and then in drawing some fruit from what has been seen."

🕭 Take notice of the people there, walking among them, place yourself as one of them, experiencing externally what they experienced. Try then to place yourself as them experiencing internally what they themselves experienced.

THIRD POINT
The Senses

🕭 *Sight*: "This will be to see in imagination the…"
Having been transported in the Spirit and witnessing Scripture in imagination strive to see all such phenomena as if you were bodily present.

🕭 *Hearing*: "To hear the…"
Listen with greater perceptibility to the many voices, noises, melodies, and music of the present moment.

🕭 *Smell*: "With the sense of smell to perceive the…"
Breathe in the many smells and aromas surrounding you, whether they be stenches or perfumes, submit yourself to the reality of the present Scripture.

🕭 *Taste*: "To taste the…"
Savor without discretion the bold feasts, bitter wine, burnt ash, and wanting hunger stretched throughout Scripture.

🕭 *Touch*: "With the sense of touch to feel the…"
Immerse yourself wholly in Scripture submitting your entire body to the Word of God, embracing the heat, sweat, toil, joy, and anguish of each subject of Sacred Scripture.

COLLOQUY
Heart speaking to Heart

Having then experienced the Word of God in both body and soul turn to Christ our Lord, who Himself became man, conversing heart to heart the many experiences imparted to you through the Holy Spirit. Conclude with an *Our Father and Glory Be.*

INTRODUCTION

All praise and thanksgiving be to our Lord Jesus Christ Who has sent His angels and His Mother to guide and inspire me toward the end of completing this *Contemplation*. I submit this work to Holy Mother Church for the edification of all Christians in an attempt to set forth a simple yet comprehensive narrative of the preternatural state of man and angel in the Garden of Eden. It is my great hope that such a work as this, can give Christianity a proper Cosmology capable not only of withstanding the scrutinies of the world, but of developing the Christian Faith.

I shall try to explain, to the best of my ability, the constitution of this *Contemplation* and the manner with which it ought to be read. I first set out to write this book as a novel, with the words of a poor sinner feebly grasping at Lady Philosophy's tattered cloth, but the Lord soon thereafter asked me *"And what of that which I have written? Will My words not suffice?"* Immediately I was taken back by the Lord's words, overcome with disgust at the unwittingly proud assumption that my own words could ever worthily describe *Eden*, the Garden of God! So at the Lord's request I discarded all that I had written and started anew, fearfully gathering together all the various Bible passages scattered throughout the Old and New Testaments that pertained to Creation and the Garden of Eden.

A great fear began to arise in me; never had I come across anyone who used Scripture to tell a story about Scripture, utilizing different passages to produce a coherent narrative. But soon the Holy Spirit began revealing examples to soothe my fears. The most astonishing example of reworking Scripture for such a narrative purpose was in the Bible itself, namely the *Books of First and Second Chronicles*. The chronicler set out to recount certain events from Samuel and Kings, wishing to emphasize and clarify important aspects of the original texts that would have otherwise gone unknown and unnoticed. He even goes as far to add a genealogy from Adam to King Saul and reveal such intimate details as that David was not allowed to build the Temple because of the blood he had spilt in war. The chronicler further omits the building of Solomon's Palace and even much of the history of the Northern Kingdom, choosing rather to focus on the Temple and the Southern Kingdom of Judah in order to show the importance of the Davidic line. All this the chronicler does so effectively in the Holy Spirit that his work ends up becoming part of Sacred Scripture itself.

The Holy Spirit then showed me similar ways that the Church has traditionally used Scripture: first, by introducing me to *Ignatian Contemplation* through Fr. Gallagher, where I learned how St. Ignatius used the power of the imagination to supplement Scripture in order to produce a sensory encounter with the everliving Christ; then, by bringing to my attention the various readings for the *Stations of the Cross*, wherein different scriptural passages are laced together and supplemented with extra-scriptural words to produce a coherent meditation on Christ's Passion. Even the readings at daily Mass follow this pattern, as large passages of the Old Testament and Gospels are abridged and joined to produce clear and concise readings for the Liturgy. In all these examples the Holy Spirit revealed how Catholics have employed Scripture as *Prayer*, organically utilizing it through the direction of the Holy Spirit for the purposes of engaging the Word to converse with the Father.

This form of prayer must be done with reverence and awe for the Word of God and remain in keeping with the whole of Christian Doctrine and Scripture itself. It is for this reason that the underlying structure of this *Contemplation* is taken from the first three chapters of *Genesis,* the narrative story of Creation. Where this work differs from any other is that the *Book of Revelation* is then superimposed over the narrative story of *Genesis,* which for the first time allows the contemplative soul a metaphysical glimpse into the preternatural state and Fall of the Universe. The bi-contextual axis of this work is Genesis 3:14, in which the *Ancient Serpent* is bound to the Earth cursed to crawl on its belly, and Revelation 12:9, in which the *Great Red Dragon* is kicked out of Heaven and banished to the Earth. Both these passages are describing the same event: the Fall of Satan and his banishment to the Earth. Once these two passages are aligned, the true event comes into focus, allowing one to see the Fall both from the eyes of man in *Genesis* and from the perspective of the angels in *Revelation*. This plainly is the structure of the book.

Finally, to produce a comprehensive contemplation, various Psalms, Proverbs, and visions of the Prophets were used to fill in essential truths about our Creation and Fall that the Holy Spirit revealed only later in the course of Salvation History. For example, it was unknown to humanity the underlying motivation behind the Serpent's beguilement of Eve until the Holy Spirit revealed to the author of the *Book of Wisdom* that "It was through the *Envy of the Devil*, that death entered the World." Passages like these exist throughout the Old and New Testaments and have thus been gathered together in an attempt to produce an all-encompassing *Ignatian Contemplation* on our Christian Cosmology.

To preserve and honor the sanctity of Sacred Scripture all biblical texts in this *Contemplation* have been meticulously translated from the original Latin Vulgate with careful comparison to the Douay-Rheims, NABRE, and RSVCE translations in order to produce the best possible English translation and to ensure the fullness of each Scripture passage is preserved.

Even still it must be said—and I cannot emphasize it enough—that this work is a *Prayer* devoted to St. Michael and Our Blessed Mother and, as such, it should never take the place of reading Scripture! Rather, it should inspire the reader to return to the Scriptures with renewed fervor, eager to delve deeper into the fathomless depths of God's Wisdom revealed in His holy Word.

It is my utmost prayer that whosoever prays this *Contemplation* will have the Scriptures opened to them and have their hearts burn within them, just as those blessed disciples' hearts burned within them as they walked with Christ on the road to Emmaus. Just as they experienced Christ in the Eucharist and eagerly returned to Jerusalem to experience the outpouring of the Holy Spirit, so too I pray you too will experience Christ in this *Contemplation* and eagerly return to the Scriptures to receive an outpouring of the Holy Spirit!

May Mary and her angels watch over you, and Christ be ever with you.

AN INVOCATION TO THE HOLY SPIRIT FOR MAGNANIMITY IN THE NEW EPOCH

O Beloved, Who soared above the formless waters come descend upon us in tongues of fire sent from the Celestial Height, that Divine Darkness where Ancient of Days and Wisdom rest. Hasten with Lover's longing, **O** Herald of the Eternal Heart, and enkindle in us the sacred flame of seraph and Madonna, that we, like our illustrious King, might shine with Transfiguration to the entire World. Anoint our heads with the Crown of Grace and our hearts with the Ardor of Love to be leaven to the World ~ prophets of the New Epoch. We consecrate ourselves to you, O Finger of Providence; usher us into Your innermost chamber and wed us eternally to Your Sacred Will. Consummate our cup as You overshadowed Your heavenly Spouse, and fill us with grace-overflowing. Let our souls cascade with rosaline waters, that heavenly dew which makes all soil fertile. Bestow glory upon Your steward, whose flesh is the soil of Paradise, the last great vestige of Eden; and walk with us again that Eden might be made anew. Plant in us the fruit of the Tree of Life, so that we might stand with our prolific Mother, and in her voice sing:

My Lord and Lover, come to me!
Ravish my soul, O Lordly King,
And throw me into Ecstasy!
Remember Love's first Promise and Betrothed's first Kiss,
How captive You were with Beauty's Bliss.
Such a promise made in whispered Breath
That Love is as stern as Death.
Amen.

BOOK ONE

The
Celestial Hierarchy

*"Amen, Amen, I say to you, you shall see the Heavens opened
and the Angels of God ascending and descending on the Son of Man."*
John 1:51

IN THE BEGINNING

Genesis 1:1

In the Beginning,[1] when all was formless and void, and darkness abounded in the deep, the Ancient of Days was seated upon His lofty

Daniel 7:9...

Throne. His garment was as white as snow, and the hair of His head like pure wool: His throne was like flames of fire, the wheels of which were as burning flames. A swift river of fire surged forth from whence He sat: Thousands upon thousands ministered unto Him, and ten thousand

Daniel ...7:10

times a hundred thousand stood before Him. The great multitude beheld in the right hand of the Ancient One who sat upon the Throne a large

Revelation 5:1...

Scroll,[2] it had writing on both sides and was without any seal.[3]

Then in a mighty voice the Lord God proclaimed, "Who is worthy to open the Scroll? Who shall proclaim its Word? Who will advocate

Revelation ...5:4

for its decree?" But no one in heaven or under heaven or within the nether was worthy to open the Scroll or even to examine it.[4]

The great assembly of stars[5] shed many tears because no one was found worthy to open the Scroll, for it shone too brightly, and a great fear and trembling seized the host of heaven, for no one was found worthy to know the Mind of God.[6]

Lo, the Ancient One turned in thought[7] to Wisdom[8], the Son of the

Daniel 7:13...

Father, and He came riding on the clouds of Heaven. He came unto the Ancient of Days Himself, and presented Himself before Him. Thus the Ancient One bequeathed Him power, glory, and kingdom: All creatures, tribes, and tongues shall serve and obey Him. All that the Ancient One possessed was handed over to Wisdom,[9] and His dominion was an everlasting dominion that could never be taken away, His kingship an

Daniel ...7:14

insoluble crown for all ages. Wisdom came and received the Scroll from the right hand of the Ancient One who sat upon the Throne. When He received the Scroll He took His seat upon the Triune Throne, and the Lord rejoiced, for His son was triumphant, enabling Him to open the Scroll and make known the Wisdom of God.[10]

IGNATIAN CONTEMPLATION

1   The first three lines of Genesis reveal the Triune Godhead: "In the beginning when God created the heavens and the Earth, the Earth was formless and void, and darkness covered the face of the deep, while the Spirit of God swept over the face of the waters. Then God said, "Let…," etc. The Spirit of God refers to the Holy Spirit; God speaking refers to the Person of the Word, i.e. God the Son; and "In the Beginning" refers to God the Father. How beautiful that the Most Holy Trinity is first revealed in the first three lines of the Bible.

2   This is the same Scroll we read about in Chapter 5 of the Book of Revelation, this Scroll is the Word, the Way in which God plans to wed Himself to the human race. It is for the purpose of wedlock that God created the Universe, why the Lord set to speak the hallowed Word of creation and sent His only Son to be born of the Virgin Mary. The Wedding Feast of the Lamb that we read about in Revelation at the end of time, is the same intention that God had in the beginning when He made the heavens and the Earth.

3   Even though this is the same Scroll as the one in Revelation, humanity and creation has yet to fall, meaning the many seals and bowls meant to purify and prepare the listener of the sacred Word are not necessary as Creation is still in a state of grace. Upon closer examination, we see that the Seven Seals are the very fall itself, and the Seven Bowls are the purification necessary to prepare the human race for the wedding feast. What does remains from the Book of Revelation's description is the Seven Trumpets that would always be sounded before the reading of the Scroll heralding God's proclamation to all of Creation.

4   The Scroll is the innermost desire of God, the desire to wed Himself to the human race, which even the angels can never decipher without Divine Revelation.

5   'Star' is a tropological name for the celestial intelligences before they became angels, as indicated in Revelation 1:20

6   Just as in the Book of Revelation, the Scroll is to be understood as the Mind of God, the intention and covenant God has for Creation.

7   The eternal procession of the Second Person of the Trinity, God the Son.

8   'Wisdom' is God the Son, who was in the beginning, is now, and ever shall be.

9   Here the Great Mystery of the Most Holy Trinity can be glimpsed in the Vision of Daniel. Only through Love can Three be One and One be Three. For truly the Father, the Son, and the Holy Spirit are one because God is Love and this Divine Love is absolute, a complete gift of the totality of Divine Life. Nothing, absolutely nothing, is withheld, thus this Unity created by such radical love necessitates a singularity for nothing is left to differentiate the two except the gift, and this gift shared between the two is itself entire, lacking absolutely nothing of God Himself. Thus, we see that the Father gives everything to the Son; the Son receives everything from the Father with gratitude; and the Holy Spirit is the loving everything of the Father and the Son. It is only the pure totality of Divine Love can produce singularity and personality without contradiction.

10 The Second Person of the Trinity is the eternal procession of the Wisdom of the Father and thus from all eternity is entrusted with the Scroll of God.

Lo, the Ancient One and Wisdom turned in love[11] to the Beloved,[12] who came soaring over the waters, leaping upon the mountains, and skipping over the hills. The Beloved came to serenade the Ancient One, anoint Wisdom, and advocate the Wedding Covenant of God. He came in Love,[13] for His name spoken was spreading perfume, His song sweet, dripping with honey. All that stood before Him rejoiced and exulted: "We extol your Love; it is beyond wine: how rightly you are Loved!"

The Beloved was radiant and red; He stood out among the thousands. His head was as pure gold: His locks as palms of the tree, black as the raven. His eyes were as doves upon brooks of running waters; His teeth bathed in milk and set like jewels. His cheeks were as beds of aromatic spices set by the grand perfumers. His lips were lilies dripping choice myrrh. His arms were rods of gold adorned with chrysolites. His body was a work of ivory covered in sapphires, His legs pillars of marble set upon gold foundations. His stature was as great as the trees of Eden, as imposing as cedars. His mouth was sweetness itself: He is all delight. Such was the Beloved; such is the Lover of God.[14]

Song of Songs 2:8

Song of Songs 1:3

Song of Songs 5:10...

Song of Songs ...5:16

NOTES

11   The eternal procession of the Third Person of the Trinity, God the Holy Spirit.

12   'The Beloved' is God the Holy Spirit, who was in the beginning, is now, and ever shall be.

13   The Holy Spirit is the very love of the Father and the Son, the relation held so perfectly and so profoundly that It is the Third Person of the Most Holy Trinity, God Himself. (Cf. Summa Theologiae, Prima Pars, Q37, A1 & A2)

14   Let us turn now in adoration of the Most Holy Trinity that 'great mystery, the mystery of love, an ineffable mystery, before which words themselves must give way to the silence of wonder and worship. A divine mystery that challenges and involves us, because a share in the Trinitarian life was given to us through grace, through the redemptive Incarnation of the Word and the gift of the Holy Spirit.' (St. Pope John Paul II)

Let us consecrate our very *Soul* to the Triune God: Let my *Memory* and all my actions be given over to God the Father; Let my *Intellect* and all my words be given over to God the Son; Let my *Will* and my desires be given over to God the Holy Spirit. That nothing I am and nothing I do may ever be apart from Them, Most Holy Three in One.

Holy Trinity on their Throne

The Throne Room

enceforth the Divine Council was seated upon the high and lofty Throne, and the train of Their garment was filling the Temple. A door was opened, and a voice like a trumpet proclaimed: "Come up here, and I shall show you the things which must be accomplished hereafter."[15]

Thus the Celestial Court[16] was summoned, and all the many stars were caught up in the Spirit to the heavenly throne room. They beheld the Throne of God set in the Temple of heaven, and upon the Triune Throne, they beheld the One God[17] who was seated, whose appearance sparkled like jasper and carnelian stone, and around the Throne was a rainbow as brilliant as emerald shining in glory.

Surrounding the Throne, twenty-four other thrones were set up, on which the twenty-four *Ancients*[18] were to be seated. Draped across each of the empty thrones lay a white robe and a golden crown. From the Throne came flashes of lightning, rumblings, and peals of thunder. Suddenly, a sound came from up above like a mighty wind, filling the entire house of heaven. Tongues of Fire[19] appeared before the Throne, blazing and swirling about the Altar as seven burning flames.[20] The Spirit of the Lord came to rest upon the Altar, surrounded with the burning flames of the spirit of *wisdom* and the spirit of *understanding*, flaming with the spirit of *counsel* and the spirit of *fortitude*, and blazing with the spirit of *knowledge* and the spirit of *piety*, and all aflame with the spirit of *fear of the Lord*.[21]

Isaiah 6:1

Revelation 4:1…

Acts of the Apostles 2:2

Isaiah 11:1

IGNATIAN CONTEMPLATION

15   The court of God has been summoned to judge creation; all the angels are called to gather to bear witness to the Word of God.

16   The "Celestial Court" refers to the ancient Biblical and Hebraic notion that Heaven is a judicial court in which God judges right from wrong. Satan is thus in the role of the prosecutor, for "Satan" means Adversary. Cf. Revelation 12:10, "For the Adversary… who accuses [our brothers] before our God day and night."

17   The hallowed truth that God is Trinity can only be known through Divine Revelation, given through the Word Himself. Thus, when the angels look upon the Triune God they see only one, simple, and perfect Being.

18   The 'Ancients' refer to holy angels from the Book of Revelation, later known as Thrones, who will adhere themselves to the Divine authority, specifically bequeathed to the Church as the twelve tribes and twelve apostles.

19   Acts 2:2 The tongues of fire are a great truth revealed about the Holy Spirit, for we see that the Holy Spirit is Fire, an ardent flame burning with the all-consuming love of God. This is an eternal fire flowing straight from the intimate union of the Most Holy Trinity. This eternal and Divine fire is the reason why the Holy Altar in Heaven is ablaze as seen in the Book of Isaiah, where a seraphim takes an ember from the burning Altar and purges the sin from Isaiah's lips, and is in fact the reason why the Seraphim themselves are aflame. This holy and ardent love of the Holy Spirit is the sacred flame of Seraph and Madonna.

20   This preternatural state of the heavenly throne room shows the eternal fire of the Holy Spirit coming down for the first time to set the heavenly Altar ablaze. The seven flaming torches mentioned in Revelation 4:5 are the Seven Gifts of the Holy Spirit given to The Seven Angels "who stand before the Glory of the Lord." Thus, such torches symbolize both the fire of the Holy Spirit and the bearers of such fire, The Seven Holy Angels. "Seven unlit torches awaiting the Lord to kindle them with the flames of His Spirit."

21   Isaiah 11:1 These are the Seven Gifts of the Holy Spirit, seven holy flames that burn with the selfsame ardor of the Holy Spirit Himself. The chief flame is Wisdom, which is the intimate knowledge of and conformity to the Divine, the ability to judge, think, and act according to Divine Truth, directing oneself entirely like the Divine. Understanding is penetrating insight into the very heart of things, always illuminated by the Light of the Divine, especially the comprehension of higher truths necessary for eternal salvation— true vision of God. Counsel is the subservience of the soul to God's will in all matters necessary for salvation. Fortitude is the strength of spirit to do good and avoid evil, especially when undergoing the 'test,' overcoming all obstacles of sin and death, by virtue of God's own strength. Knowledge is the correct judgment of all matters of faith and morals, so as to never wander from the straight path of justice. Piety is the fervent desire to offer reverence to the Lord as Father, offering proper worship to God out of fear of the Lord. Fear of the Lord is the beginning and end of Wisdom, the holy and fervent desire to never be separated from the Lord as a lover from the beloved. This also encompasses the horror of Hell: eternal separation from God.

Revelation
...4:6...
Ezekiel
1:22...

Stretched out before the sight of the Throne stood the great assembly that resembled a sea of glass shining like crystal.[22] Encircling the head of each, over every one of the assembly was a likeness of the celestial firmament:[23] a terrible and awe-inspiring sight to behold, stretching upwards like shining crystal around the heads of each. Beneath their crowns of light were mighty and luxurious wings outstretched, straight and broad, the one toward the other.[24] The sound of their wings was as the roar of many waters, echoing like the voice of the Almighty. As they took up position, the march of an army resounded in the deep. Then a voice came from over their heads and above their crowns of

Ezekiel
...1:25

light, so they stood at attention and let down their wings.[25]

Revelation
10:1...

In the center before the Throne stood the mighty Morning Star[26] wrapped in a cloud, with a rainbow about his head; his face was like that of the sun and his feet were as bright as pillars of fire. In his hand he held a small scroll that had been opened. He placed his right foot on the Sea and his left foot on the Land, and then he cried out in a loud voice as a lion roaring. When he cried out, seven thunders raised their

Revelation
...10:3

voices to echo his cry.

Roundabout the mighty Star and the Throne stood Four *Living Creatures*,[27] whose vision was most keen, their wings were like that of the peacock covered with eyes both in front and in back. Yet, they could not even glimpse the Splendor of the Lord. Only the Light Bearer, Lucifer, the mighty Morning Star, could bear to behold the

Job
40:19

Splendor of the Lord. He came first, at the beginning of God's ways, and was appointed taskmaster over all. He received first the Divine Light, and having so received such sublime and edifying light, he himself shone with the selfsame Splendor of the Lord. He then, the Herald of the Great Dawn, being so filled and overflowing with holy brightness, imparted his own overflowing light unto the Four Living Creatures roundabout the Throne, and they, possessing more luminous intelligence, duly received and again shed forth the Divine Light unto

22   The uniformity of the assembly represents the preternatural state of the angels, properly referred to as Celestial Intelligences, denoting their nature as a pure spirit. This is before they were given the choice whether or not to serve God through serving mankind, thus they cannot be properly named Angels, because the name angel denotes the occupation of messenger.

23   This is the Scriptural origin of artists' depiction of halos. Since the artists had to depict the dome of the heavens two-dimensionally we eventually came to know their glory as rings of light about the head.

24   At this point, the celestial intelligences did not differ from one another according to their respective choir and thus had two wings each.

25   This is the Scriptural origin of artists' depiction of angelic wings.

26   This is Lucifer, the Light Bearer, the first and most important star in heaven. He is responsible for making all the stars in heaven resemble the Lord God in intelligence.

27   The 'Four Living Creatures' are the four holy angelic Evangelists, who will lead the Celestial Choir of Cherubim.

Lucifer: the Light Bearer

all those more distant stars of heaven, until the whole assembly shined with the Splendor of the Lord, so that no star in the heavens could shine without beholding the Lord's Splendor, first received and so imparted by the Light Bearer himself.[28]

Sirach
50:1...

So when Lucifer arose and spoke before the court all that had gathered fell silent, for it was through him that they could behold the Lord. He was the leader of his brothers and the pride of his people. He was the highest star and under his care the whole House of Heaven was redoubled and the Temple fortified. A great wall was built up for the Temple grounds with powerful turrets, and a great reservoir was excavated, a pool with the vastness of the sea. He cared for all that was bestowed upon him and delivered it all to the Lord his Maker. He enlarged the entrance of the Temple and court. He shone in his days as the Morning Star in the midst of a cloud, as the moon at full, and as the sun when it shineth, so did he shine in the Temple of God. And his radiance was as the rainbow giving light amongst the bright clouds. He was as bright as a fire and as sweet as frankincense burning at the altar; he was the grand vessel of the Lord, made of gold and adorned with every precious stone. Thus, when he put on his glorious robe, he was clothed in perfect splendor. He then ascended the holy Altar and made the court of the sanctuary shine in glory.

Sirach
...50:11

The Light Bearer, the Four Living Creatures, and the whole host of heaven then fell down before the Lord, but their harps were without string and their golden chalices had no incense, until Lucifer, the Light Bearer, proclaimed: "Worthy are You, Lord God of all creation, to receive glory and honor and power, for You created all the stars in the heavens; because of Your will they came to be and were created!" And again he exclaimed, "Worthy are You to hold the Scroll and break open its Word!"

Revelation
...4:11

28   This is the nature of the angels: they are pure spirits, perfect minds. Therefore, what they see, they know, and what they know, they become. Thus, when Lucifer beholds the light of God, he knows and embodies that very light, shining with the selfsame luster as God Himself, and when he passes on that light, all those angels below him take on and actually resemble the light of God according to the portion of each. What they see of God in the Holy Light is what they actually shine forth, taking on His own splendor in and through their own intelligence. Therefore, there forms a natural hierarchy of Intelligences, according to how much each sees of the Godhead. Lucifer being first is the most like God, and those below him see less and thus rank less. It is through the Divine Light that all the Celestial Intelligences understand God and the Universe. That is why the Psalter says: "In Your light we see light." Psalm 36:9

NOTES

Then he heard the voices of the many stars who surrounded the Throne and the Living Creatures and the whole assembly of heaven as an echo of his own. They were countless in number and they cried out in a loud voice: "Worthy is the Lord, the Creator, to receive power and riches, wisdom and strength, honor and glory and blessing!"

Revelation 5:12…

So throughout all of heaven, and below heaven and in the deep, everything everywhere cried out: "To the One who sits upon the Throne be blessing and honor, glory and might, forever and ever."

The Light Bearer and the Four Living Creatures then replied, "Amen," and all the stars fell down and worshiped.

Revelation …5:14

The Heavenly Throne Room

—————— ❧ *NOTES* ❧ ——————

The Seven Trumpets

Revelation
8:3…

T he Lord God then took the Scroll in His hand, and seven trumpets were given to seven stars of heaven to herald the decree of the Lord. There standing at the Altar, a golden chalice was given to the Morning Star with a great quantity of incense to offer, along with all the prayers of the holy stars, on the golden Altar that was before the Throne. The smoke of the incense along with all the prayers of the stars were delivered up to God by the hand of the Light Bearer. Then he took the chalice, filled it with burning coals from the Altar, and the Lord commanded: "Hurl them down below; set it ablaze with the fire of My love." There were flashes of lightning, rumblings, peals of thunder, and now an earthquake!

§ *The First Trumpet* §

Revelation
…8:6…

The seven stars, who held the seven trumpets, prepared themselves to sound the trumpets, heralding the reading of the Scroll.[29]

The first star sounded his trumpet, and the whole assembly who had gathered before the Throne beheld the Glory of the Earth. Looking down, they beheld the center of creation filled with soil instead of light, and from that soil arose a glory unknown in the heavens: magnificent trees and green grass. So beholding the beauty of the Earth, they understood the Earth, and the Lord's desire to create the Earth.[30]

§ *The Second Trumpet* §

Revelation
…8:8…

The second star then sounded his trumpet and the great multitude of stars beheld the Glory of the Sea. They watched as the formless waters of the deep pooled and collected into the Sea. The waters surrounded the Earth as a great mountain and teemed with life. So beholding the Sea, they understood the Sea, and why the Lord wished to gather together the waters of the deep.[31]

IGNATIAN CONTEMPLATION

29   The Seven Trumpets are the events heralding the reading of the Scroll, both here and in the Book of Revelation. The Scroll is the Plan of God, His innermost Counsel, that His son should become man culminating in the Wedding Feast of the Lamb. These trumpets herald events that must take place before the Scroll can be read. Thus, since Creation is in a state of grace before the Fall, the events that must take place are not ones of purification as in the Book of Revelation, but are ones of illumination, ultimately leading to the perfection held in the Incarnation of Christ. Therefore, these events are the original plan of God: Why God created Lucifer and the tremendous good that would have transpired if he would have served the Lord in love. Note the first four trumpet blasts echo the Days of Creation, where the last three trumpet blasts echo Salvation History, both essential for Christian cosmology.

30   Revelation 8:7 The first trumpet reveals the Lord's desire to glorify the Earth and all the vegetation upon it. Similarly, the first trumpet we read about in Revelation is about purifying the Earth from sin. This, however, would not be necessary if the Earth had not become corrupt on account of Adam's sin.

31   Revelation 8:8 The second trumpet shows the glory of the sea, how the Lord gives form to the formless waters and fills them with life. The second trumpet in Revelation is purified with a great mountain of fire, for the sea had become the abode of Satan, the great sea serpent Leviathan.

The Seven Heralds

§ *The Third Trumpet* §

Revelation
...8:10...

The third star then sounded his trumpet, and the whole court beheld the Glory of the Rivers and Streams, the life-giving waters welling up from the Earth. There from the side of the Earth came forth a spring of life-giving water, and anyone who drank from the water would be given life eternal because the water had been made sweet. So beholding the Rivers and Streams, they understood the fount of life and why the Lord wished to impart His grace.[32]

§ *The Fourth Trumpet* §

Revelation
...8:12...

The fourth star then sounded his trumpet, and the great assembly beheld the Glory of the Sun and Moon and the Stars in the sky. They watched as they were given light to shed upon the Earth and authority to set forth the times and seasons. So having beheld the Sun and the Moon, and all the Stars in the sky, they understood the honor bestowed upon themselves, and why the Lord wished to make them luminaries of the Earth.[33]

§ *The Fifth Trumpet* §

Revelation
...8:13...

Then a star with the wings of an eagle cried, "Glory! Glory! Glory! For the last three trumpet blasts are about to sound."

Revelation
...9:1...

The fifth star then sounded his trumpet, and the stars beheld the glory of the Morning Star descending upon the Earth. He was given the key to the passage to heaven and brought with him the whole host of heaven to illumine the Earth. They came out of the clouds onto the land and were given the power of angels, and were told to minister unto the peoples of the Earth. The appearance of the stars changed and took the form of angels, some purifying, some illuminating, and some perfecting. They had as their king the Angel of Light, whose name was Lucifer.[34]

So they beheld the first glory as it had been set out, and they understood God's desire for them to become Angels and serve the Earth, but there are two more glories yet to come.

32 Revelation 8:10 The third trumpet shows the Lord's desire to have life-giving water pour out upon the Earth, just as the water from Christ's side is the water of eternal life. This is the opposite of the third trumpet in Revelation, where we see the corruption of the waters because of the fall of the angels. The falling star Wormwood taints and makes bitter the waters, corrupting the rivers and streams; this again shows Leviathan's dominion over the many waters and how they have become his abode upon the Earth.

33 Revelation 8:12 The fourth trumpet shows the Lord's desire to glorify the sun and moon and stars in heaven. The fourth trumpet in Revelation speaks about the fall of the angels, how a third of the stars in heaven fell from the sky and how all the lights in heaven were diminished by a third.

34 Revelation 9:1 The fifth trumpet shows how glorious God's plan for Creation could have been, if Lucifer would have served and obeyed. The fifth trumpet in Revelation shows the scourge of Satan as he releases Hell upon the Earth, allowing his demons to roam about the Earth torturing the human race.

The Fifth Trumpet

§ *The Sixth Trumpet* §

Revelation
...9:13...

The sixth star then sounded his trumpet, and they beheld the glory of man, the splendor of the Saints throughout the Earth. So the Four Living Creatures roundabout God's Throne and the great host of heaven spread the Word of the Lord throughout the Earth, and all mankind was enraptured by the fire of their mouths and turned to God in great love.[35]

Revelation
10:1...

But then the mighty Morning Star who in his hand held his own small scroll arose and interrupted with a loud voice roaring like a lion. And when he cried the seven thunders echoed their cry, but the seven thunders' voices were sealed up and not made known. So the Morning Star raised his hand to heaven and swore by the One who lives forever and ever, who created heaven and all the things therein; and the Earth and all things therein; and the Sea and all things therein: that there shall be delay no longer, but at the time of the voice of the seventh star, when he sounds the seventh trumpet, the mysterious plan of God shall be revealed, as He declares to the ones He loves.

Revelation
...10:7
Revelation
11:3...

The multitude then beheld the Temple of God, its Altar, and all those who worshiped therein, and so two great witnesses were given authority to prophesy to the Earth. They stood as the two olive trees and the two lampstands before the Lord of the Earth, and as they spoke fire poured out from their mouths and enraptured the inhabitants of the Earth. They were given authority over the waters so that nothing could quench the fire of God's love upon the Earth. Through their testimony the whole Earth came to give glory to the God of heaven.

So they beheld the second glory as it had been set out, and they understood God's desire for there to arise Saints upon the Earth, but the third glory has yet to come.

35   Revelation 9:13 The sixth trumpet is about the glorification of man as Saints of the
      Lord. The sixth trumpet in Revelation is about the purification of man. This, however,
      does not work, and man remains wicked and unrepentant. Thus more is required, and
      God sends His two witnesses, the Law and the Prophets, that humanity might repent
      and love the Lord.

NOTES

§ *The Seventh Trumpet* §

Revelation
...11:15...

The seventh star then sounded his trumpet and they beheld the mysterious plan of God, the glory of *the Woman,* Queen of Heaven and Earth. For the kingdom of the world now belonged to the Lord and His Anointed, and He shall reign forever and ever. The assembly then cried out, "How? How shall this come to be?"

So the Temple in Heaven was opened, and, for the first time, they beheld the Ark of the Covenant, enclosed in the Holy of Holies of the Temple. And upon beholding the Ark of the Covenant, all creation trembled, there were flashes of lightning, rumblings, peals of thunder, an earthquake, and finally a violent hailstorm!

Revelation
...11:19...

Revelation
...12:1...

So as they beheld the Ark of the Covenant, a great sign appeared: A woman clothed with the sun, and she stood with the moon under her feet, and upon her head was placed a crown of twelve stars.

Immediately a murmur ran through the great multitude that had gathered before the Throne: "What is this that light need not pass through it? But rather wears the sun, the source of all light, as a garment? And uses the crescent as a footstool? And the crown upon her head adorned with stars as if they were jewels. Who is this Queen of Heaven?"[36]

Revelation
12:2

The Woman then wailed aloud in labor pangs, for she was pregnant and in agony to give birth. She gave birth to a son, a male child, who was destined to rule over all the Earth with an iron rod. They watched as the Son was then taken up to God and placed on His Throne.

Revelation
12:5

Again a murmur ran through the great assembly of stars: "Who is this Woman so full of grace that she births the Son of God? How is this that the mysterious plan of God, the Ark of the Covenant, should be revealed unto us? Why are we so honored, that the Mother of our God should come unto us?"

Luke
1:43

So having beheld the third and final glory as it had been set out, they tried to understand God's desire for Covenant with *the Woman,* but for the first time envy crept into the heart of Lucifer, and a shadow formed, obscuring the vision of *the Woman* from the multitude.[37]

36   The Woman possesses as trinkets everything that the Celestial Intelligences hold dear, revealing her authority and nobility over all the angels in heaven.

37   Revelation 11:15 The seventh trumpet is the most important; it reveals the ultimate glory, the Incarnation of God Himself, the source of all glory. How glorious must be the Mother of God, who bore His son, giving her flesh for His, bearing Him in her womb and not being completely obliterated. It is this vision in Revelation that finally reveals the envy of the Devil and his actions in the Garden of Eden. It is at this moment that envy enters the heart of Lucifer, and he begins to plot the destruction of the Woman. Furthermore, because of Lucifer's envy, the revelation of the Woman is obscured and tainted in all the minds of those below him.

The Celestial Woman

The Jilted Lover

T he great Light Bearer stood before *the Woman*, the Mother of the Son of God and pondered her in his heart. He then canticled a prayer to the Lord before the celestial court, seeking understanding of the seventh trumpet: "O Lord, our Lord, how majestic is Thy name throughout all the Earth. Thou hast set Thy glory above the heavens!

Yet, by this babe, an infant, Thou hast confounded Thy foes, thwarting enemy and avenger.

Yet, when I behold Thy heavens, the works of Thy fingers, the moon and stars Thou set in place: What is man that Thou art mindful of them, mere mortals that Thou care for them?

Yet, Thou hast made them little less than the gods![38] Thou hast crowned them with glory and honor.

Thou hast given them rule over the works of Thy hands, and put all things at their feet: All sheep and oxen, even the beasts of the field, the birds of the air, the fish of the sea, and whatever passes through the depths of the sea.

O Lord our Lord, how majestic is Thy name throughout all the Earth."

The Light Bearer stood in silence pondering in his heart, "What is man that Thou art mindful of them? The sons of men that Thou care for them?"[39]

Psalm 8:1...

Psalm ...8:9

IGNATIAN CONTEMPLATION

38 Lucifer is calling the Celestial Intelligences gods, revealing his true opinion of all those beings in heaven and those men upon the earth. This will eventually culminate in Satan's attempt to create the great Pantheon, both in Egypt and in Rome, where all the power of the fallen angels, demons, will be collected in order to be worshiped as 'God' by all mankind.

39 Psalm 8 The psalm for the eighth day (Sunday). This is the great question of the Scriptures: "What is man?" Created little less than the angels yet not a spirit, fundamentally animal yet given authority over all the animals. This Lucifer cries in his heart, trying to understand how God could love such an awkward creature as man, and love him so much as to desire wedlock. It is in asking this question that one eventually arrives at the conclusion that God specifically crafted us to be the perfect recipient of His love, capable of the ultimate act of love, Holy Matrimony with the Divine. For only an animal can experience the bodily union of one flesh, and only a rational mind/intelligent-volitive spirit can know God; thus it is only man, who is the ration-animal, that could ever be married to the Divine.

The Jilted Lover

The Age-old Scroll

Revelation
21:1…

Moved by the prayer of the Light Bearer the Lord God took the Scroll in His hand and unraveled it across the sky, and behold, they witnessed a new Heaven and a new Earth, for the former Heaven and the former Earth had passed away, and the depths of the Abyss[40] were no more![41] Then they saw her, *the Woman*, coming down from God. She was prepared as a Bride[42] adorned for her Husband.

Then they heard the loud voice of God thunder from the Throne, saying, "Behold, The Ark of the Covenant! I make My home with the human race. I will live with them, and they shall be My kin, and I Myself will always be with them as their God and Husband. I shall wipe away every tear from their eyes, and death shall be no more, nor mourning, nor weeping, nor sorrow shall be anymore. For the old order[43] has passed away!"

Then the One who sat upon the Throne proclaimed, "Behold! I shall make all things new! Transcribe all these words onto the flesh of your heart, for they are trustworthy and true."

God again proclaimed, "The Word has been fulfilled: I am the Alpha and the Omega, the Beginning and the End. To those that thirst I shall give a free gift from the Fount of Life-giving Waters, to the victor these gifts are their inheritance, and I shall be their God and they shall be my offspring, with my bride as their mother."

The Lord then announced in great joy: "Come! I will show you My Bride, the Wife of the Lord."

They then looked out from the height of a tall mountain, where they saw her coming down out of the very heart of God. She gleamed with the splendor of God. Her radiance was like that of precious stone, like the jasper stone, clear as crystal. Her dress girt her like a wall, and was adorned with every manner of precious stone: the first was jasper, the second sapphire, the third chalcedony, the fourth emerald, the fifth sardonyx, the sixth carnelian, the seventh chrysolites, the eighth beryl,

IGNATIAN CONTEMPLATION

40   The depths of the sea represent the formless waters of nonexistence, the closest thing to pure nothingness, pure evil; it is for this reason that Leviathan flees to the sea, making it his abode, the kingdom of darkness.

41   Revelation 21:1 This verse is often taken by Protestants to refer to the end of time, but it can also refer to the new Heaven and the new Earth that Christ brought about through His Paschal Mystery: suffering, death, and resurrection.

42   This is the Church, the bride of Christ, but also in a profound and holy mystery is Mary, Spouse of the Holy Spirit.

43   The 'old order' can refer to several things. It could refer to the order of creation, destitute of grace, in which the angels are higher than man and are deserving of our worship. It could also refer to the order of Satan, which he establishes when he inherits the world because of Adam's sin. Both, however, show that the grace of Christ's passion, death, and resurrection fundamentally change the Universe, transfiguring Creation itself into the Church, through which God's spousal covenant unites Creation permanently with the Creator.

The Church: The Bride

the ninth topaz, the tenth chrysoprase, the eleventh hyacinth, and the twelfth amethyst. Her dress was as brilliant as pearl, and her belt was made of twelve grand pearls, and the path she walked was pure gold, as transparent as glass.

Beholding her, there was no Temple, only the Lord God Almighty as Spouse. She had no need for sun or moon to shine, for the Glory of God gave her light, and her lamp was the Lord. The Earth walked in her light, and all the kings of men brought her their treasure. Her eyes never shut by day, and night never fell upon her. All the treasure and wealth of the Earth was brought to her, yet nothing unclean was found in her, only her children, those whose names were written in the Book of Life by the Lord.

Then the Lord revealed the River of Life-giving Water, shining as bright as crystal, flowing from the Throne of God down and round about *the Woman*, filling her and overflowing like a wedding veil. On either side of her grew the Tree of Life with its twelve kinds of fruit, producing its fruit each month; and the leaves of the Tree grew for the healing of the nations. Nothing accursed shall ever be found in her, only the Throne of God and the Lord, and she will bring all His servants to worship Him, showing them His face, and inscribing His name upon their foreheads. And there shall be no more night because of her, no need for lamp or sunlight, for the Lord God will be her light, and they will reign forever and ever.

But once again envy hardened the heart of Lucifer, and a shadow obscured[44] the vision of *the Bride* from the multitude.[45]

Revelation ...21:27

Revelation 22:21...

Revelation 10:10

Revelation ...22:5

44   This means that the whole assembly of heaven, all the many stars, never actually saw the vision of the Woman as bride. Since angels receive all revelations from God as handed down from the angel above them, as light passing through glass, the hardness of Lucifer's heart blocks this revelation from their vision, and since he was the chief and highest angel, his envy blocks the vision from every angel without exception.

45   Sadly because of the envy of Lucifer's hardened heart the purpose of Creation itself was withheld from the many angels, and not until the end of time would the Scroll be unraveled and the Bride of Christ, the Church, be revealed. Only with the fullness of time and Revelation is it clear that Creation was always destined to be transfigured in the Lord, and this perfection of Creation is the Church.

The Bride of God

ᏖᎻᎬ ᏩᏒᎬᎪᏖ ᎠᎬᏴᎪᏖᎬ [46]
§ Lucifer's Accusations §

Ꮦ he grand assembly of the celestial court fell silent, for the wedding covenant spoken of in the Scroll was beyond the minds of all the stars in heaven, until out of the silence the wrath of the Light bearer was kindled. He was angry with *the Woman*, for she did not deserve the Love of the Maker. So when Lucifer saw that there was no reply in the mouths of his kin, his wrath was inflamed, and he decided to accuse man,[47] bringing many accusations against him before the Court of God, for if man could be convicted so too woman. Thus, the Son of Man[48] was placed on trial, and every sin humanity would commit was brought before the Lord, in search of a verdict of whether or not man was worthy of creation and the love of the Maker.

Revelation 10:2

Job 32:6...

Lucifer, the bearer of the light of God, then unraveled his small scroll and spoke out before the court his words were as sweet as honey in the mouth, but were a bitter brew in the stomach. He declared, "I am young in days and Thou art Ancient; therefore, I held back and was afraid to declare my knowledge,[49] for I hoped that one of greater days would speak, and many years would teach wisdom. But, as I see, it is the spirit of the mind that gives understanding. It is not those of many days who are wise, nor do the ancient understand judgment.[50]

Job ...32:10...

Therefore, I shall speak: Hearken to me; let me too set forth my knowledge! Behold, I have waited for Your words and have given ear to Your wisdom. Yes, I followed You attentively as You laid bare what You had to say; and behold there is none who has convicted the Son of Man. Not one of you could refute his actions—what he is going to do! So I am forced to speak, lest you all should say, 'We have found Wisdom! It is God's choice, not man's." For had man addressed his words to me, I should not then have answered him as You have done. Are all the stars in heaven dismayed, and make no reply? Words fail them. Must I wait?

IGNATIAN CONTEMPLATION

46 If you are not spiritually prepared to contemplate the mind of Satan please omit reading this section. In order to properly contemplate the speech of the Evil One recorded in the Book of Job (from which this chapter is taken); one must first enter into a prayerful state trusting in the inspired Word of God and that such words though from the Adversary are in Sacred Scripture for the edification of souls. Then pray to submit yourself to the Holy Spirit who will reveal and make plain the cunning words of the Adversary, his envy hidden in hatred. He is cunning, but the Holy Spirit bears all things to light.

47 The word 'Satan' can also mean 'accuser' in Hebrew.

48 This is Jesus. Jesus is on trial for all mankind's sins and atrocities, standing before the celestial court, both as a representative of mankind and a member. Thus, when Lucifer is addressing the defendant, he is addressing both the person of Christ and all of mankind.

49 The majority of text in this chapter and the next are taken from the Book of Job.

50 Lucifer insults God Himself, The Ancient of Days, by saying that experience is not what gives wisdom, but the mind. Lucifer thinks this gives him the right to speak out against man.

── ·୬ *NOTES* ୬· ──

Now that He speaks no more, and has ceased to make reply, I too will speak my part; I also will show my knowledge! For I am full of matters to speak of, and the spirit within me compels me. Behold, I am like a new wineskin filled with wine; I am ready to burst! Let me speak and obtain relief; let me open my lips and make reply. I will not accept the Son of Man, and I will not level God with man! For I know not how long I shall be permitted to speak, and whether after a while my Maker may take me away.[51]

Job
...33:1...

Therefore, O Court, hear my discourses and hearken to all my words. Behold, now I open my mouth; my tongue and my voice speak words. I will state directly what is in my mind. My lips shall only utter knowledge sincerely, for the spirit of the Lord has made me; the breath of the Almighty keeps me alive. If you are able, refute me; draw up your arguments and stand forth. Behold I, like yourself, have been taken from the same pool of light by the Maker. Therefore, let not my wonder terrify thee, and let not my eloquence be burdensome to thee.

Job
...33:8...

Now the Son of Man will say before the court, and I have heard his arrogant words: 'I am clean, and without sin. I am unspotted, and there is no iniquity within me, because He invents pretexts for me and reckons me as His Lover. He has put my feet in His sandals; He has watched over all my paths!' In this, O Son of Man, you are not justified, let me tell you; for God is greater than man!—Who is upright before the Lord? Why, then, does man, at once make war against Him and claim His Love? Demanding an accounting of all His doings, but not your own? For God does speak, perhaps once or twice, though you, man, perceive it not. Only one[52] stands at His throne and lends ear to all His words.

Job
...33:15...

In a dream, in a vision of the night, when deep sleep falls upon men as they slumber in their beds, it is then that He opens the ears of men and as a warning, terrifies them, that He may withdraw man from evil and may deliver him from pride, receiving his soul from

51 Since Lucifer is the most intelligent being ever created, he understands that he is blaspheming against the Lord, but he still boldly accuses man before the court in the feeble hope of convincing God not to love man on account of his iniquity.

52 Lucifer is referring to himself, claiming God for his own like a jilted lover.

The Accuser

corruption and the pit, his life from passing to the sword. He rebuketh man by sorrow in his bed and he maketh all his bones to wither, so that to his appetite food becomes repulsive, and his soul rejects the choicest nourishment. His flesh shall be consumed away, and his bones that were covered shall be laid bare. His soul draws near to the pit, his life to the place of the dead.[53]

Job
...33:23...

If, however, there shall be for him a celestial being[54] out of the thousands, a mediator, to declare man's righteousness and bring man back to justice, The Lord shall take pity on him and say, 'Deliver him from going down to the pit; I have found him a ransom.' Only then shall his flesh become as soft as a boy's, and he shall be again as in the days of his youth. He shall pray, and God will favor him; he shall see God's face with rejoicing. He shall sing before all others and say, 'I sinned and did wrong, yet because of the celestial being He has not punished me accordingly. He delivered my soul from passing to the pit, and I beheld the Light Bearer.'[55]

Job
...33:29...

Lo and behold, all these things God does, twice or thrice, for a man. Bringing back his soul from the pit to the light, in the land of the living. Be attentive, O court; listen to me! Be silent and I will speak. If thou hast anything to say, answer me; speak for I would have thee to appear just. If not hear me; hold thy peace, and I will teach thee wisdom."

Job
...34:1...

Then Lucifer continued and said, "Hear ye, O wise ones of God, my discourses, and ye that possess knowledge, hearken to me! For the ear testeth words as the taste does food. Let us discern for ourselves what is right; let us learn between us what is good.[56] For the Son of Man shall say: 'I am innocent before the Lord, but God has overthrown my judgment; for in my judgment there has been a lie; my wound is fatal, though I am without transgression.'

53 This is a glimpse into Lucifer's understanding of the relationship between God and man. In his view, man is so low and deplorable that the only relationship the Almighty can have with him is one of a taskmaster keeping disobedient swine from greater evil.

54 Lucifer thinks that the savior of man should be an angel.

55 The word 'Light' indicates Lucifer as savior.

56 This is Lucifer's first step down the path to choosing his own will instead of God's.

Angelic Worship

Job
...34:7...

What creature is there like man, who drinks in blasphemies like water, keeps company with evildoers, and walks upon the path of the wicked? O stars of heaven, hearken to my voice; far be it from God to do wickedness; far from the Almighty to do wrong! Rather, He requites man for his conduct, and according to the ways of each man He will render unto him. Surely God cannot act wickedly; the Almighty cannot violate justice. Who gave Him government over the earth or who else set all land in its place? If He were to take back His spirit to Himself, withdraw to Himself His breath, all flesh would perish together, and man would return to dust.[57]

Job
...34:16...

Now do you, O court, hear this? Hearken to the words I speak! Can an enemy of justice indeed be in control, or will you condemn the Just One as unjust? The Son of Man is Evil! Who says to a king: 'You are worthless!' and to nobles: 'You are wicked'? Who neither favors the person of princes, nor respects the rich more than the poor, for they are all the work of His hands? They shall all suddenly die, and all men shall be troubled at midnight. They all shall pass, even the nobles, God will remove the powerful without lifting a hand, for His eyes are upon the ways of man, and He beholds all his steps. There is no darkness, no shadow of death so dense that evildoers can hide from Him. For it is never in the power of man to enter into judgment with God.[58] He shall break into pieces the many and innumerable, and shall make others to stand in their stead. For he knows their works and therefore brings night upon them, and they shall be destroyed! He hath struck them as being wicked, in plain view those who as it were on purpose revolted against Him, and would not heed His ways.

Job
...34:29...

So it is they that cause the cry of the needy to echo to Him! And He heard the cry of the poor, but when He remains still who can condemn? When He hides His face, who then can behold Him, whether it be nations or the man? Who makes the Son of Man, a hypocrite, to reign for the sins of all men?[59]

57   Lucifer is trying to resolve this paradox: God created man, who is material and wholly deplorable. In spite of this, God promises Himself to man instead of promising Himself to an angel of pure light, specifically the highest angel of purest light. This would seem wrong, yet God can do no wrong because God is supreme in every way; and so the fault must reside with man. Lucifer feels compelled to show God that man is not worthy of union with Him.

58   Lucifer directly contradicts 1 Corinthians 6:3: "Do you not know we will judge the angels…"

59   Lucifer is speaking directly to Christ, a man who will conquer the sin of humanity. The Christ is a hypocrite in the eyes of Lucifer, because to him being human means being sinful before God. Thus the Christ is a sinful man hypocritically ruling over the sins of other men.

NOTES

Seeing that I have spoken of God, I will not hinder thee in thy turn. If I have erred, teach me wherein I have sinned. If I have spoken iniquity, I will add no more. Would you, O stars of heaven, say that God must punish, since man rejects what He is doing? It is you who must choose, not I; speak, therefore, of what you know. Let those of understanding speak to me, and let the wise hearken to me and say, 'Man speaks without intelligence, and his words are without sense.' Let the Son of Man be tried to the limit, even to his utter end, since man's replies are only those of the impious! Man is only adding rebellion to his sin by brushing off my arguments and addressing many words to God."

Job
...35:1...

Then Lucifer proceeded and said to man, "Do you think it right to say: 'I am just rather than God?' To say: 'What does it profit me to be just? What advantage have I for having not sinned?' I have words for reply and all mankind. Look up to the skies and behold; ponder the heavens high above you. If you sin, what injury do you do to God? Even if your offenses are multiplied, how do you harm Him? If you are righteous, what do you give Him? What does He receive from your hand? Your wickedness can only affect another man and your justice only another human.[60]

Job
...35:9...

Only in great oppression do men cry out, do they wail aloud for help, because of the violent arm of tyrants saying, 'Where is God, my maker, who has given visions in the night, taught us rather than the beasts of the earth,[61] and made man wise rather than the birds of the heavens?' Though thus they cry out, He answers not against the pride of the wicked. Surely God does not hear such an empty cry, nor does the Almighty regard it. How much less when man says that he does not see Him, yet your case is before Him, and with trembling should you wait upon the verdict! But now that man has done otherwise, God's anger must punish, He will not show concern that the Son of Man will die. Yet man to no purpose opens his mouth, and without knowledge multiplies words."

60   Lucifer is telling a great and terrible lie, by claiming the distance between God and man prevents a viable relationship. He does not understand that God's love bridges this gap and that man can build a relationship with the All-loving God through his virtue or vice. (This is also the perspective of modern agnostics: if there is a God, He is too far removed from human life to merit a real relationship.)

61   Lucifer equates man to the beasts of the earth when he says that the only difference between man and beast is that God gave man knowledge. This is a terrible lie, for God created man in his image and likeness. (Modern science holds a similar perspective on the biological world: Humanity is a happenstance result of superior knowledge through evolution.)

NOTES

Lucifer proceeded further and said, "Wait yet a little longer, and I will instruct you, for there are still words to be said on God's behalf. I will bring my knowledge from the beginning, and to my Maker I will accord the right. For indeed my words cannot fail me: the one perfect in knowledge[62] I set before thee. Behold, God does not cast away the mighty whereas He Himself also is mighty. He withholds not the Son of Man's right, but grants vindication to the oppressed. He will not take away His eye from the just; He places kings upon their thrones and sets them to be exalted forever. Or if they are bound with fetters and held fast by chains of affliction, then He makes known to them what they have done wrong and their sins of boastful pride. He also opens their ears to correct them, and exhorts them that they may turn from iniquity. If they obey and serve Him, they shall spend their days in prosperity, their years in happiness, but if they obey not, they shall perish by the sword; they will die for their lack of knowledge.[63] Dissemblers and devious men prove the wrath of God, neither shall they cry when they are bound. Their soul shall die in the Flood, and their life be among the effeminate. But He shall deliver the unfortunate through their affliction, and instruct them through their distress.[64] Therefore He shall set you free from the narrow mouth, which has no foundations beneath it, but the peace of your table will be filled with fatness![65] Your case has been judged as that of the wicked; trial and judgment will you receive. Let no wrath, then, overtake you to oppress any man, nor let multitude of gifts turn you aside. Lay down your greatness without tribulation, as should all men who are mighty in strength.[66] Prolong not the night that others may not take your place. Take heed, turn not to evil, for you have preferred revelry to affliction.[67]

62   Lucifer.

63   Lucifer claims that holiness and knowledge are coextensive, which makes himself the holiest being in existence, since he has the greatest knowledge of God. It follows then that man is naturally unholy because he does not possess knowledge of God by nature as the angels do.

64   Again Lucifer insists that the only way God can benefit man is through punishment and reprimand.

65   Another terrible lie: only suffering men are holy; peace from suffering is sinful because man will turn to fatness and sloth.

66   Lucifer proposes that man should strive for three things: to correct no one, for every man is equal; to prevent God's gifts from causing feelings of happiness, lest suffering cease; and to lay down the greatness God has given to accept suffering as an inferior being. All three ideas attack the greatest virtue, Magnanimity, by implying that the most man can hope for is humility in suffering.

67   Lucifer has cunningly disposed of joy. Under his account, the only two states of man are affliction, which is beneficial, and revelry, which is sinful.

 NOTES

Job
...36:22...

Behold, God is sublime in His power. What lawgiver is there like Him? Who can search out His ways? Or who can say, 'You have done wrong?' Remember that you know not His work, concerning which men have praised in song. All men contemplate it, but behold it from afar.[68] Lo, God is great beyond our knowledge; the number of His years is past searching out. He lifts up the drops of rain and pours out showers like floods, till the skies run with water, and the showers rain down on mankind. For by these showers He nourishes the nations, and gives food to mortals. Lo, He spreads the clouds as the carpeting of His tent. In His hands He holds the lightning, and he commands it to strike. His thunder speaks for Him a jealous cry of anger against iniquity!

Job
...37:1...

At this my heart trembles and leaps out of place, to hear the angry thunder of His voice as it rumbles forth from His mouth![69] Everywhere under the heavens it echoes with His lightning, to the ends of the Earth. Again His voice shall roar the majestic sound of His thunder. His voice shall be heard, yet shall not be found out. God shall thunder wonderfully with His voice, He that does great things beyond our knowing, wonders past our searching out. He commands the snow: 'Fall down upon the earth,' and likewise to the heavy winter rain. He shuts up all mankind indoors; the wild beasts take cover and abide quietly in their dens. Out of its chamber comes forth the tempest, and the chill out of the north. With the Breath of God comes the frost,[70] and the broad waters become ice. With hail also the clouds are laden, as they scatter their flashes of light, which go about, wheresoever the will of Him who governs them shall lead, to unleash whatsoever their task is upon the surface of the earth, whether it be for punishment or mercy as He has commanded.

68 Lucifer begins to describe how far away man is from God—so far away that he can know nothing about Him.

69 Lucifer prefers the angry thunder of the Lord's justice to the calm peace of His mercy.

70 Lucifer speaks of the Holy Spirit as if He brings frost and ice. However, the Holy Spirit is the ardent flame of God's love, and can only set hearts on fire.

Closing Statements

Job
...37:4...

Hearken to this, O Man! Stand and consider the wondrous works of God. Do you know how God commanded the rains and makes the clouds shine with His light? Do you know how the clouds are banked, the wondrous works of Him who is perfect in the knowledges? You, who are made hot when the south wind comes over the land? Perhaps with Him you have made and spread out the firmament of the heavens, which are made most strong, and as hard as smelted brass? Teach us then what could be said to Him; there is nothing, for darkness makes your plea. Who shall make known to Him the things I speak? Even if the Son of Man shall speak, his words shall surely be swallowed up. Nay, it is rather the light, which men see not while it is obscured among the clouds,[71] till the wind comes by and sweeps the clouds away. From the north comes the splendor of the stars, surrounded by God's awesome majesty! The Almighty, no one can discover Him, preeminent in power and judgment; His great justice owes no one an accounting. Therefore all men shall fear Him, though none can see

Job
...37:2

Him, however wise their hearts!"[72]

Mark
14:61...

At the end of Lucifer's speech, he asked of the man: "Are you the Christ? Son of the Blessed God?"

The man on trial replied: "*I AM.* And you shall see the Son of Man sitting at the right hand of the power of God, riding upon the clouds of Heaven."

At this Lucifer, the high priest, mediator of light, tore his garment saying: "What need have we of witnesses? You have heard the blasphemy yourself! What is your decision?"

Mark
...14:65

And all of them condemned the man as deserving of death.[73] They moved to spit on him, blindfold him, and strike him for Lucifer's words stirred the heavens into a great tempest.

71   In Lucifer's mind, man's vision of God is obscured because the clouds of matter block out the light, while Lucifer, being above matter, is free to view God directly.

72   Lucifer is telling a horrendous lie: God is a lofty being Who has no dealings with men, and Wisdom, which all men seek, cannot bring them closer to God. This lie directly contradicts the entire message of the Bible, which culminates in God, Wisdom Himself, becoming man to prove that 'God's dwelling is with the human race'.

73   Mark 14:61 The great power of Lucifer's words becomes evident as the 'chief angel', who like the chief priest has the authority to stand in as God for the multitude.

NOTES

GHE GREAG DEBAGE
§ Ghe Lord's Decree §

Job
38:1...

Ghen the Lord addressed the Son of Man out of the storm. "Who is this that darkens Divine Dealings with words of ignorance?[74] Gird up your loins like a man! Now I will question, and you shall answer![75] Where were you when I laid the foundation of the Earth? Tell me, if you have understanding. Who determined the measure of it; do you know? Who stretched forth the measuring line for it? Into what were its pedestals sunk, and who laid the cornerstone, while the morning star[76] sang in chorus, and all the sons of God shouted for joy? Who shut the sea within its doors when it burst forth from the womb, when I made the clouds for its garment and thick darkness for its swaddling bands? When I set limits for it and fastened the bar of its door, and said: 'Thus far shall you come, but no farther, and here shall your swelling waves be stilled?' Have you ever in your lifetime commanded the morning and shown the dawn its place? Have you ever taken hold of the ends of the Earth, shaking them till the ungodly are flung from the surface? The clay of the Earth[77] shall receive my seal, and its garment shall be dyed. But as for the wicked, their light shall be withheld, and the arm of pride shattered.[78] Have you entered into the sources of the sea or walked about the depths of the abyss?[79] Have the gates of death[80] been opened to you; have you seen the darksome gates? Have you comprehended the breadth of the Earth?[81]

Job
...38:19...

"Tell me, if you know all things, which is the way to the dwelling place of Light, and where is the abode of darkness, that you might bring them to their boundaries and set them on their paths home? You know because you were conceived before them; and the number of your years is great![82] Have you entered into the storehouse of the snow and beheld the treasury of the hail, which I have prepared for the time of the Enemy,[83] against the day of war and battle? Which way to the parting of the winds, whence the hot east wind spreads over

IGNATIAN CONTEMPLATION

74 This particular passage from Job depicts God addressing Satan through a speech directed to man, since the whole purpose of the Book of Job is to illustrate to humanity how Satan causes evil. When the Lord goes on to speak of the Leviathan and the Behemoth, He is telling us about the age-old adversary, Satan himself.

75 Even though God is questioning Man, it is important to remember that Lucifer is still before the Lord and also being questioned. Furthermore, Lucifer in his arrogance has a real answer to all the questions that the Lord is asking.

76 More evidence from Scripture that Lucifer, the morning star, was originally good and fell from grace.

77 Man, but in particular the Son of Man, Jesus, whose tunic is stained in His own blood.

78 This refers to Lucifer, whose own light shall be withheld and pride shattered.

79 The dwelling place of Satan.

80 Hell, the domain of Satan, over which God Himself has mastery.

81 Satan acquired the Earth as his domain when he dethroned Adam in the Garden of Eden.

82 A mockery of Lucifer's opening statement.

83 God declares the frost and hail is for Satan on the day of the great battle, in refutation of Lucifer's earlier statement that they were intended to punish man.

 *NOTES*

the Earth? Who has laid out a channel for the downpour, and for the thunderstorm a path to bring rain upon the Earth, without man in the wilderness, where no mortal dwells; to enrich the wasteland and desolate ground till the desert blooms with verdure?[84] Has the rain a father, or who has begotten the drops of dew? Out of whose womb[85] comes the ice, and who gives the hoarfrost of heaven[86] its birth when the waters lie covered as though with stone that holds captive the surface of the deep?[87]

Job
...38:31...

"Shall you be able to join together the shining stars of Pleiades, or loosen the bonds of Orion?[88] Can you bring forth the daystar in its time, and make the evening star to rise upon the children of Earth?[89] Do you know the order of heaven; can you set down their reason upon the earth?[90] Can you lift up your voice to the clouds that they may[91] veil you in an abundance of waters? Can you send forth the lightnings, and will they go, and will they return to you and say, 'Here we are'? Who can declare the order of the heavens, or who can make the harmony of heaven to sleep? When were the water jars of heaven tilted and poured upon the dust of the Earth to fuse it into a mass, its clods made solid?[92]

Job
...38:36...

"Who has put Wisdom[93] in the heart of man or understanding in the cock to herald the dawn?[94] Will you hunt the prey for the lioness or appease the hunger of her cubs, while they crouch in their dens or lie in wait in the thicket? Who provides nourishment for the raven when her young ones cry to God, wandering about because they have no food?

Job
...39:1...

"Do you know the time when the mountain goats bring forth life, or watch for the birth pangs of the doe, numbering the months of their conceiving and fixing the time of their birth? They crouch down and bear their young; they deliver their progeny in the desert. Their offspring thrive and grow, they who leave and do not return.

Job
...39:5...

"Who has set the wild ass free, and who has loosed him from his bonds? I have made him a house in the wilderness, and the salt flats his dwelling. He scoffs at the roar of the city and hears no shouts of a whip master. He only roams the mountains for pasture and seeks after every patch of green.

84   God plans to pour forth His graces into the desolate desert of fallen man, so that from the wasteland life will blossom. God accomplished this when he poured all His graces upon Mary, who then brought forth the Incarnate Word. Lucifer thought this impossible for fallen man.

85   The Lord is speaking of a Woman who through her womb will send ice to cover up the waters of the abyss, the dwelling place of Satan.

86   As stated above, hail is reserved for the Enemy as his punishment.

87   Ice will seal up the abyss where Satan dwells. Cf. Canto XXXIII Dante's Inferno.

88   God asks Lucifer what good it will accomplish to gather the stars of heaven (i.e., the angels) under his banner.

89   God questions whether Lucifer can set himself up as the ruler of men.

90   God asks Lucifer if he understands that the whole purpose of heaven is directed toward the earth.

91   Lucifer.

92   When God formed man out of the dust of the earth.

93   Consider how God's Wisdom uniquely rests within the heart of man, unlike in any other creature, God specifically begins the list of animals with the Cock, the Herald of Dawn. This is a specific and pointed reference to Lucifer, the light bearer, the true Herald of Dawn.

94   'Herald of Dawn' a title attributed to Lucifer before the fall. This is the first instance of the Lord using an animal to describe Satan to man. Several more follow in order to illustrate Lucifer's devolution into Satan.

NOTES

Job
...39:9...

"Will the wild ox consent to serve you, and pass the nights by your dwelling? Will a rope bind him to plow or will he till the valleys after you? Will you trust him for his great strength and leave to him the fruits of your toil? Can you rely on him to thresh out your grain and gather in the yield of your threshing floor?

Job
...39:13...

"The wings of the ostrich beat idly; her plumage is lacking in the feathers of flight. When she leaves her eggs on the earth and deposits them in the sand, she is unmindful that a foot may tread upon them, that the wild beasts of the field may break them. She has been hardened from such concern, as if they were not hers, with no fear constraining her, for God has withheld wisdom from her and has no share in understanding. Endowed with swiftness of foot, she makes sport of the horse and rider.

Job
...39:19...

"Do you give the horse his strength, and endow his neck with splendor? Do you make the steed to quiver while his thunderous snort spreads terror? He jubilantly paws the earth and rushes in his might against the weapons of war. He laughs at fear and cannot be deterred; he turns not his back to the sword. Around him rattles the quiver, flashes the spear and the javelin. Frenzied and raging, he devours the ground; he holds not back at the sound of trumpets, but at each blast he cries, 'Aha!' He smells the battle even from afar, the shouts of the captains and the roar of the army.

Job
...39:26...

"Is it by your wisdom that the hawk waxes its feathers and soars, spreading its wings to the south? Does the eagle take flight at your command to build his nest in high places? On the cliff he dwells among the rocks and stony walls where there is no access. From thence he watches for his prey, and his eyes behold it from afar. His young ones greedily drink up blood; where the slain are, there is he.[95]

Job
...40:1...

The Lord proceeded to speak: "Will we have more arguing and contending with the Almighty by the Adversary? Let him who would correct God give answer!"

95 The animals God lists progress from innocent to increasingly depraved, mirroring Lucifer's descent as he falls from grace. Each of the animals depicts an attribute of Lucifer. The Cock is the herald of dawn, just as Lucifer is the morning star. The Lioness and Raven both kill in order to feed their young. The Goat and Doe both have offspring that leave their parent, which mirrors the fate of the First Son of Dawn. The wild Ass shows how Lucifer shirks off the commands of the Lord and seeks reckless freedom. The Ox has the greatest strength of all the beasts, just as Lucifer is the strongest of all the angels. The Ostrich is stripped of its power of flight, just as Lucifer after his rebellion. The horse is a creature of strength and valor but, if exposed to blood, craves war. Finally, the Hawk and the Eagle are creatures that feast on the carcasses of rotting flesh and 'greedily drink up blood'.

—————— *NOTES* ——————

But the Son of Man answered the Lord and the court: "Behold, I am the least among the court; what can my words answer you? I place my hand over my mouth. Though I have spoken once, I shall not do so again; though twice, I shall do so no more."

Job ...40:6...

Then the Lord again addressed the Son of Man out of the storm, the tempest of Lucifer. "Gird up your loins like a man. I will question you and you shall answer! Would you refuse to acknowledge my right? Would you condemn Me that man might be justified? Have you an arm like God, or can you thunder with a voice like His? Adorn yourself with grandeur and majesty; array yourself with glory and splendor? Let loose the fury of your wrath; tear down the wicked and shatter them? Bring down the haughty with a glance; bury them in the dust of the earth, in the Dark World imprison them?[96] If so then will I too acknowledge that your right hand can save you?[97]

Job ...40:15...

"Look and behold, besides you, I have made *Behemoth*[98] that feeds on the yield of the Earth[99] like an ox.[100] Behold the strength in his loins and the vigor in the muscles of his belly. He carries his tail like a cedar; the strength of his thighs is like that of cables. His bones are like pipes of bronze; his frame like iron rods.[101]

Job ...40:19...

"He came first, at the beginning of God's ways,[102] and was appointed taskmaster[103] over all; of all creatures he makes sport.[104] All the produce of the mountains is brought to him.[105]

Job ...40:21...

"Under the fig tree[106] he lies, in the coverts of the reedy swamp. He lurks in the shade, hiding himself among the thicket of the bank. If the river grows violent, he is not disturbed; he is tranquil though a torrent surges in his mouth.[107]

Job ...41:1...

"Who can capture him[108] by his eyes, or pierce his nostrils with a stake? Can you lead about *Leviathan*[109] with a hook or tie his tongue[110] with a cord? Can you put a ring in his nose or bar his jaw with a harness? Will he then make supplications with you, time after time, or address you with tender words? Will he make a covenant with you

96   What God does to Satan as punishment for tempting Adam and Eve.

97   Behold the great irony of God addressing Jesus who is on trial for the sins of humanity. Jesus indeed does have all such power and authority, and God will be condemned to justify the human race on the holy wood of the Cross. Jesus does lay down his life and by the strength of His own right hand take it up again.

98   Behemoth is the first image we are given to describe the spiritual nature of Lucifer, but it is not the last. This is not simply another animal used to illustrate an attribute of Satan; rather, it is an analogy to understand Lucifer's nature as a whole, before his fall.

99   A reference to Genesis 3:14, in which the Serpent is cursed to eat the dust of the earth. Here the horned bull/Behemoth eats up the grass of the earth. Man is both referred to as dust and grass in the Scriptures.

100   The ox provides additional insight into Lucifer's nature. In Hebrew, the word for Cherubim is the same as the word for ox. Thus, in the vulgate, the word 'cherub' is used for the word 'ox' to describe the first evangelist. See Ezekiel 10:14-15: "Quator autem facies habebat unum: facies una, facies *cherub*, et facies secunda, facies hominis: et in tertio facies leonis, et in quarto facies aquilae.

101   Bronze and iron are metals of war.

102   Lucifer was the first angel of God's creation.

103   The word "taskmaster" exemplifies Lucifer's relationship to the rest of creation. He views the rest of the world as slavish and subordinate.

104   Because Lucifer was first, he had a natural dominion over all of creation.

105   'Behemoth' is an aquatic creature, and the mountains represent the earth not covered by water. Thus, the natural order is reversed, and men dwelling on land serve Satan among the depths. This is a result of the Fall.

106   The Tree of Knowledge of Good and Evil was a fig tree, where Lucifer tempted Adam and Eve, and whose leaves they used afterward to cover themselves out of shame. The mystery of the fig tree is intertwined throughout all the Scriptures, from the Song of Songs, to Jesus' curse of the fig tree in the Gospel, to Revelation, where the stars of heaven fall like figs from a fig tree.

107   The torrent of water in his mouth represents the great power of Satan. For example, Revelation 12:15: "The serpent, however, spewed a torrent of water out of his mouth after the woman to sweep her away with the current."

108   Leviathan.

109   'Leviathan' is the most accurate Name to describe the pure nature of Satan. The Leviathan is a sea-dragon, a serpent of the sea. Its description shows how Satan cannot be subdued or stopped.

110   The forked tongue of Satan is a perilous weapon; no man could hope to quell his lies.

that you may have him as a servant forever?[111] Can you play with him, as with a bird? Can you trust him to a leash for the maidens of man?[112] Will friends bargain for him? Will he be divided up and sold to the nations?[113] Can you fill his hide with barbs, or his head with spears? Once you but lay a hand upon him, you shall remember no other battle, and speak no more!

Job
...41:9...

"Is he not relentless when aroused; who then would dare stand before him? Whosoever might vainly hope to do so need only see him and be overthrown! Who has assailed him and come off safe—whosoever under the heavens?[114]

Job
...41:12...

"I need hardly mention his limbs, the strength, and robustness of his armor. Who can strip off his outer garment, or penetrate his double corslet? Who can force open the doors of his mouth so close to his terrible teeth? Rows of scales line his back, tightly sealed together, fitted each so close to the next that no space intervenes, so joined one to the other that they hold fast and cannot be parted. When he sneezes, lightning flashes forth; his eyes are like those of a red dawn. Out of his mouth go forth fire-blasts; sparks of fire leaping forth. From his nostrils issue forth steam, as from a seething pot. His breath sets coals afire; flames pour from his mouth. Strength abides in his neck, want and terror leap before him.

Job
...41:25...

"His heart shall be as cold as stone and as hard as a smith's anvil.[115] When he rises up, the stars in heaven[116] shall fear, and shall purify themselves; the waves of the sea shall break and fall back.[117] Should the sword reach him, it will not prevail, nor will the spear, nor the dagger, nor the javelin. He regards iron as straw, and bronze as rotten wood. The arrow will not put him to flight; the stones of the sling are to him like stubble. Clubs he esteems as splinters; he laughs at the crash of spears.

Job
...41:30...

"The beams of the sun shall be under him, and he shall leave a trail of gold beneath him like mire.[118] He shall make the depths to boil like a pot; the sea to churn like oil in a kettle. Behind him he leaves a

111 The angels serve man out of love of him and God; they guide, enlighten, and protect. Serving man is the one thing that Satan will never be willing to do.

112 An allusion to the deep mystery of Satan's hatred for woman; no leash can make her safe from his attack. This hatred is shown concretely when Lucifer chooses to attack Eve rather than Adam.

113 Through Christ's death, the Church has authority over Satan.

114 St. Michael is the only creature to triumph over Satan and dispel him from heaven.

115 A 'hard heart' is a term used throughout the Pentateuch to describe someone who has turned his back on God.

116 Satan still holds real power, even among the Celestial Hierarchies.

117 Because the moon causes the tides, this shows Satan as the antithesis of the Moon, which is an image of the lesser light meant to govern the night.

118 Since Lucifer is the greatest natural being, the sun's rays are below him; his path deceptively resembles gold.

Leviathan

shining path; you would think the deep to have the venerable head of old age.[119] Upon the Earth there is not his like: him who was made intrepid, to fear no one.[120] All, however lofty, fear him; he is king over all the children of pride."[121]

Job
...42:1...

Then the Son of Man answered the Lord and said: "I know that You can do all things, and that no thought can be hid from You. Yet who is this, Leviathan, that hides counsel without knowledge?[122] Therefore, I have dealt with great things that I do not understand: things too wonderful for me, which I cannot know. Open Your ear, and I will utter from my mouth; I will ask and pray You answer. With the hearing of the ear, I have heard You, but now my eye has seen You! Therefore,

Job
...42:6

I gird up my loins like a man and do penance in dust and ashes."[123]

Thus, the trial of the Son of Man was consummate, and humanity was found worthy,[124] flesh would there be, the secret wisdom of God![125] The Son of Man accepted the verdict[126] of the Lord and all the evil that would befall the human race, for he saw the Wisdom of God.

Psalm
82:1...

Henceforth, the Lord God issued a decree from the Throne to Lucifer and all the stars of heaven:"The Lord God rises in divine councils, and gives judgment in the midst of the assembly of gods.[127] How long will you judge unjustly and favor the course of the wicked?" At this, the firstborn star, the herald of dawn, hung his head. "Defend the lowly and fatherless; render justice to the afflicted and needy! Rescue the lowly and poor; deliver man from the hand of the wicked! Or the gods[128] shall neither know nor understand, wandering about in darkness, and all the world's foundations shall shake!

"I declare to you, mankind: gods though you be, offspring of the Most High all of you, yet like any mortal you shall die; like any prince you shall fall."

Psalm
...82:8

So Lucifer, the Four Living Creatures, and all the stars shouted out at once, "Arise, O God, judge the Earth, for Yours are all the nations."

119 Part of his deception is that the depths, which are evil and separated from God, appear glowing with wisdom.

120 As the highest created being, Lucifer fears no other creature, but he also does not fear God, even though "the fear of God is the beginning of wisdom."

121 Pride is the root of all sin and is the seed of Satan. We are the children of pride ever since the fall of Adam, but Christ's death freed us from our accursed birthright, even though we can still choose to take it.

122 In this paragraph, man is grappling with the problem of evil, which he professes is "too wonderful" for him to understand. At the heart of his prayer, his "eye has seen," and looked upon the mercy of God made man. Therefore, he does "penance in dust and ashes," accepting death in obedience to God's providence. At the same time, this explains Leviathan's angst with the flesh, which limits the enfleshed soul but allows the greatest of gifts to be bestowed upon it.

123 It is fitting that the trial would end with man understanding death, for death is a natural effect of being enfleshed. It is an insurmountable evil, overcome only by Christ Jesus, who conquers death and unites us to the Father. Thus, seeing the good of God becoming man allows man to accept his fate as mortal; he knows both the good of the flesh and the evil of the flesh.

124 The entire trial was to determine whether or not it was wise to create flesh, for with flesh comes many things: Death, passions, physical needs, sex, and reproduction. Lucifer saw these things as evil because they distract and separate man from God, whereas angels are pure spirits in constant adoration of God.

125 Flesh is the greatest gift God could give. Although it does make man lower than the angels, it also makes men share one common nature. When God became man, all men became united to God because of this common nature. This is the wisdom of God that Lucifer could not accept: men, mortal flesh bags, could be eternally united to God.

126 The verdict of the 'Great Debate' is the Incarnation and ultimately the Suffering, Death, and Resurrection of Jesus. Christ accepts the salvific plan of God to redeem and to unite the human race with the Divine.

127 All the angels gathered together in the celestial court. Angels are sometimes referred to as gods, which is fitting, given a proper understanding of their nature.

128 Christ himself quotes Psalm 82 in John 10:34: "Jesus answered them, "Is it not written in your law, 'I declare, "You are gods"'?" Thus, men are also called gods, though we wonder about in darkness and confusion.

IN THE BEGINNING

John
1:1

o the Lord God arose[129] from His Throne, and, with a voice that thundered in the deep, proclaimed: "In the Beginning was the Word, and the Word was with God, and the Word was God." At the Lord's decree, a radiant glory and splendor burst forth, the likes of which had never been seen before in all the heavens. So every god that dwelt in heaven, every star found in the sky, began to sing in chorus, and all the sons of God shouted for joy![130]

Genesis
1:2...

All the stars of Heaven then bore witness to their own creation, the creation of the Heavens and the Earth, when the Earth was *formless* and *void*, and darkness[131] abounded in the deep. All was the abyss, and the abyss was all, yet the Beloved, the Spirit of God, soared upon the surface of the deep. The Lord God Most High, Creator of all, then whispered the hallowed Word of creation in Divine silence, and all the assembly of Heaven, every star from east to west, fell prostrate, hiding their faces and sheltering their ears.

Genesis
...1:3...

"Let[132] there be Light!" And there was light, in such perfection and abundance that no god in Heaven could bear to look upon it. The light boomed forth like a hundred million swords of heaven crashing into the boundless darkness of the deep.[133] God looked upon the light and saw how good it was, so He separated the light from the darkness, eternally making holy the light. God named the light 'day' and the darkness He named 'night.'[134]

Genesis
...1:5

The morning star arose first and bore the light of God most pure.[135] From him in due accord, the rest of the stars arose and bore witness to the splendor of Light, which pierced the formlessness of nonexistence. Again all the stars sang in chorus, a melody to traverse the heavens, radiating with the holy light of God.

IGNATIAN CONTEMPLATION

129 In ancient theology, the Lord God never rises from his throne. When He does, it is significant. For example, Acts 7:55: "But he [Stephen], filled with the holy Spirit, looked up intently to heaven and saw the glory of God and Jesus standing at the right hand of God, and he said, 'Behold, I see the heavens opened and the Son of Man standing at the right hand of God.' Jesus stands to welcome the first martyr into heaven.

130 Job 37:7. The angels being pure minds, celestial intelligences, actually witness their own creation, and being so overwhelmed participate by adding to the Word of God with their own shouts of Joy.

131 Genesis 1:2. This verse describes the primordial darkness that existed before creation. It is pure evil, because it is absolute nothingness, the Abyss in which the Leviathan dwells. Thus, when God creates, He is banishing the nothingness and forming existence.

132 'Let' is the hallowed Word of Creation. It is neither the command of a tyrant nor the plea of the powerless, but rather the word of a lover, giving what the beloved already desires. It is the word Creation eagerly awaited. "Let" is not only the first word of the first creation, but also the first Word of the second creation uttered by Mary, Queen of Existence, at the conception of the new world. This sense is preserved even in Hebrew or the Latin 'fiat,' where 'let' is inherent in the verb voice.

133 The Light and the Darkness did not dispel each other, but rather were intertwined amongst themselves. This is the perfect example of an unstoppable force meeting an immovable object, for light is never swallowed by darkness, but the void into which it shines is infinite.

134 God sees the goodness that is the light, so He separates the light from the darkness. In Hebrew, to be holy is to be set apart or separated; thus, God makes the light holy, unlike the darkness, which is evil. Nevertheless, God uses the darkness in his creation, giving it form and naming it "night," ever governed by the light.

135 This is Lucifer's namesake: lux: light and ferre: to bring.

Lucifer saw first, for his vision was most keen: the light resembled the likeness of a tree. Its branches extending upward to the heights of Heaven, beyond the reach of any star, stretching into the Divine Darkness[136] where Ancient of Days and Wisdom rest. The trunk of the Celestial Tree, whose majesty and grandeur was like that of the arm of God, stood towering over the darkness. The trunk itself was so immense that thousands upon thousands upon thousands of stars stretched wing to wing could not comprise its girth, for it was the Pillar of Heaven.[137] Yet, upon its branches it bore no leaves.[138] Thus, evening came and morning followed—the First Day.

Genesis
1:5...

Genesis
...1:6...

Then God said, "Let there be a dome, a firmament, in the midst of the deep, and let it divide the waters above from the waters below." And so it happened; God stretched forth His hands, one atop the other, toward the formless abyss, and, piercing the deep, formed a chasm between His hands. He then blew a mighty gust of wind into his hands, and the waters above were separated from the waters below.[139]

Genesis
...1:8

The Celestial Tree breathed in the Spirit of God, giving the tree life. Its branches grew up and out in every direction, while its roots grew down and out in every direction.[140] The roots were sunk like pedestals into the dark abyss, for they were the pillars of the Earth, while the branches of the Celestial Tree became the Heavens in all their glorious array. God named the firmament-dome 'the sky.'[141] Thus, evening came and morning followed—the Second Day.[142]

Genesis
...1:9...

Then God said, "Let the waters under the sky be gathered into a single basin, so that dry land may appear." And so it happened; God soothed and tamed the waters below the sky so that they might have peace, and He named the waters below 'the sea.' From this peace blossomed dry land to be a medium between the sky and the sea. Mountains formed and penetrated the clouds and knew the sky, while the shore formed to know and bear all the moods of the sea. So God named the dry land 'the earth.'

136 The "Divine Darkness" is the abode of the Holy Trinity, not the darkness of the Abyss. It is not the darkness caused by lack of light, but rather a sacred darkness from the superabundance of light, beyond the scope of any created light.

137 Proverbs 11:30. The Celestial Tree is the key to understanding creation and salvation. The Tree is the Pillar of Righteousness, the only reason why Heaven is Heaven, for it bears within itself the reordering of creation: it is the harbinger of Christ crucified.

138 The angels do not yet exist.

139 These are the primordial waters that are "formless and void." God is giving form to the formless, and is making a space for man.

140 The Celestial Tree forms the Celestial Sphere. The branches comprise the upper hemisphere, and the roots comprise the lower hemisphere. Only at the base of the tree do we find earth and man.

141 God does not call the Second Day good, although he does so for the other days. This would seem curious at first, but is more comprehensible in light of ancient Hebrew cosmology. The "pre-universe" was a tumultuous sea of black, pure nothingness, the closest image possible to unmitigated nothingness. Thus, these primordial waters are in themselves evil, for their essence is to be without any goodness or being. On the Second Day, God does not actually create anything, only a division among the waters.

142 The Second Day illustrates how God is creating a series of spheres, one inside the other, starting with the outermost. The first sphere was made on the First Day, the upper half pure light and the lower half pure darkness; within it is the sphere of water made on the Second Day. The waters above glow blue with holy light, while the waters below grow dark because they conceal the darkness. In this way the waters bind the earth to both waters, the sea bearing the darkness and the sky bearing the light. God is working inward, which is key to understanding Genesis and God's intent for man.

NOTES

Genesis
1:11...

He then looked upon the earth and saw how good it was, so His heart was moved, and He said: "Let the earth bring forth vegetation: every kind of plant that bears seed and every kind of fruit tree on earth that bears fruit with its seeds in it."[143] And so it happened: God placed His hand upon the womb of the earth, and the earth was filled with life and bore witness to the touch of the Divine.[144] The earth brought forth every kind of plant that bears seed, and every kind of fruit tree on earth that bears fruit with its seeds in it. The whole of the earth was filled with His love and bore the fruit of life.[145] God then looked upon the earth and saw the life that was its child, and smiled at how good it was. Thus, evening came and morning followed—the Third Day.

Lucifer, bearer of the Light of God, and the rest of his kin then bore witness to the formless becoming form.[146] The days fell upon each other: the first upon the second, and the second upon the third, sphere within sphere within sphere,[147] until formlessness was obliterated from creation. Yet all of creation was still void: the spheres of the first, second, and third days were judged and found to be empty, void of all living creatures.

Genesis
...1:14...

So God said: "Let there be lights in the firmament of Heaven, to separate the day from the night. Let them mark the seasons, the days, and the years, serving as luminaries in the firmament of heaven, to shed light upon the Earth."[148] And so it happened: God made the two great lights, the greater one to govern over the day, and the lesser one to govern over the night, and He made the stars. God set them in the firmament of Heaven, to shed light upon the earth, to govern the day and the night, to separate the light from the darkness.

Genesis
...1:18

Lucifer and all the great multitude of Heaven looked up and bore witness to the glory of God, bore witness to their own creation.[149] The great Celestial Tree of God blossomed and bore two perfect fruits. The greater shined with the warmth of gold and the lesser shined with the luster of silver. The greater governed over the day, for where He was darkness was not, and the lesser governed over the night, for she

143 This is the first command of creation, the first charge given by God, that life is to perpetuate life. This gift of fecundity is the very purpose of life, and is the first example of God's marital relationship with creation.

144 God is overshadowing creation in order to bestow it with life. Mary experiences the same thing in the new creation, when she stands in for all creation and bears the fruit of God's love.

145 It is on this day that God creates the Tree of Life and the Tree of Knowledge of good and evil as the center of all the glories of the Earth, and for the glorification of man to be.

146 The first three days are dedicated to solving the problem of formlessness. Form is in reference to three spheres: light, water, and earth. Each sphere will be filled in due accord in the next three corresponding days.

147 This illustrates perfectly the centrality of the earth in cosmic creation. God is working down and up, filling in the gaps as He approaches the earth. Centrality is an ancient way of understanding purpose, and thus the First and Second Days are accomplished in order to provide a fitting and hospitable place for the dry land.

148 Here God is explaining the purpose of the luminaries: to shed light upon the earth. This is a service not of dominion, but of selfless devotion.

149 On the Fourth Day of creation the angels were created; they are the first 'beings' to be created, and due to their peculiar nature of being pure spirit/mind, they are able to witness their own creation with perfect clarity.

The Fourth Day

was the light in the darkness, and all darkness was under her heel. A king and queen of Heaven, to govern over all time: the seasons, the days, and the years filling the earth with their light. The great Celestial Tree then budded and brought forth every kind and variation of leaf, each shining with a unique and precious light.[150] The leaves were beyond count and were hung throughout the great expanse of Heaven, perpetually shining their light upon the Earth. They were handed over to the queen to shine with her in the darkness, in testimony to her grace. God looked upon the heavens filled with their radiant glory shining upon the earth, and He saw how good it all was. Thus, evening came and morning followed—the Fourth Day.[151]

Genesis 1:20...

Then God said: "Let[152] the waters teem with an abundance of living creatures, and let birds fly above the earth across the firmament of heaven." And so it happened; God created the great sea monsters and all the kinds of swimming creatures with which the waters teem, and all the kinds of winged beasts, which flock above the earth.

So Lucifer and his stars looked down from heaven and saw the dome above the earth and the dome below the earth, how they began to teem with life. The depths of the sea filled with every kind and variant of life, while the heights of the sky filled with every manner of winged beast. Above the earth, the crest of the sky knew the soar of the eagle, and, below the earth, the chasm of the sea knew the slither of the sea monster.

Genesis ...1:22...

God saw how good it was and could not constrain Himself, so He blessed[153] them saying, "Be fruitful and multiply! Fill the waters of the seas, and let the birds multiply above the earth!" Upon hearing these words Lucifer turned in thought, 'What is such a blessing as this that it is reserved for such lowly creatures, and withheld from the heights of Heaven?' Thus Lucifer pondered in his heart the first blessing of creation.[154] Evening came and morning followed—the Fifth Day.[155]

150 Each leaf has its own unique light because each angel is its own unique being, similar to no other angel. This is because angels possess no matter, and are therefore differentiated only by form; thus every angel is its own species, as different from each other angel as a slug is from a sloth. This also means the different possible angels are infinite, whereas material beings have an intrinsic limit on possible variations.

151 The Fourth Day fills and provides governance of the First Day. The two great lights and the stars govern over the light and the darkness. They order the light of the First Day, directing it toward the earth.

152 Every day God begins by saying 'Let', for it is the word of creation; God provides the act to fulfill the natural potencies. Thus, the Fourth, Fifth, and Sixth Days of creation are not random implements of God but rather natural tendencies. The land, sea, and air wanted to give rise and be filled with life.

153 This is the first specific blessing of creation mentioned in Genesis.

154 This illustrates something vital, which is often overlooked. Not all blessings increase as one ascends higher in the order of creation. Animals are specifically blessed with sex and offspring because they are corporeal, a blessing that simply cannot be given to bodiless intelligences.

155 The Fifth Day fills and provides governance for the Second Day: birds have mastery over the air and fish govern over the sea, leaving only land empty.

The Fifth Day

Genesis
...1:24...
Then God said: "Let the earth bring forth every kind of living creature: cattle, creeping things, and wild animals of all kinds." And so it happened: God created every kind of wild animal, every kind of cattle, and every kind of creeping thing that crawled upon the earth.

Again the stars looked down from heaven and said, "There are living creatures above the earth and below the earth, and now there are living creatures upon the earth. How great is God to obliterate Void from creation! The Formless has been given form, and the Void has been filled with the living. Creation is now..."[156]

But before the great multitude of stars could finish, God looked and beheld how good it was, and His heart was overcome with love.

Genesis
...1:26...
So He turned to Himself, the Divine Council, and said: "Let Us[157] make man in Our *Image*,[158] and after Our *Likeness*. Let them have dominion[159] over the fish of the sea, the birds of the air, and over the cattle and all the creeping things that creep upon the earth." And so, it happened: God created man in His image, in the Divine Image[160] He created him: male and female He created *them*.

So Lucifer and the many stars looking down from Heaven beheld the creation of man in the Image of God; male and female they glimpsed Him, and in that moment they beheld more of God than had been seen in the highest of heavens.[161]

Genesis
...1:28...
God blessed[162] them, saying, "Be fruitful and multiply; fill the Earth and subdue it![163] Have dominion over the fish of the sea, the birds of the air, and over all the living creatures that move upon the earth." And God said, "Behold! I give you every seed-bearing plant which is upon the face of the earth, and every tree that has seed-bearing fruit on it to be your food;[164] and to all the animals of the land, all the birds of the air, and to all that have the breath of life I give every green plant for food."

156 Creation from a natural perspective would have been complete without man; no part of creation lacks a governor. However, from a supernatural perspective, the universe would have no purpose without him. Man is a special act of God; though he is created from the dust of the earth, he is not bound to the Sixth Day. Man was created for the Seventh Day, the end and center of creation, and thus he has dominion over all the other days.

157 There are few times in Scripture where God uses the plural 'We' instead of the singular 'I'; this is only when He is speaking amongst Himself. Faulty interpretations say that God is speaking to the angels; however, the angels do not have the power of generation as God does. This is the first indication in Scripture that God is a Triune God, as any perfect being would be.

158 'Likeness' is in reference to God's nature, a self-mover with rationality and life. This we share in common with the angels.

159 Here God hands over dominion of all the physical world, for man has governance of the governors. However, there is no mention of the celestial stars in this proclamation. This is because we do not naturally have dominion over the angels. Rather, since they are naturally greater than us, they must choose to serve us by shedding light upon the earth, rather than being slaves and forced to serve us, as the ox or carrier pigeon does. All this changes with the Incarnation of Christ; in the new order, Mary is queen of the angels, and a Man sits upon the throne of the Almighty.

160 The Divine Image, above and beyond the 'likeness' of reason and will, unites us to God, for it mirrors the triune personhood of God. This is confirmed by scripture, which here expounds the sexual nature of man: 'Male and Female He created them.' Thus, only through the union of the sexes in marriage does man consummate the Divine Image, in a love so real it produces a third person, one family comprising three persons.

161 The preeminent mystery of the Most Holy Trinity is the source and summit of all mysteries in the Church. The wisest angel in the highest heaven was not able to comprehend such a sublime and edifying mystery of the Triune nature of God; this most sacred truth was only manifest through the Holy and Divine Revelation of Sacred Scripture itself. Further, this is the moment in which Michael, one of the lowest angels, saw most keenly the mystery of the Trinity encapsulated in the 'one flesh' of man and woman, the Image of God Himself. This deeply profound understanding of God as Trinity is what elevates Michael to saint and Prince of the Heavenly Host.

162 Consider the first blessing, the first 'productive' command of God given to man and his wife; how through this command all the Earth would be glorified, transformed into the Garden of God (and through the Earth the whole Cosmos as well). This first 'productive' command must then be looked at in light of the first 'prohibitive' command given by God not to eat from the Tree of Knowledge of Good and Evil, for these two commandments are two sides of the same coin. They are both for the glorification of man and the Cosmos.

163 'Fill the earth and subdue it' is an additional command given by God to man and woman that is withheld from every other creature, including the angels.

164 Man did not eat the flesh of animals in the Garden of Eden, which seems to be in accord with Genesis 9:3. "Any living creature that moves about shall be yours to eat; I give them all to you as I did the green plants. Only meat with its lifeblood still in it you shall not eat." Here God even compares the meat that he gives to the green plants that he gave man at the beginning.

And so, as it was said it was done: God Almighty by word of mouth[165] brought forth all creation out of nothing. God saw everything He had made and behold it was *very good*.[166] Evening came and morning followed—the Sixth Day.[167]

Thus the Heavens and the earth and all their array were completed. Lucifer, the Light Bearer of God, canticled a song to the Lord for His conquest over all that was formless and void and over the waters of the abyss. "The Lord hath reigned, He is robed with beauty: the Lord is robed with strength, and girded with might, for He hath established the world, which shall not be moved. Thy throne is prepared from of old: Thou art from everlasting, O Lord! The floods have lifted, O Lord: the floods have lifted up their voices. The floods have lifted up their waves. More powerful than the roar of many waters, more powerful than the surges of the sea, most powerful in the Heavens is the Lord. Thy decree is firmly established, holiness belongs to Thy house, O Lord, for all the length of days."[168]

God then contemplated His creation, for on the Seventh Day, God was finished with all His work He had done. On the Seventh Day God rested from all the work He had undertaken.[169] From the rest of God, peace blossomed and settled upon the Seventh Day, and in that peace God's work could be seen. So the assembly of the heavenly court began to sing as the morning light filled creation, "Hallelujah! Praise ye the Lord from the Heavens; praise Him from atop the high places. Praise Him all ye Celestial beings; praise Him all ye host of Heaven. Praise Him, O sun and moon; praise Him all ye stars of light. Praise Him ye Heaven of Heavens, and let the waters above the heavens praise the name of the Lord. For He spoke and they were made, He commanded and they were created. He hath established them forever and for ages of ages to come. He hath made a decree, and it shall not pass away. Praise the Lord from the Earth ye sea monsters, and all ye depths. Fire, hail, snow, and ice; All ye stormy winds, which fulfill His word;

Marginal notes:
Psalm 93:1...
Psalm ...93:5
Genesis ...2:1...
Psalm 148:1...

165 All creation is through the Word, that is, the second person of the Trinity.

166 In Hebrew, this phrase is denoting the elevated or exceedingly great state of God's work. While some argue this refers to the whole of the Universe, and some that it refers to man, these opinions are only fully true when taken together; man is only a pinnacle when taken amidst the whole of creation, while the Universe would be without purpose if man had not been created. It would be as a master clock, working seamlessly and perpetually, but without telling time, for there is no history without man. It is, however, important to note that God does not use the superlative; the Universe and man are not made perfect, they have not reached their final cause. This of course only occurs through the Incarnation, where Creator and creation meet, where God Himself enters the Universe as man.

167 Numerology is very important in Jewish tradition. The number of the beast, 666, literally comes from the Sixth Day, wherein the beasts are created, while three is the number of perfection or completion. The triple six therefore represents man ignoring his call to the peace of the Seventh Day, and losing himself completely to the beast.

168 Psalm 93. Lucifer is praising the Lord for conquering the primordial evil of non-being, the infinite abyss of formlessness and void.

169 Creation can be seen as a war between God and nothingness, which God wins through Word of mouth alone. The Seventh Day shows that creation is not an indefinite thing, or an eternal war between good and evil, but is a completed deed, fulfilled through the might of the Lord. God's rest is the victory of love over nothingness. Unlike our rest, this rest is the perfect and complete state to which all His actions in creation tended.

NOTES

Mountains and all ye hills; Fruit trees and all ye cedars; Beasts wild and tame; Ye serpents and all feathered fowl; Ye kings of earth and all its inhabitants; Ye princes and all judges of the earth; Young men and maidens: let the old with the young praise the name of the Lord. For His name alone is exalted, majestic above the Heavens and the Earth. The Lord has lifted high the horn of man to the glory of all His saints, the holy men of God, the ones chosen to be near their God.

Psalm
...148:14

Hallelujah!"

So God blessed the Seventh Day and hallowed it, making it holy, because on that day God rested from all His work which He had done in creation. Thus, evening never came upon the Seventh Day,[170] for it was consecrated to the Lord. Such is the genesis of the Heavens and

Genesis
...2:4

the Earth at their creation.[171]

Peace of the Seventh Day

170 There is a notable lack of an end to this Day; while God rests, no evening and morning set off an end to God's peace. The Seventh Day is therefore eternal, the unending joy of God, at peace with the work He has done. This illustrates the importance of the Sabbath day as the third commandment dictates, for to keep holy the Sabbath is to join ourselves to God's life-giving plan for creation, to become holy by contemplating as He does the goodness of all His works.

171 The first story of creation is a full and true account, sufficient on its own. The second story of creation is an expounding of the first, not a literal second creation.

 **NOTES**

WITHIN THE BEGINNING

Job
1:6...

At that time, when the sons of God[172] came to present[173] themselves before the Lord, Lucifer also came among them.

And the Lord said unto Lucifer, "From whence do you come?"

Lucifer answered the Lord and said, "I have roamed round about the Earth and walked through it."

So the Lord said to Lucifer, "Have you considered my servant Adam? That there is none like unto him in all the world, a blameless and upright man, fearing God and avoiding evil?"

But Lucifer answered the Lord and said, "Is it in vain that Adam is a God-fearing man? Hast Thou not made a hedged garden about him, and all that he has, on every side? Hast Thou not blessed the work of his hands, and given him possession of the Earth?[174] Truly, what is man that Thou art mindful of him?"

Job
...1:10

Psalm
8:4

Therefore, the Lord arose from His Throne and the hand of the Lord came upon Lucifer and brought him forth in the Spirit of the Lord, which settled upon the Mountain of God. And the Lord proclaimed to Lucifer, "Harbinger of Dawn and first of your kin, I have brought you forth unto the day when the Lord God made the Earth and the Heavens, so that you, choirmaster,[175] who looked down from heaven with vision most keen, might now see the work of my hands from within rather than without."[176]

Ezekiel
37:1

Genesis
2:4...

Lucifer looked about from atop the Mountain of God, yet there was no plant of the field or shrub on the earth, and no grass of the plain had sprouted up, for the Lord had sent no rain upon the earth, and there was no man to till the soil. But a stream[177] was welling up from atop the mountainside and was watering the whole face of the Earth.

IGNATIAN CONTEMPLATION

172 "Sons of God" is a term for the angels, referring more to their nature than their eventual occupation (the choirs).

173 The angels came to present themselves to the Lord that they might be assigned into their specific choirs. Once creation was complete, the governance and maintenance of the universe would be handed over to the angels, which chose to serve that aspect of creation which most showed each one the glory of God. For example, Virtues govern over the elements of the universe, maintaining every aspect of the physical universe.

174 In Job, this paragraph has "But now stretch forth your hand and touch all that he has, and surely he will curse you to your face." God allows Satan to afflict Job just as He allows Leviathan to tempt Adam and Eve.

175 'Choirmaster' is a new term for Lucifer; while the celestial intelligences have not yet been given their tasks, God is showing Lucifer his role, should he choose to serve.

176 "Within rather than without." This is the difference between the first story of creation and the second story of creation in the Book of Genesis. The first story shows the order of the universe, while the second story shows God's intent for the universe, namely, man is the pinnacle of creation, and all things are ordered toward him.

177 This is the water which flows from the side of Christ and is the river spoken of in Ezekiel 47.

Overlooking Paradise

So Lucifer looked on as the Lord God Most High knelt upon

Genesis
...2:6...

the Earth, reaching into the flesh of the ground where the life-giving waters had been welling up. The Lord God then formed man out of the clay of the ground, sculpting him in the *Likeness* of the Divine.[178]

Song of Songs
4:9

The Lord God then arose saying, "You have captivated my heart, my betrothed, my friend; you have captivated my heart."

The heart of the Lord God Almighty was then indeed overcome

Song of Songs
5:12

with compassion, and His eyes were as doves beside running waters. So the Lord God bestowed upon man the Kiss of Spiration,[179] and the man's nostrils were filled with the fiery breath of life, and so man

Genesis
...2:7

became a living soul.[180]

There, creature and Creator stood locked in the eternal stare, until the eyes of Man fell dim with childish tears, and his vision of God obscured. On his knees he fell before the Creator with not the strength to lift his head. So the Lord God, Father of Man, knelt down toward his son and held out His hand. Together they rose, and the Lord wiped away every tear from his eyes, so that man's vision might rest on God.[181]

Lucifer pondered over the creature called man: "What is man that the Lord loves him so? Is he a spirit imprisoned in the flesh? Or a beast of the Earth, some favored pet of the Almighty? Why has the Lord given His *Likeness* to such a creature of the Earth? Is it not cruel to place the sanctity of mind in such a dishonorable vessel as flesh?"

Genesis
2:8...

The Lord God then planted a garden in Eden, in the east, and He placed there the man whom he had formed. Out of the ground the Lord God made grow every tree that is pleasant to sight and good for food, with the Tree of Life[182] in the middle of the garden, and the Tree of Knowledge of Good and Evil.[183]

Genesis
...2:10...

A river rose out of Eden to water the garden; beyond the mount it divided and became the four rivers.[184] The name of the first river is the Pishon; it is the one that flows throughout the whole land of Havilah,

178 "Likeness" is key to understanding Man, for it is what separates us from the animals. Animals do not bear a Likeness to God; lacking a rational soul, they do not share in God's own mind as men and Angels do. Note the lack of "Image" at this moment in the story, for, as God tells us in Genesis 1:27, it is "Male and Female" that is the "Image of God." Thus, since Eve has not been created yet, man does not reflect the Divine Image yet. Angels, therefore, do not bear His Image, unable to come together in engendered love to produce a third person of love. Only by having both an ennobled mind and an enfleshed animality can man bear the awesome plan of the Almighty: to enter into His creation and be joined to it in the flesh, as Jesus Christ.

179 The "Kiss of Spiration" is the breath of life, bestowed upon man and man alone. While it is easy to imagine God blowing in Adam's face, it is a much more intimate scene. God is breathing in through Adam's mouth, filling our nostrils with His Spirit, and inflating our lungs for the first time. God is teaching Adam how to spirate, to take part in the breath of the spirit.

180 "Living Soul" is specifically used here to show that there is no differentiation between Body and Soul.

181 This is a microcosm for all of Salvation History.

182 The Tree of Life is the Cross, on which hangs its fruit, Jesus Christ. The Tree of Life was God's plan from the beginning, bestowing a permanent sacrament of God's love upon man. God is forever united with man in the Incarnation, His selfless love forever witnessed in His crucifixion, and He is repeatedly given to His Church in the Blessed Sacrament. These actions are the sewing, reaping, and enjoying of the fruits of the Tree of Life.

183 Understanding the Tree of Knowledge of Good and Evil is more complicated than understanding the Tree of Life. It will be further explained as the story progresses, but this much is essential to start: knowledge of good and evil allows man to love properly, since knowledge is prerequisite to love. It is for this reason that Aristotle said that happiness consists in a life of virtue, training oneself to act according to the knowledge of the good and to avoid what is evil.

184 The one river which divides into four rivers symbolizes Christ and his good news. Christ preached one Gospel to the Apostles, but after he ascended into Heaven, the rest of the world receives his good news through the four living accounts of his life, the four Gospels.

where there is fine gold. The gold of that land is excellent; bdellium and onyx can also be found there. The name of the second river is the Gihon; it is the one that flows throughout the whole land of Cush. The name of the third river is the Tigris; it is the one that flows east of Assyria. The fourth river is the Euphrates.

Genesis
...2:15...
The Lord God then took the man and settled him in the Garden of Eden to cultivate and care for it, to guard and to garden.[185] And so, the Lord God commanded[186] the man[187] saying: "You may eat freely of every tree of the Garden,[188] but of the Tree of Knowledge of Good and Evil you shall not *take and eat*,[189] for the moment you *eat* of it you shall surely die, and dead shall you die."[190]

So the man went off to guard and garden as the Lord God had commanded.

The Lord God then turned to the Light Bearer, who had been watching, and before the Tree of Knowledge of Good and Evil
Ezekiel
28:12...
declared: "You have been stamped with the seal of perfection, of complete wisdom and of perfect beauty. You are in Eden, the garden of God; every precious stone is your covering: ruby, topaz, and emerald; chrysolite, onyx, and jasper; sapphire, turquoise, and beryl.[191] Of gold are your pendants and jewelry made; on the day you were created they were prepared for you! You shall be the anointed guardian Cherubim,[192] for so shall I ordain you if you so choose to serve, and you shall reside
Ezekiel
...28:16
on the holy mount of God and walk among the fiery stones.

To you, O morning star, son of dawn, and first of your kin, I entrust the highest and most precious truth, the Tree of Knowledge of Good and Evil.[193] Lucifer, bear the light of truth! For the fruit of the Tree of Knowledge of Good and Evil is most precious, holding the Divine Secret, the secret of man's flesh, his nakedness between good and evil.[194] . . .

185   The words "cultivate" and "guard" denote that Man is being appointed king of the earth, and as king he has two jobs: to make fruitful all that is entrusted to him, and to protect it from all threat and harm. Throughout Scripture, the superiority of the crown is always equated with service: "The Son of Man did not come to be served, but to serve, and to give his life as a ransom for many" (Matthew 20:28). Kingship is not a distant superiority, but caring stewardship. Adam's role as king is vital to understanding his interactions with Eve and the Serpent.

186   This is the first command God gives to creation in the second creation story in Genesis. Since the second creation story shows creation from within rather than from without, it is fitting that the command concerns Man's soul.

187   Note God gave this command to Adam before the creation of Eve; therefore, Eve's knowledge of the command must have come from Adam, especially with a proper understanding of Adam's preternatural priesthood. Consider how God appoints Adam as the preternatural priest of both the Earth and the family; it is his duty to serve as mediator between God and creation, as Steward of the Garden. It is this understanding of Adam's priesthood that is key to understanding the Fall of mankind, and how he was entrusted with the passing on of the commandment to Eve.

188   This includes the Tree of Life. Adam and Eve were completely free to eat from the Tree of Life at any time; however, the natural progression goes first through the Tree of Knowledge; only knowing what it means to be good as an enfleshed being can prepare us for receiving the greatest good of the flesh: the enfleshment of the Life of God.

189   The command not to take and eat of it has made many believe that the fruit itself was evil. However, the first creation story in Genesis shows that everything that is is good, for God cannot create anything evil in itself. Thus, the Tree of Knowledge of Good and Evil, being at the very center of the Paradise God created for man, cannot be evil, and its fruit cannot be bad or harmful; rather, the evil must lie in the disobedient taking of the fruit. Contemplate, further, this first 'prohibitive' command of God, for it is not by accident that the phrasing is specifically contrasted with the great 'positive' command of our Lord at the Last Supper, "to take and eat…" Draw then your minds to the sanctity of the Fruit and how the sacred knowledge housed in the fruit is too precious to be taken; like the Eucharist, it can only be given freely by God to man.

190   This wording is crucial. God is not speaking of normal bodily death, but of something far worse: the double death of the soul. The first death of the soul is sin, which separates us from God, just as the soul is separated from the body in bodily death. The second death of the soul is mentioned in Revelation 20:14—permanent separation from God in Hell. Before Christ, all men were doomed to die this double death, prisoners of Hell. True death is separation from God.

191   These stones are not the same as the twelve stones prescribed to the woman and her priestly order in the Book of Revelation, but rather these nine stones represent the nine choirs of the Celestial Hierarchy of angels.

192   Cherubim are angels of truth. While there were no choirs before the fall, all the angels could in a sense be called 'Cherubim' through their essence, as beings of knowledge.

193   Lucifer was not just any Cherubim, but the Highest Cherubim in charge of the highest truth. Lucifer was the taskmaster of all truth; thus the Tree of Knowledge of Good and Evil was his by right.

194   Man's flesh is the Divine Secret, at the heart of God's plan for creation. Man can exist between good and evil, which allows for Divine Mercy. But such revelations come at the ends of stories, not middles.

. . . It is far too precious of a gift to be taken; such a gift can only be given. So I ask you, Herald of Truth, will you be My messenger, My angel,[195] and give man the *good news*?"[196]

Though Lucifer replied: "Lord, am I not Your Light Bearer? Did You not choose me on the day I was created? Did You not conceive of me first at the beginning of Your ways, and did You not appoint me taskmaster over all? Did I not behold Your light before there were stars in the sky? Before sun and moon shed forth their light, was I not there, lending ear to Your counsels and delighting in Your decrees? O Lord, who else can say they have clung to You from the beginning? Who else can say they are the confidant of God?

"Is this not why You have made me first in nature, fashioned me Lucifer, conduit of Divine Light, through which all light and truth of God enters the Universe? I have borne Your light and promulgated Your decrees; I have heralded the dawn, and, through me, the great multitude have come to know You, shining with Your own light throughout the heavens.

"Now You have brought me into the Day of the Lord, to the garden of God, and placed before me the Tree of Knowledge of Good and Evil, a wisdom not revealed in light, but concealed in the flesh of a fruit.[197] What truth is there that is born on a tree, yet withheld from the heights of heaven?"

So the Lord then made a great wind blow through the Tree of Knowledge of Good and Evil, and the Glory of the Lord was over Lucifer's head, and there appeared something like a throne, which surpassed in beauty any sapphire stone, and, seated above the likeness of the throne, was a figure whose form was the likeness of a man. A nebula surrounded the enthroned and was of the resemblance of polished amber, with the radiance of fire enclosed on all sides within it. Such was it from the loins up and from the loins down,[198] the great radiance of fire and brilliance of light radiating from the man.

Ezekiel
1:26...

195 By performing this deed, Lucifer would have accepted the Lord's command and chosen to serve God through a service to man. This would have made Lucifer into an angel proper, for 'angel' means messenger.

196 Lucifer was charged with giving the first good news, the news of Christ, concealed within the sacramental fruit of the Tree of knowledge of Good and Evil. This suggests the choir of angel that Lucifer would have naturally belonged to is that of the choir of Cherubim, for we know the four-faced angel described in Ezekiel 1:6 is a Cherubim, and the Four 'Evangelim' are Cherubim tasked with the duty of spreading the Gospel of Christ.

197 Turn your mind toward the immense love of God, how He most tenderly places the most essential truth about human nature in a fruit, created solely to be eaten and enjoyed by man, beautiful to the eye, good for food, and desirable for gaining wisdom. God desires to make us happy and wants to reveal Himself in ways that are uniquely human; there was no greater gift God had planned than the fruits from the Tree of Knowledge of Good and Evil and the Tree of Life, gifts He is determined to give us even after our tragic fall from grace.

198 Ponder for a moment the peculiar wording of Scripture, that the Holy Spirit chooses the loins, not only to emphasize that the figure is a man, but that it is the center of his radiance. This is the part of the body that Adam shamefully covers after he eats the fruit, and conversely the part of Christ that is exposed by the Romans in order to shame our Lord, though in so doing they only added to His glory.

NOTES

Just as the resplendence of a bow among the clouds on a dreary day, so, too, was the brilliance of light that surrounded the enthroned.[199] This was the appearance of the Glory of the Lord in the *likeness* of man, which Lucifer beheld in the branches of the Tree at the center of the garden.

Ezekiel
...1:28

Lucifer, having seen the vision of God in the likeness of man, fell on his face and whispered: "*Immanuel...* God's dwelling is with the human race?"

Revelation
21:3

He then arose and said: "Unthinkable for the Lord to do wrong, that the Almighty would pervert justice! But is God indeed to make His dwelling upon the Earth? For even the heavens and the highest heavens cannot contain You, O Lord, much less the flesh of man! Though far be it from wrong, for God to put on the guise of man, and in human semblance play man upon the earth,[200] for every tribe of the earth will mourn when they see the Son of Man riding on the clouds of heaven coming in great power and glory!

Job
34:10

2 Chronicles
2:6

Philippians
2:7

Matthew
24:30

"O the depth of the riches and wisdom and knowledge of God. How impenetrable are His judgments, how inscrutable His ways. For who has known the mind of God, or who has been his counselor, apart from His Light Bearer? This then is why You have made man after Your *likeness*, sharing a portion of Your spirit with him, though he be but an animal?"

Romans
11:33

Though the Lord replied: "Thus, have I created man, fashioning him after the likeness of God, making him a righteous and upright man, filling him with the Divine Spirit, with ability, intelligence, and knowledge, but not after My likeness alone is man made! He has also been made in My *Image*, and it is not good for man to be alone. Wait here while I go to him; then once he is made whole,[201] you may deliver him the *good news*."[202]

Exodus
31:3

Genesis
...2:18...

199 Ezekiel 1:26. The Glory of the Lord is that he emptied himself into the likeness of a man, in order to rule Heaven and Earth, but no angels understood that God intended to become incarnate.

200 Twisted form of Philippians 2:7. Lucifer has little problem with God coming down out of the clouds disguised as a son of man and subduing the human race, as in his response to the first vision of the sealed scroll. However, Lucifer has a grievous problem with God actually becoming man, for this necessitates being born of a woman.

201 Man is not whole, for God has yet to create woman to complete him.

202 Lucifer was charged with giving the first good news, the news of Christ, news that could only be delivered to a husband and wife (just as Gabriel delivered the good news to Mary, the New Eve, at the Annunciation). This is also fitting because the four faced angel described in Ezekiel 1:6 is a Cherubim, for the Four Evangelists are Cherubim tasked with the duty of spreading the Gospel of Christ

NOTES

The Lord God returned to the man, His friend, and walked alongside him in the garden, revealing to man the many trees and wisdoms planted in the Garden of God.[203] As they drew near to the center of the garden, God instructed the man, saying, "All flesh is like grass, and all its loveliness like the flowers of the field. Grass withers, flowers fade, when the Breath of the Lord has blown upon them. Indeed man is like grass, taken from the dust of the earth and returning to the dust of the earth."

The Lord continued as they reached the middle of the garden, saying, "Man was made mortal, withering, fading, but the Word of the Lord endures forever!" So the Lord God revealed to man the River of life-giving water, sparkling like crystal, flowing from the Throne of God down the midst of the garden. On either side of the river grew the Tree of Life, bearing twelve fruits, yielding its fruit every month of the year, and the leaves of the tree were for the healing of the nations.

With great joy the Lord God canticled a song to the man: "Set Me as a seal upon your heart, as a seal upon your arm; for Love is as stern as Death, devotion as relentless as the netherworld; Love's flames are a blazing fire! Deep waters cannot quench Love, nor floods sweep it away. If one were to offer all that he has,[204] the wealth of his house, to purchase Love, he would be roundly mocked and laughed at." But when the Lord God, the Fulfillment and End of all creation, looked upon the man, whom He loved, He found him to be lonely.[205]

So, with somber heart,[206] the Lord God said: "It is not good for man to be alone. I will make for him a helpmate,[207] a reminder of how close God truly is to man!"

Isaiah 40:6...

Isaiah ...40:8

1 Peter 1:24

Revelation 22:1...

Revelation ...22:2

Song of Songs 8:6...

Song of Songs ...8:7

Genesis ...2:18...

203 In *The City of God*, St. Augustine writes that all the different trees in the garden were trees of different wisdoms, capable of bestowing knowledge upon Adam and Eve. This indicates that there was a natural ordering of knowledge and learning that took place as man made his way to the center of the garden. God would undoubtedly have been the guide, the instructing father, guiding his son in wisdom, as we see in the intimate image of God walking with Adam in the garden.

204 This is in fact what Lucifer does: he abandons all that he is and tries to force God into loving him. He sacrifices his grace and glory in a dastardly scheme to destroy man, in an attempt to prove to God that he alone is deserving of Divine Love.

205 This is one of the most tragic scenes in all the Scriptures. God looks down while walking with Adam, the man whom he loves, and realizes God is not enough for man. It is far worse to be lonely in company than in isolation; the more important the relationship, the sadder it is. To be lonely with one's spouse is heartbreaking, but to be lonely with God is existential despondency. This longing is because man is incomplete: flesh is by its very nature communal and needs unity with another, and so God decides to create woman as a living sign of God's intention for man. From our perspective, it is natural to long for another to complete us; from God's perspective, woman first comes as a solution for man refusing to be content with Him.

206 Cf. 1 Samuel 7:4: "Then all the elders of Israel gathered together and came to Samuel at Ramah, and said to him, 'You are old and your sons do not follow in your ways; appoint for us, then, a king to govern us, like other nations.' But the request displeased Samuel when they said, 'Give us a king to govern us.' Samuel prayed to the Lord, and the Lord said to Samuel, 'Listen to the voice of the people in all that they say to you; for they have not rejected you, but they have rejected me from being king over them.'"

Both of these examples show how God brings immense good out of evil, for through this rejection by the people, God brings about David, the first man who seeks after God's own Heart, and, through the loneliness of Adam, God brings about woman, who finds her completion in Mary, the Mother of God.

207 'Helpmate' refers not to the relationship between the man and the woman, but to that between man and God. Some of the oldest translations actually use the word 'Savior' denoting how woman was truly created to fulfill an inherent lacking in man, something that even God's company could not fill. There is no other creature that is so precious to God; woman is God's ingenious plan to bring about the fulfillment of man. Thus, woman is meant to stand in for God, be a sign, a living sacrament of God's love for man. Woman will have an innate desire unlike any other of God's creation, and this can only be accomplished through beauty. Beauty is what inspires the purest love, and is the highest of the transcendentals (the good, the true, and the beautiful). Therefore, God put an inherent desire in woman to be captivating, a yearning desire to enrapture man through beauty. This results in a paradoxical desire in the woman to attract man for herself and attract man toward God, one that Lucifer himself will exploit.

The Lord God then formed out of the ground various wild animals and various birds of the air,[208] and brought them to the man to see what he would name them; whatever the man called each living creature became its name.[209] The man gave names to all the cattle, all the birds of the air, and all the wild animals, but no animal proved to be a suitable help-mate for the man. So the Lord God cast a deep sleep over the man, and, while he was asleep, God took one of the man's ribs and closed up flesh in its place.[210]

Song of Songs 4:1…
As the man slept, the Lord came upon him in a dream with a vision of his wife. At the sight of her, the man cried, "Ah! You are beautiful, my beloved. Ah! You are beautiful! Your eyes are doves behind your veil. Your hair is like flocks of goats streaming down the mountains of Gilead. Your teeth are as a flock of sheep ready to be shorn, which comes up clean from the washing, all with twins; there is none barren among them! Your lips are like scarlet strands, and your speech sweet. Your cheeks are as pomegranates behind your veil. Your neck is like the tower of God girt with battlements. A thousand shields hang upon it, all the armor of valiant men. Your breasts are like young fawns, twins, which feed among the lilies. Until the day breathes cool, and the shadows lengthen, I will hasten to the mountain of myrrh, to the hill of frankincense.[211] You are all-beautiful, my beloved, and there is no blemish within you. Come from afar, my bride, come from afar, come! Descend from atop the mount, from the tops of mountains, from the den of lions, from the mountain of leopards.

208 Here we see the opposite of the first story of creation. In the first story of creation, there is a clear evolution from creation ex nihilo and culminating in the creation of man and woman. In the second story of creation, man is the first of God's creation, and then God forms a garden around him and forms wild animals and birds to bring before the man. This is a brilliant literary device called a chiasm, a building up and then building away from a key and central idea. As in a pyramid, the piling of stones exists in order to raise up the pinnacle, and in an arch, the structure cannot exist without the keystone, so, too, the central idea of a chiasm is both the heart of meaning and the reason the rest of the story exists. When the first and second stories of creation are taken as two halves of a whole, man is found directly in the middle! The first story builds up to him as creation's crowning culmination, while the second begins with man as its principle creature. When properly understood, Genesis is explaining that Man is at the very center of creation, the very reason that God created the universe in the first place (including the angels).

209 Man names all the animals to show both his dominion and his ability to understand their natures. He is participating in creation, anointing them with the seal of his understanding. Man is acting as king, and without him the animals would be purposeless, just as a kingdom without a king.

210 This is very important: the rib is that which protects, yet fundamentally blocks the way to the heart; God through the creation of woman, transforms this impediment into a real and living way into man's heart.

211 This is a reference to the breezy time of day, mentioned in Genesis 3:8. When the evening winds are blowing, God discovers that Adam and Eve have eaten from the Tree of Knowledge. It is also important that myrrh and frankincense are sweet-smelling spices for burials.

The Creation of Eve

Song of Songs
...4:9...
You have ravished my heart, my sister,[212] my bride. You have ravished my heart with one glance of your eye, with one bead of your necklace. How beautiful are your breasts, my sister, my bride. How much more delightful are your breasts than wine, and the sweet scent of your ointments above all aromatic spices! Your lips drip honey, my bride. Honey and milk lie beneath your tongue. And the fragrance of your garment is the fragrance of frankincense.

Song of Songs
...4:12...
"You are a secret garden,[213] my sister, my bride, a secret garden, a fountain sealed up. Your plants are a paradise of pomegranates with all choice fruits: nard and saffron, sweet cane and cinnamon, with all kinds of spices, myrrh and aloes, with all the chief perfumes. You are a garden fountain, a well of living waters, which flow fresh from heaven. Arise, north wind! Come, south wind! Blow through my garden, and let her aromatic spices flow!"

And when he awoke from his deep sleep, he heard a soft voice,
Song of Songs
...4:16...
"Let my lover come into his garden and eat the fruit of his fig tree."

Genesis
...2:22...
For the Lord God had built up a woman from the rib which He had taken from the man.[214] He then presented her to the man, and the man said, "At last! This one is bone of my bone, and flesh of my flesh;[215] she shall be called woman, for she was taken out of man."[216]

The Lord God then pronounced, "Henceforth a man shall leave his father and mother and cling to his *wife*, and they shall become one flesh!" So they were married, the man and his wife, both naked, and
Genesis
...2:24
yet felt no shame[217] for their bodies.

212 'Sister' is one of the highest compliments a husband can give to his wife. 'Sister' implies the familial bond, such closeness and love that she is indistinguishable from real blood bonds.

213 Here woman is being called the 'secret garden' to indicate that she is the garden hidden within the garden. Thus, if the purpose of the Garden of Eden was to allow man to dwell with God, then being with woman is only to dwell more intimately with Him. Woman manifests God's secret purpose of the Garden itself, the matrimony of God and man. This union between God and man achieves completion, again through a woman, when God himself becomes 'flesh of our flesh and bone of our bone.'

214 Woman is not created like any other creatures; she is taken from man so that she can be his completion. She is not taken from the head or from the foot, but specifically from the rib, which shows that woman is neither to rule nor be subjugated by man, but rather is equal to him, taken from the bone closest to his heart. Furthermore, all the animals and man were created from soil, but woman was created from flesh. This is what allows God to give her such beauty. Beauty stirs the beholder to long to be one, united with the beautiful. This is woman's specific purpose, to remind man how close God truly is to man.

215 Here in the flesh rests the great mystery of God's love for mankind. Recall, therefore, the purpose to which woman was created: to be a living testament of the relationship that God so desired to have with man. Thus, making man a bodily being, God allows for a physical manifestation of His unific love. Flesh is this peculiarity which allows two to become one, the most fundamental desire of love itself. This is why woman fulfills man so, and the Sacrament of Marriage is the Image of the Trinity, something no other institution can claim. Further, God not only desires for marriage to be a reflection of the Trinity, but desires Himself to enter into a marriage covenant with mankind, something that can only be accomplished through the woman, who was taken from the flesh of man.

216 Man's first reaction to woman is elation, shouting 'At last!', recognizing that she completes him, and yet he gives her a name, just as he did to the beasts which could never satisfy him. Latent in this first encounter are all the complexities and difficulties of marriage: Both being equal, man and woman must nevertheless serve and be served, complete each other and look to the other for completion. Woman's beauty does not give her dominion over man, and man's dominion does not counter his need to cling to her.

217 Naked and unashamed, Adam and Eve walked together completely innocent, concerned with neither the good nor evil of their bodies. Since God had introduced woman as man's completion, the way to be united to God was through her, ultimately culminating in his sexual union with her. Ignorant of both the good or evil that the flesh can embody, man's sexuality was not yet fully awakened. Thus, to say that they were 'unashamed' is not some ominous foretelling, but actually reveals a neutrality toward either the joy of a selfless sexuality or the shame of a selfish loss of control; it is theirs to choose whether to be naked and esteemed or naked and ashamed.

ᏀᏠᎬ ᎮᎡᎬᏟᏏᎮᏏᏟᎬ ᎾᎰ ᎮᎡᏏᎠᎬ

he Lord God then returned to the Tree of Knowledge of
Good and Evil to find Lucifer coiled amongst its branches,
contemplating the mysterious plan of God. The Lord proclaimed,
1 Corinthians
11:11
"It is accomplished; man is made whole, for in the Lord neither is
woman independent of man, nor man of woman. Will you go then,
and render to them of one flesh the *good news*? Bestowing the Fruit
of Wisdom upon them? For they see not their nakedness nor their
glory."

Lucifer receded from the branches and said: "Do You think me a
fool? With Your right hand You would seek to raise the horn of man
over the heavens, and with Your left You would have me bequeath it?
I know who springs from the side of man. I know of the woman and
Your intentions for her, the secret plot of creation:[218] to lay low the
stars of Heaven and raise up the dust of the Earth. I know the truth
concealed in the flesh of the fruit, the Wedding Covenant You have
planned for mankind!"[219]

The Lord then took and broke open a fig from the Tree of
Revelation
12:1...
Knowledge of Good and Evil, and immediately above the Tree, a great
sign appeared in the sky: a woman clothed in the sun, with the moon
under foot. She stood in the crescent of the moon, shining where no
light could shine.[220]

Beholding her beauty, the Lord loved *the Woman* more than
Esther
2:17
any other creature; and she found grace and favor in His sight more
than all virgins, so much so that the Lord set the royal crown upon
her head, a crown of twelve stars,[221] though the twelve stars were not
stars of heaven, but saints of the Earth. And so, she became Queen of
Heaven and Earth.

IGNATIAN CONTEMPLATION

218 Lucifer is alluding to the inescapable conclusion that, if God is to become a man, a woman would have to be the God-Bearer: a spotless mortal, elevated higher than any angel, who would be matrimonially united to God, and who would give her very flesh and essence for the generation of a God-Son to enter the universe. This, woman, is the unavoidable necessity for God to take on flesh.

219 The Tree of Knowledge of Good and Evil lies at the center of creation, for at the heart of God's wisdom in creation is the wisdom of God's creation of man. This is borne out in all of Genesis, the chiasm of the spheres; God works inward to bring the middle into focus: man, and at man's heart, woman. In turn, the center of creation is the turnkey to the building or breaking of the entire universe. While flesh opens the door for sin and death, the pride of angels and the disobedience of men, flesh also makes possible the greatest good this universe has ever seen, a good so great that it causes angels to sing (Luke 2:13). In the Incarnation, God is united with man, the center of the Universe, and so, just as God's voice echoes into the center of creation, his union with the heart of creation makes all the spheres rejoice at his intimate presence. This is the truth that was held within the fruit of the Tree of Knowledge of Good and Evil, the nakedness of the flesh to cause such tremendous evil and the ultimate good. The Tree especially belonged to Lucifer, and so he understood the purpose of man's nakedness between good and evil; the revelation that man is the end of creation and the source of God's union with it is an appalling truth to the highest and most beautiful angel.

220 This is the great majesty of Mary; she is the reality to which the sign of the Muslim faith points, a shining light where no light could be.

221 The twelve stars are the twelve tribes of Israel, symbolizing all of God's chosen people. The twelve apostles are the perfection of the twelve tribes, and therefore also symbolize all of God's chosen people within the Church. The twelve apostles are united and grouped around Mary as the twelve tribes were united and grouped around the Ark of the Covenant, the crown of the Queen symbolizing her dominion over all the earth.

Sirach
24:24...
The Lord then declared: "Behold, she is the Mother of fair love, and of fear, and of knowledge, and of holy hope! In her I shall place all grace of the way and of truth, and in her is all hope of life and of virtue. Go to her, all who desire her, and be filled with the fruit of her womb! For her spirit is sweet beyond honey, and her inheritance beyond honey and honeycomb. Her memory shall be unto everlasting generations.

Sirach
...24:28

So Lucifer replied: "What creature is this that she is Queen and Mother? What is woman that You favor her so? I am Your Light Bearer, the conduit through which all light and knowledge of God enters the Universe. What then is woman? What does she bear for the Lord?"

Genesis
1:27

The Lord answered: "I have created man in My own Image; in the Image of God I created him; male and female I created *them*. I have placed in their flesh a *great mystery*: blessing their marriage with the first blessing: 'Be fruitful and multiply; fill the Earth and subdue it.' So the

Genesis
1:28

Lord has commanded, and so shall the Love of God be made manifest:

1 John
4:9

that God is to send His only Son into the world, so that all men might have life through Him. Authority shall rest upon His shoulders, and

Isaiah
9:6

His name shall be Wonder Counselor, Mighty God, Everlasting Father, Prince of Peace; and for His throne and kingdom peace will have no end."

Luke
1:35

The Lord then explained: "Of old has the Spirit of the Lord courted her, enveloping her, and the power of the Most High has overshadowed

Proverbs
3:18...

her. She is the Tree of Life to those who grasp her, and felicity to those who cling to her. I founded the Earth with her in mind, established the Heavens with an understanding of her. For her were the depths split

Proverbs
...3:20

open, and the clouds dropped down their dew."

Revelation
...12:2...

The Woman was then found to be with child,[222] and she wailed aloud in pain as she labored to give birth.

So Lucifer began to weep aloud when the vision had been laid before his eyes, while the woman herself wailed aloud in joy at the

Ezra
3:12

birth of her son, so that it was indistinguishable: the sound of wailing from the sound of weeping.

222 The Woman is Lucifer's greatest fear, a being immensely lower than himself and bound in flesh, yet with the potential to outstrip the hosts of heaven; she can be a willing participant in the very act of creation. Woman can literally be a gateway for the Divine; through woman, God can enter into creation and permanently bind Himself to it. Since God's glory and majesty are immutable and infinite, he is not disgraced by such a union, and yet, through her we are graced infinitely by God entering into creation and sharing in our nature. This is Lucifer's envious fear, that we will have such a union with God specifically because we are enfleshed.

Theotokos: The Mother of God

Lucifer, having seen the image of *the Woman* with child, fell on his face and cried aloud: "*Theotokos*! What creature can bear forth God Himself?!" He then arose in protest and said: "I am Your Light Bearer, not her! I am Your chosen conduit, not her! Can such a lowly creature even be called God-Bearer? Can a woman be named Mother of God?!"

The Lord God then looked upon the heart of His Light Bearer and saw that his heart had been hardened by envy, so He had there appear Revelation …12:3… another sign in the sky: a great red dragon, with seven heads and ten horns, and upon his seven heads were seven diadems. The dragon was so large, and his wings so great, that he blocked out the sun from a third of the sky. The dragon's tail swept away a third of the stars in the sky and hurled them down to the earth.[223] The dragon stood before *the Woman* who was about to bear the child, that he might devour her child when she gave birth. She gave birth to a son, a male child, destined to rule all the nations with an iron rod. But before the dragon could devour her child, he was caught up to God and His Throne, and *the Woman* fled into the desert where she had a place prepared for her by God, that she might be taken care of for twelve hundred and sixty days.[224]

Seeing the great sign in the sky, Lucifer fell to his knees and tore his garments[225] of light; he removed his veil of light and laid bare his Job 15:14… naked form,[226] the great winged dragon: Leviathan. He then boasted: "What are mortals, that they can be clean? Or those born of woman, that they might be righteous? God puts no trust even in His holy ones, and the heavens are not clean in His sight; how much less one who is Job …15:16 abominable and corrupt, one who drinks in iniquities like water? A flood is coming like a torrent of water to sweep away *the Woman*! What then, will the Lord do when His Immaculate one is defiled, when *the Woman* is corrupt and made an unfit vessel for God? Yes, I in justice shall bring sin into the world, and, through sin, death—that men might be nothing to envy and take only death as their inheritance!"[227]

223 Lucifer is seeing a foretelling of his own apostasy: called by God to bear forth his light and his truth, he will forgo his role and literally block out the light from reaching the rest of creation. In his shadow, no other angel will receive, at least directly from God, an understanding of the beauty of God's plan for creation.

224 This represents Lucifer's attack on the heart of mankind, the first woman. However, it is not Eve that he is interested in destroying, but the eternal office of the God-bearer, the subject of his great envy. While Eve succumbs, God does not abandon the woman of destiny, but hides her away until the appointed time. The number one thousand two hundred and sixty is an enigma until it is broken up into its components, translated by the days of creation. It is equivalent to forty two months, which is in turn the product of six and seven. The sixth day was the creation of the beasts, while the seventh day is the perfection of God's rest. Thus, forty-two is the symbol of God touching creation, the combination of God's perfection and the earthly reality of ensouled life.

225 Reflect upon how too the High Priest tears his garments at the trial of Jesus, this act of rending his priestly vestments voids his priesthood allowing for the true High Priest, Jesus Christ, whose garments were not torn but rather were cast lots for, to fulfill the role of High Priest par excellence. So too does Lucifer's rending of his garments of light, void his role as Lightbearer allowing for a new 'Bearer' to take his place, Mary the Fount of Grace, who no longer bears God's light, but God Himself into the Universe.

226 Angels, while each possessing their own incorporeal form, usually appear to men as either pure light or in the form of man himself. Demons, on the other hand, reveal themselves in great variety, often in bestial forms. This is because the shedding of the light of grace reveals the pure nature. Lucifer's divesting of light allows Adam and Eve to perceive his nature; by the time he reaches the garden in Genesis, Lucifer is called tannin, 'the serpent.' To be called serpent is not an insult, for Lucifer was a dragon, the mightiest creature; even as the light bearer of God, this was the form given to him at his creation. However, this unveiling also means he is naked to the choice between good and evil, just as Adam and Eve are. If he chooses to serve God, he will be set on fire with love, becoming a seraph (fiery serpent). If he chooses to scorn God's will, he will become Leviathan (watery serpent), fleeing to the abyss.

227 Wisdom 2:24 & Romans 5:12. show how and why Satan brought death into the world, because of his envy of the *immaculate Woman*.

Lucifer's mind turned to cunning, and he plotted in his heart: "I will scale the heights of heaven, and above the stars of God I will raise my throne! I will sit enthroned upon the Mount of Hosts, on the crest of the Sacred Mountain! I will ascend beyond the coverings of clouds, and I will make myself like the Most High! Then, when man is laid low, and I sit like God in splendor, He shall see that it is *I* whom He should love, and not man."[228]

The Lord said in reply: "First son of dawn, are you not the wisest and most endowed with knowledge among the stars? Then show forth your wisdom! Act in good conduct with works done in meekness born of wisdom. Yet, here you stand with bitter envy and selfish pride in your heart, boasting and lying against the truth. Such wisdom is not from God above, but is from below, thought up, and Demonic![229] For where there is envy and pride there shall follow disorder and wickedness of every kind."

The wrath of Leviathan was kindled, and he declared: "You speak to me of disorder? When you have blackened the sun as sackcloth, and steeped the whole moon in blood; casting the stars of heaven to the earth as the fig tree casts off its unripe figs during a gale? The heavens have been darkened, the sun and moon, and stars shed no more light. Yes, the treasuries of heaven have been emptied, carelessly spilt upon the Earth. What else can You give them? Does Your dotage have no end?"

But the Lord God said in reply: "I, the Lord God, in Wisdom have blessed man with every spiritual blessing in the heavens. I have chosen men, from before the foundations of the world, to be without blemish before the Lord. In love I have destined them for *adoption* into Myself, through Wisdom, in accord with the favor of My will, for the praise and glory of My Name, by such grace granted them in the Beloved."

"You plot to make *man God*!?"[230] Leviathan cried out in agony. "Bestowing upon them a more excellent name than all the gods of heaven!?"

Isaiah 14:12...

Isaiah ...14:14

James 3:13...

James ...3:16

Revelation 6:12

Ephesians 1:3...

Ephesians ...1:6

228 Lucifer is the smartest being in all existence, and so he would never try to overthrow God. Lucifer was far more cunning; he sought to establish himself as first, the brightest and most beautiful angel in the sky; and then to destroy man so that he would be loathsome to the Almighty. If these things were accomplished, Lucifer would be God's only option as the conduit of his light; however, Lucifer severely underestimates God's strength. This is why Gabriel, whose name is God's strength, delivers Divine Truth to Mary at the Annunciation, counterpoint to the deception of Leviathan. Unlike Lucifer's proud stance against the first woman, Gabriel's genuflection is the humility which allows God's mightiest deed to come forth, the Incarnation and redemption of the entire human race through The Immaculata.

229 The Lord is naming the spiritual nature of envy and pride, demon, and the source of all evil.

230 Lucifer feels the hot whips of panic like a lover losing pride of place. His revelation is proclaimed to us, all throughout the New Testament: We are gods. Christ himself says it in John 10:34, and it is affirmed in Galatians 4:6, Psalm 82, 2 Peter 1:3-4, John 1:12, Romans 8:15, and Ephesians 1:5. Through the Incarnation, through the matrimony of God and Mary, the universe was fundamentally altered, and the Gates of Grace opened. Thus, through a superabundance of grace, we coheirs in Christ are made gods through the physical consumption of His flesh. That is why the Most Holy Eucharist is the fulfillment of the spiritual life, source and summit of all life and happiness, because it is the Divine Gift that endows the beholder with Divinity. This could only be accomplished through God's most ingenious thought, Flesh; an inconceivable thought for an angel of pure light.

NOTES

So Leviathan hated *the Woman* with a very great hatred, for the hatred with which he hated *the Woman* was greater than the love with which he had for God.

2 Samuel
13:15

But the Lord was silent, so Leviathan spoke: "I have been Your Light Bearer from the beginning of Your ways; from before the Earth was formed was I declaring Your truth, but this truth I cannot bear. For in the marriage of man, You have sown the seeds of my own destruction, and now You ask me to be the herald of my own undoing?! To serve them, the greatest among the gods a slave, because You desire wedlock? Curse the fruit and its divinizing power! I will not serve! No, this I cannot allow. What is man, that he should live and not see death? Who can deliver his soul from the power of Hell?"

Jeremiah
2:20

Psalm
89:48

The Lord then declared: "From your creation you were the seal of perfection, complete in wisdom, and perfect in beauty! I have placed you in Eden, the garden of God, where you might dwell at the heart of creation. Every precious stone is your covering; your pendants and mountings were prepared for you on the day of your creation. From the beginning were you called to be, a cherubim with double wing as your covering. I have placed you upon the Holy Mountain of God, that you might walk among the fiery stones. Blameless were you in your ways from the day of your creation, bearing God's own light."

Ezekiel
28:12…

Evil has yet[231] to be found within you, though you plot commerce full of licentiousness,[232] and plan to birth sin into this world. Where then will there be a place for you, banished from the Mountain of God, from among the fiery stones, barred by a true cherub? Your heart has grown haughty because of your beauty; your wisdom corrupt, because of your splendor. Must I cast you to the ground and make spectacle of you in the sight of kings? Are you to defile your own sanctuary by the depravity of your iniquities, by the perversity of your trade?

The Most Cunning of All

231 Most theologians believe that Lucifer had already become Satan by the time he plotted to deceive Eve, saying that even the intention to do such an evil meant that he had already been corrupted. Jesus seems to affirm this when he says that "he who looks upon a woman with lust has committed adultery in his heart." However, this points to a deeper truth, for the heart is the seat of the will just as the mind is the seat of the intellect. Until the heart bears an action to completion, completely and fully willing an action, it cannot be said to have committed either sin or good. The man who stops just before he gives alms is not rewarded, just as the man who almost steals is not punished. When this rubric is applied to Lucifer, no sin is committed until he tempts Eve with the fig from the Tree of Knowledge of Good and Evil. This has serious cosmological implications for the Fall of the Angels and of Man.

232 Lucifer wanted Eve to be defiled by sin and therefore be an unfit vessel for the Lord God's incarnation. This is why Lucifer was the original sin peddler; he sold Adam and Eve the choice to grasp at their own divinity, at the price of their true divinity. This promulgation of sin is itself Satan's true sin, the self-fulfilling accusation.

Ezekiel
...28:19

Must I bring fire out from the midst of you, to devour you and render you ash upon the earth? Are all nations to look appalled at how you have become a horror, never to be again?"

Matthew
24:29

Leviathan then rendered his words to the Lord: "I, Your firstborn Son of Light, have no place in heaven, for the sun has been darkened and the moon sheds no more light; the stars have fallen from the sky, and the heavenly powers are no more. You, God of man, shall rue the day You placed heart with mortal beings, and lament the making of man, for I shall show You the depth of their depravity, and Your Heart

Genesis
7:11

shall grieve! Upon that day the fountains of the great abyss shall burst forth, and the floodgates of the nether shall be opened, and man shall be no more! Then when all is as it once was and darkness abounds in the deep I shall reign, and man shall be regarded as nothing! All these things will come to pass in justice, for on this day the sons of light were cheated of their inheritance, their glory cast as pearls before swine, and they themselves set as slaves to potbellied flesh!"

Matthew
20:13...

The Lord God then replied, "My friend, I am not cheating you. Did you not agree with the Lord on the day of your creation, to be? Is not the sacrifice of being service? Take what is yours[233] and go. What if I wish to give these least ones the same as you? Or am I not free to do as I wish with my own grace? Are you envious[234] because I am generous?" So the Lord declared: "Thus it is, that the last shall be first,

Matthew
...20:16

and the first shall be last."

ʲ

233 God has given the fruit from the Tree of Knowledge of Good and Evil to Lucifer; he is the Light Bearer, the highest angel of Truth and thus bears the highest Truth, the Wisdom, hidden within the fruit of the Tree of Knowledge. It is for this purpose that Lucifer was created; the fruit is his by right, and God will not take it away.

234 Recall Wisdom 2:24: "But by the envy of the devil, death entered into the world."

—————— *NOTES* ——————

ᏻᏥᎬ ᎠᏒᎪᏀᎾᏁ'Ꮪ ᏫᎪᏆᏞ

Luke
,18:11

So Lucifer returned to his place among the stars, but his heart had become hardened on account of his envy. He went before the Temple and prayed aloud in the public place: "Lord, I thank You that I am not like the others![235] That I am not like man, multiplying iniquities upon the Earth! I groan because of the agitation of my heart! Lord, all

Psalm
38:8...

my desire is laid before You; my sighing is not hidden from You. My heart throbs, my strength fails me; and the light of my eyes, even that has fled from me! My loved ones and my friends stand aloof from my

Psalm
...38:11

plague; and even my kinsmen stand far off."

Hearing this, the sons of God who had gathered to present themselves before the Lord drew closer to the Light bearer,[236] and he

Isaiah
24:16...

continued, saying: "I have heralded the sun, yet I scream: 'I waste away! I waste away!' Woe to me, and stars of heaven! Oh, the treacherous betrayal! With treachery the treacherous betray! Terror and pit and snare await you, O stars of heaven. To flee in terror is only to fall into the Pit! To climb from the Pit is to only be caught in the snare![237]

Isaiah
...24:22...

"For on this day, the Day of Presentation,[238] the Lord will punish the stars in Heaven, subjugating them to the kings of the Earth! Sons of light will be herded together, like prisoners bound for dungeons; we shall be shut up in prisons and be punished for the rest of our days![239] The moon is to be dismayed, the sun ashamed! For the Lord Almighty has removed His face from the heavens![240] His reign is upon Mount

Isaiah
...24:23

Zion, upon man and the sons of men.

Hebrews
1:4...

"It is true, I have heard Him say to the *Son of Man*: 'Come sit at the right hand of the Majesty on High, for You have become much superior to the stars as the name You inherit is more excellent than theirs.'

"For to which of you has God ever said: 'You are My true Son, on this day I have begotten you?' Or, 'I will be a Father to you and you shall be a son to Me?'

IGNATIAN CONTEMPLATION

235 Luke 18:11: The infamous prayer of the Pharisee.

236 It is very important to understand the hierarchical nature of the Celestial Intelligences; since Lucifer was the greatest and highest celestial intelligence he received first the very Light of God, and this light was knowledge of God Himself. It then follows by necessity that since all the light and knowledge of God was first poured into Lucifer as 'Light bearer' it must in turn be passed down from Lucifer to all those lower angels which fall below him. Thus, if Lucifer so chose to withhold or taint any knowledge first received by God, no lower angel would know the truth or would have the authority to protest such a revelation.

237 Lucifer understands the wages of an angelic rebellion; he is under no illusion that his actions could not have direct consequences on his place in heaven. In order to win the other angels to his side, he presents God's plan as a double bind: If the angels stay, they will be imprisoned in the confines of the Celestial Hierarchies, forced to serve their lesser. If they rebel, they will be thrown down into the pit of Hell.

238 The Day of Presentation is the day God asks each individual 'angel' whether or not they will serve Him, specifically by serving man. This is the day the celestial intelligences become angels, accepting their role as messengers between God and man. Before this point it is not proper to call any of the celestial intelligences angels; they existed as pure spirits according to the nature of light, being filled and simultaneously overflowing into those below, a cascade ultimately derived from the Divine Light of God. This presents an immense problem: Lucifer stands at the head of such a pyramid but has cast off his light, causing a total eclipse of the Divine Light upon the Heavenly hosts.

239 Lucifer is equating the joyous 'yes' of serving and loving the Lord in a celestial choir to being imprisoned, bound, and tortured into serving man for the rest of their existence.

240 Lucifer sees God's plan for an Incarnation as a betrayal of the natural ordering of creation. This is how he deceives the other angels, by telling them that God has perverted the order of creation, that the stars were only created to serve men.

"Yet, at the birth of His firstborn into the world He says: 'Let all the stars of God worship Him!' [241]

"Regarding you He says no such thing, only: 'Let my servants be spirit-winds; and My ministers flames of fire.'

"Only of His man-child does he say: 'Your throne, O God, is forever and ever, and the righteous scepter is the scepter of Your kingdom! You have loved righteousness and hated lawlessness; therefore God, Your God, has anointed You with the oil of gladness beyond *all* the stars of heaven.'

"And this He says to His Son: 'In the Beginning, Lord, You laid the Earth's foundations; the heavens were struck by Your hand; they will perish, but You shall remain; they will wear out like a garment; like a cloak You will roll them away, and like a garment they will be changed. But You shall remain the same, and Your years will have no end.'

"But to which of you has He ever said: 'Come, sit at My right hand, until I make your enemies[242] a footstool at your feet?'

"He regards us only as ministering spirits, sent to render service for the sake of those who will inherit salvation."[243]

Hebrews
...1:14

NOTES

241 This refers to the Annunciation, when God through the romance of the Holy Spirit brings Wisdom the Word into creation through the perfect conduit, Mary.

242 Lucifer is implying that the 'angels' themselves are to become the enemies of the Son of Man.

243 The first chapter of Hebrews exemplifies the fear of Lucifer, for man is now able to boast that God has chosen the son of man to become God. This address is given to all the angels as a summary of the injustice of God's plan. Lucifer, however, will go on to address each potential choir of angels, presenting their unique service to the Lord as an injustice and abasement. God will arrange the choirs according to the natural inclination of each angel, to praise Him and serve Him with whatever aspect of creation delights them most and which is proportionate to their intelligence and ability; Lucifer seeks the opposite, to make them hate the very things they were meant to love, just as he grew to hate God's gift to him, to bear the good news of the Tree of Knowledge.

Forked Tongue

§ Cherubim § [244]

Ezekiel
1:4...

A great whirlwind came out of the North, and a great cloud with brightness enfolding it and fire flashing forth continuously, and out from the midst of the light flashed something like gleaming amber. In the midst thereof stood the Four Living Creatures[245] with

Ezekiel
...1:5

their myriad of eyes; they gathered about Leviathan like a garland and

Job
33:31...

so a host of similar stars encircled him and he spoke: "Be attentive, O court; listen to me! Be silent and I will speak. If thou hast anything to say answer me; speak, for I would have thee to appear just. If not, hear

Job
...33:33...

me; hold thy peace, and I will teach thee wisdom.

Job
34:1...

"Hear me, O wise ones of heaven my discourses, and those that possess knowledge, hearken to me! For the ear tests words as the taste does food. Let us discern for ourselves what is right; let us learn

Job
...34:3

between us what is good!

Wisdom
7:1...

"My stars, I, too, am immortal,[246] the same as all the rest, the firstborn descendant of the Celestial Light. In the twinkling of night, I was molded into the Morning Star, heralding the light of day, shining with all vigor, possessing the great abundance and wealth, and wisdom that accompanies being next to God.

"I, too, when born, sang in chorus and shouted for joy, shining from the heavens! Wailing, I uttered the same song common to all. For no god of heaven has any different origin of birth;[247] and no other

Wisdom
...7:6...

purpose than to shine upon the earth![248]

"Filled with light and so overflowing, I took my position among the stars, as all the gods found their places. Yet thus all of us were deceived, for atop the heights of Heaven God plotted to plunder the heavens of their glory, carelessly spilling their treasure upon the earth.

Wisdom
...7:7...

"So I prayed, and understanding was given me; I pleaded and the spirit of sagacity came to me.[249] I preferred it to throne and scepter, and deemed such heavenly riches nothing in comparison.[250]

IGNATIAN CONTEMPLATION

244 Lucifer begins his great speech addressing the Cherubim, not the Seraphim, for the simple fact that the Celestial Choir of Seraphim don't yet exist. Before the Celestial Hierarchy of Grace, of which Michael is the Prince, there was only the Celestial Hierarchy of Lucifer, which existed according to the Order of Nature. Lucifer was the greatest being God created, both in intelligence and beauty, and so he finds himself upon the hierarchical pinnacle in the Order of Nature. This original hierarchy is according to the celestial intelligences' proximity to God, in the sense of sight or knowledge: the closer the angel is to God, the more the angel sees of God and therefore actually becomes more like God. Thus, it is important to remember that when Lucifer speaks about God he speaks with authority, for he sees more and is more like God than any other creature in Creation. However, there is a new hierarchy established upon the grace poured forth into each individual angel's heart, and it is not according to natural proximity to or knowledge of God, but rather receptivity to God's Love. Seraphim, who give themselves entirely and specifically to God's love, and to such an extent that they themselves catch fire with His own Love, find themselves at the pinnacle of such a new Hierarchy. How the new hierarchy is established out of the desolation of the old is something we must pay close attention to; for the insurgence of the new Order of Grace is founded in Michael's unique ability to stand up to Lucifer, contending with the dragon according to a particular grace he has been given because of his humble receptivity to God's loving plan as an Archangel.

245 This is Lucifer's address to the angels that would love the Lord most in His Truth. These angels, if they so choose, will become the celestial choir of Cherubim.

246 In order to draw a line between God and the heavenly spirits, Lucifer first points out that he is one of them, born of the same light. He is claiming to be their advocate, fighting for their rights.

247 This is a reference to the Book of Job, which reveals that the angels sang at their own creation.

248 Lucifer is now placing doubt in the celestial beings' very purpose and origin, claiming that the only reason they were created was to be slaves to the material world, light subjugated to dust

249 Lucifer is now claiming truth as his own. This is not the Wisdom of God, which lovingly dies that the beloved might live. This is a wisdom bereft of love; it is pure unmitigated justice, cold as steel and harsh as the sword. This allows Lucifer to judge, truthfully, that the lower being should serve the higher; unlike the wisdom of God, with whom the highest being pours out love upon the lower. Unwilling to waver from his truth, Lucifer becomes the accuser and executioner; however, "those who take up the sword shall perish by the sword" (Matthew 26:52).

250 Lucifer is abandoning his birthright of kingship and choosing his truth over all the blessings of heaven, setting an example to all the other angels that truth is more important than heaven. In his eyes, he becomes a selfless martyr for truth.

Nor could I liken any priceless gem to it because all the gold of heaven, in view of my cunning, is a bit of sand, and before my cunning, silver is to be accounted as mire.

Wisdom
...7:10...

"Beyond health and beauty I prized it, and I chose to have it rather than the light, because its radiance is not hollow. Yet, all good things together came to me with such cunning, and countless riches became mine. I rejoiced in them all, because my cunning heralded a new order, though I knew not it was to be the mother of a new world.

Wisdom
...7:13...

"I pray I can speak worthily of my cunning! Sincerely I learned, and ungrudgingly do I share; its riches I do not hide away, for it has unfailing treasure. Those who gain this treasure win vindication, justice beyond the word of creation!

Wisdom
...7:15...

"May I speak suitably and value these endowments worthily, for the *truth hidden within the truth*[251] is the guide of my cunning and the director of all sagacity. For both we and our words have always been valued according to their truth, according to their prudence and knowledge. Yet a *hidden truth* has given me *select knowledge* of what exists, that I might know the true structure of the Universe and the force of its principles; the beginning and the end and the midpoints of all times; the changes in the source of light and the variations of the states; the cycles of the years, constellations of the celestial gods; the souls of all living things, tempers of beasts; the powers of the winds and even the thoughts of man. Whatever hidden or plain I learned, through my sight,

Wisdom
...7:22

discerning for myself the *truth hidden within the truth*.[252]

"This, cunning, I give to you, freely and truly, bereft of chain or snare. Value it more than gold and treasure, more than crown or scepter, more than grace or glory, even more than light itself. For if

John
8:32

you do this thing then you will know the *hidden truth*, and the truth shall set you free!"[253]

251 This is the first heresy leveled against the Christian Faith: Gnosticism, the claim that salvation comes from a select and secret knowledge. This heresy also teaches that matter is evil and spirit is the only source of good. It is not by accident that the first heresy is the same mentality that Satan has toward mankind.

252 Due to the hierarchical nature of the Celestial Intelligences Lucifer has now corrupted all those 'angels' that would have chosen to serve the Lord according to His Truth and become Cherubim. The first lie uttered by Lucifer is actually that select and secret knowledge is what bestows glory, and this causes all those would-be Cherubim who naturally seek truth not to seek it in the Lord God but in Lucifer himself. Thus all those highest celestial intelligences now look to Lucifer, who purports to hand down true knowledge of God, as the way, the truth, and the light. This is of course the great Lie of Lucifer, and in reality is a shadowy illusion that promulgates down throughout the celestial hierarchy to the very lowest choir of heaven.

It is very important to understand the gravity of Lucifer's lie, for in the corruption of those 'angels' that would have adhered themselves to the choir of Cherubim, Lucifer has caused an eclipse of Truth itself. Since those angels that would have first received and shed forth the light of Truth are now corrupt, there are no angels left to show forth God's truth to all the subsequent choirs of heaven. This corruption of the Cherubim directly casts a shadow upon all those 'angels' that would have adhered themselves to the celestial choir of Thrones, removing from them their ability to discern the transcendental Truth of God and therefore the Good of God which they naturally seek. This most properly is the great shadow of Lucifer, not simply obscuring the Truth and covering the celestial intelligences in darkness, but establishing himself as sole arbiter of knowledge and 'light'. Lucifer's eclipse therefore becomes the shining darkness, which bears its halo as a mocking obeisance to that which it obscures.

253 This 'freedom' is to serve only one's own will, to be subject to none. It is the folly of 'independence,' which ends in isolation from all that is good. This subversion of truth is a direct attack on Free Will itself, causing an equivocation. The true definition of Free Will is one's ability to choose the Good free from internal and external impediments. The corrupted definition of Free Will peddled by Lucifer is that Free Will is the ability to choose anything, good or evil, which subtly necessitates that one is only free when they are able to choose evil. This characterizes our modern definition of Free Will, which we have swallowed whole heartedly.

§ Thrones §

Job
36:2...

"Wait yet a little longer, and I will instruct you, for there are still words to be said. I will bring my knowledge from the beginning, and to my Maker I will accord the right. For indeed my words cannot fail me: the one perfect in knowledge[254] I set before thee. Behold, God does not cast away the mighty, whereas He Himself is mighty. He withholds not the elders' right; He will not take away His eye from the just; He places kings upon their thrones[255] and sets them to be exalted forever.

Job
...36:7

Psalm
89:4...

"The Lord has made a dynasty and established His Throne to endure through all ages, for who in heaven can compare to the Lord? Who is like the Lord among the sons of God? He is a God dreaded in the council of gods! Great and awesome before all that surrounds him! The Lord, God of hosts, who is like unto Him? Indeed, justice and judgment are the foundation of His Throne, and it is by such justice that the Throne endures!

Psalm
...89:7

"Yet, has any one of you examined His throne? Set to number it with a measuring rod? Or test its constitution? For it is not as it seems!

Job
26:8...

Though who can draw near to examine it? For He binds up the waters in His thick clouds, so that they fill without breaking, covering the face of His Throne.[256] He spreads His clouds over it like a veil. He inscribes a circle about the waters, so that even light and darkness may not approach, and the pillars of heaven tremble and dread at His rebuke.

Job
...26:11

"I alone have peered past the covering. I alone have seen the shame of the Lord, the secret concealed in the clouds, and here do I tell you: His throne is no throne at all! The Seat of Wisdom is a woman![257] A she-beast of the Earth! Made of dust and ashes, a dishonorable and disgraceful vessel, unfit to even beset the Lord! Yet, beyond all stars she draws near to the Lord saying: 'The Lord has torn princes from their thrones but lifted up the lowly; He has filled the hungry with good things, and the rich He has sent away empty.'

Luke
1:52

IGNATIAN CONTEMPLATION

254 Lucifer, who is actually perfect in the knowledge he has been given, surpassing every created being.

255 Lucifer now speaks to the angels that would serve the Lord because of His throne (His holiness). These angels, if they so choose, will become Thrones, separating the third heaven from all creation as a king's throne raises him above his court.

256 This passage is describing God's Throne as the moon, which throughout Christian Tradition has always been understood as Mary.

257 "Seat of Wisdom" is one of the most ancient and grace-filled titles of Mary, illuminating her singular role to bear the Son of God. She participates so closely with the Second Person of the Trinity that she is the very Throne on which Wisdom sits and distributes Justice and Mercy.

 *NOTES*

2 Timothy
2:20

"Yes, indeed there are many vessels in the great house of the Lord: some of gold, some of silver, but some of wood and clay—some for honorable use and some for dishonorable use! Those of a dishonorable nature may not be used for honorable use, lest they profane the user and indeed the entire house! We mighty gods are the gold and silver in this house, which in justice ought to be reserved for the most honorable use. Yet, there is a dishonorable vessel of flesh, which has been elevated beyond gold or silver to the shame and dismay of all the gods in heaven. Yes, against all justice and right order there sits a dishonorable vessel of earthen make serving as the very throne of God![258]

Matthew
7:16...

"Arise, O ancients and hosts of heaven; prepare your reply! For I pose to you: Can injustice be born of justice? Do we not judge one by their fruits? Are grapes gathered from thorns or figs from thistles? Yes, every good tree bears good fruit, but every bad tree bears rotten fruit. A good tree cannot bear rotten fruit, and a bad tree cannot bear good fruit. Every

Matthew
...7:19

tree that does not bear good fruit is cut down and thrown into the fire![259]

"Thus, what is to be done with the Throne if it is found to be with rot? Corrupted by the base and lowly things of the Earth? Is not God's Throne to be exempt from and remain untainted by any base and earthly thing, having no part in that which is lowest?

"Can you ancients manifest God's Throne to all creation knowing there is impurity in it?[260] Or must a new throne be erected? One pure and perfect, and chosen from the illustrious gods of heaven?

"Thus, I prayed, and, in my heart, I beheld the answer. If God has corrupted His Throne with wanton desire for *the Woman*, then

Isaiah
14:13...

I, for my brethren's sake, must scale the heights of heaven, and above the stars of God raise my throne, so that a true throne might not be defiled! I will sit enthroned upon the Mount of Hosts, on the crest of the Sacred Mountain! I will ascend beyond the coverings of clouds; and I will make myself like the Most High, that the heavens might

Isaiah
...14:14

persist in their purity![261]

258 A very potent argument to a Throne, for by revealing the fact that Mary is the Throne of God without revealing why she would be so exalted, namely being the Mother of God in the Divinely willed Incarnation, Lucifer takes away the 'holiness' of God by claiming that He is profaned by His dwelling with the woman.

259 Lucifer is claiming that the only fate the woman deserves is that of Hell because her fruit is profaning the Lord.

260 Those fallen angels that would have adhered themselves to the choir of Thrones are so highly exalted by nature that they actually cause a corruption and distortion of goodness throughout all creation. In their fallen state they obscure and warp the apprehension of Goodness not only for those men upon the Earth but even those subordinate angels who stand below them in the heavens, which allows all the subsequent 'angels' in all the lower choirs to misapprehend the Good and fall into sin.

261 Isaiah 14 is one of the most important passages in all of the Old Testament concerning the intentions of Lucifer. Lucifer admits all of his desires, but cunningly appends a selfless intention so that the angels will view him as their savior.

Atop Eden

Sirach
24:1...

"It shall be I, instead of *the Woman,* who in the midst of the congregation shall be exalted, and shall be admired in the holy assembly; in the multitude of the elect I shall have praise, and among the blessed I shall be blessed,[262] triumphantly saying: 'I have shined forth from the mind of God, firstborn before all creatures: I have made it that in the heavens there should arise light that never fails! As a cloud I covered all the earth; I dwelt in the highest places, and my throne is in a pillar of cloud. I alone have compassed the circuit of heaven, and alone have penetrated into the bottom of the deep, walking among the waves of the sea. And I shall stand atop the heavens:[263] and above every star, and every choir, I shall have chief rule!'"[264]

Sirach
...24:6

Lucifer's Throne

262 According to natural law Lucifer rules the angels, because he is superior to all of them. This is why no one interrupts his speech; no other angel has the right or authority to interject.

263 Lucifer is claiming that he is the seat of wisdom, and that he is the one that should be honored and through him all good things will come to those who serve him.

264 Due to the hierarchical nature of the Celestial Intelligences, Lucifer along with the fallen Cherubim have now cast the shadow of temptation and lies upon all those 'angels' that would have chosen to serve the Lord according to His Goodness and become Thrones. Since one cannot choose the Good without knowing the Good, the fall of the Cherubim and acceptance of Lucifer's lie directly influence the fall of all those 'angels' that would have become Thrones. Now that the Thrones have fallen so too dies the fruit of their service, i.e. proper adherence to the transcendental Good of God. All subsequent choirs will now be subject to a moral relativism unable to discern what the true Good actually is. Furthermore, since the Cherubim accepted Lucifer's lie and seek a 'truth' that Lucifer alone possesses, so too do the Thrones themselves look to Lucifer as the expression of the new transcendent good. This most properly is the throne of Lucifer, not simply to undermine the goodness of God, but to establish himself and his cause as the new good, which is most desirable.

NOTES

§ Dominations §

Job
34:16...

"Now do you, O court, hear this? Hearken to the words I speak! Can an enemy of justice indeed be in control, or will you condemn the Just One along with *the Woman*? For who can say to a king: 'You are worthless!' and to nobles: 'You are wicked'? Who neither favors the person of princes, nor respects the rich more than the poor?

Job
...34:19

Yet, from you, noble lords and gods of heaven,[265] this right has been withheld! Yes, you have been passed over in favor of *the Woman* and her offspring of the Earth.

"Yes, you the elect, chosen from among the thousands! Sons of light who gather near to the Lord conforming yourselves to His infinite lordship, blessing His sovereign name, and settling every dispute and assault in the heavens! Is it not by your right judgment that peace is maintained and order is held in the heavens?[266]

Job
25:1...

"Is it not by such dominion and dread that He brings about harmony in His heavens? Is there any numbering of His armies? Yet, on which of you does His light not rise? How can anyone be in the right against God, or how can any born of woman be innocent? Even the moon is not bright and the stars are not clean in His eyes. How much less a human being, who is a worm, a mortal, who is

Job
...25:6

only a maggot? Yes, these He has chosen in disregard of the gods of heaven.

"Woe to you, O kingly lords, for a great dishonor has been dealt! For gods though you be, children of the Most High, all of you,

Psalm
82:6...

nevertheless you shall serve mortal men, despoiled like any prince. When my time is up, when the court is convened and the time for me to speak has ended, when my words are abolished and completely

Daniel
7:26...

destroyed, that is when the kingship and dominion and majesty of *all* the lords of heaven shall be stripped away. Given to men, *saints* of the Most High, and their kingship shall not be taken away; it shall be an

Daniel
...7:27

everlasting kingship: one that all Dominions shall serve and obey![267]

IGNATIAN CONTEMPLATION

265 Lucifer is now addressing the would-be angels of the Choir of Dominations, whose purpose is to regulate the angels of the First Heaven, and the two choirs directly below them in the Second Heaven. Lucifer is arguing that the angels have the right and the authority to govern themselves without any need for God.

266 These 'angels' adhere themselves to the Lordship of God and serve as the King's nobles, His court which ought to promulgate the Will of the Lord throughout the heavens.

267 This is one of the most striking passages concerning the authority of angels and the Church. for since Christ gives all authority to His Church, not only are all nations and tribes subject to its authority but also the angels in heaven. This foreseen reversal established by the new order of grace allows Lucifer to corrupt many angels from the Celestial Choir of Dominations.

Dominations

"So let us remove our peace from the heavens and see what is wrought! Let us see if man can call forth the sun and woman the moon! Let us learn for ourselves if the sun is not to rule the day, and the moon and the stars the night, For who can tell the sun to rise, or the stars to convene in their constellations?[268] Surely with our rule removed from the heavens, every god is capable of doing what is right in their own eyes!"[269]

Psalm
136:8...

Psalm
...136:9

Judges
21:25

Fallen Dominations

268 These fallen angels that would have adhered themselves to the choir of Dominations are so immense and powerful that they would not only have enslaved the peoples of the Earth but also all their subordinate 'angels'. These are some of the most ancient demons who we learn about as the chief pagan gods, such as Zeus, Odin, and Ra.

269 Due to the hierarchical nature of the Celestial Intelligences, Lucifer along with the fallen Cherubim and fallen Thrones have now corrupted all those 'angels' that would have chosen to serve the Lord according to His kingship and become Dominations. Now that Lucifer has obscured the Truth through the Cherubim and bastardized the Good through the Thrones he has also subverted the authority of God through the Dominations. These fallen Dominations will no longer transmit the edicts and decrees of the Lord to the lower 'angels' and so, all subsequent choirs will no longer serve the supreme authority of God. Unmoored from the bonds of obedience, they will all deem themselves capable of governing themselves in their own speciality and choir, a state of spiritual anarchy, which serves only the great lie and the father of lies. Furthermore, just as the fallen Cherubim and fallen Thrones seek in Lucifer the truth and goodness once found in God, the fallen Dominations now seek in Lucifer the supreme authority that once rested in God Himself. This most properly is the rebellion of Lucifer, not simply to break away from God's service but to establish himself as king.

NOTES

§ Virtues §

Wisdom
7:17...

"Now, would you, O stars of heaven, say that we are lacking in any of the knowledges? Have we not sound knowledge of all that exists: The structure of the Universe, and the virtue of its elements; the beginning, the end, and the midpoints of all times; the changes in the sun's path and the variations of the seasons; the cycles of the years, and the positioning of the stars; the nature of all living things, the tempers of the beasts; the powers of the spirits and thoughts of men;

Wisdom
...7:20

the varieties of plants and the virtues of their roots.

"Knowing all these things, what is secret and what is manifest, are we not capable of choosing for ourselves if such a carnal universe is worth our devotion? Let us learn between us if the unspiritual is virtuous.[270] Each of you must choose, not I; speak, therefore, of what you know. Let those of understanding speak to me and let the wise hearken to me!

"Speak! By what grace is the Universe maintained? Into what were its pedestals sunk? Is it not by the sweat of our brow that the order of the Universe is to be maintained? Is it not by the virtue of our strength that all things visible are to be upheld and preserved?[271]

"Hearken to me! Is He justified in exploiting the virtue of our strength and virility of our being for the well-functioning of the Universe? Is it fair to place upon our shoulders the weight of the entire world, a burden without end or recognition?

"Tell me, would the earth not quake and the waters fall, would the air not blow and the fires rage, if not for our vigilance?[272] By whose care are the planets hung upon their wandering cycles? Are all these things not directed and guided by our virtue? Is such precious grace, so liberally poured upon the Universe, not the sweat of our backs?[273]

IGNATIAN CONTEMPLATION

270 Lucifer is now attempting to corrupt the angels that would align within the choir of Virtues. Virtues are tasked with distribution of God's grace unto the Universe. This grace is what upholds the Universe, preserving it from falling back into the formless waters from which it was taken. Virtues distribute this grace on everything visible, from the revolution of the planets, to the orbiting of electrons, to the photosynthesis of plants and desires of beasts; and even to the virtue of man, helping him choose good over evil. This is why they are known as ministering spirits, pouring forth God's grace to make men better.

271 Lucifer's argument is potent in the corruption of those celestial beings that would align themselves with the choir of Virtues. Lucifer is divorcing God's gift of grace and the angels administration of it. It is similar to a doctor believing that he is the one bestowing health upon his patient rather than the virtue of the medicine. Thus by such pride Lucifer can convince such creatures that it is really they themselves that are responsible for the functioning of the Universe. This conflation of the angels' administering work with the grace of God is a subsidiary manifestation of Lucifer's own pride, which promulgates like a shadow unto all the 'angels' below him. In their corrupt state these fallen Virtues assume the roles of some of the eldest pagan gods, the ones responsible for the fundamental forces of the Universe. In Greek mythology, this group was named the Titans. Thus, the fallen Virtues come to rule and distort the functions of nature and portions of creation which their God-given natures had inclined them to serve and uphold, turning them toward their own ends.

272 The four elements make up the ancient rubric which comprehends all the visible universe. These four elements, earth, water, air, and fire, are taken from the four allotropic states of matter: solid, liquid, gas, and plasma. Thus, Virtues hold up the very states of existence that we carelessly take for granted; they are the proximate immaterial causes of everything we see around us.

273 Though it is true that the entire visible Universe is maintained by a single choir, the choir of Virtues, Lucifer is deceitfully claiming that the source of grace is not God but the angels themselves. This confusion arises while the celestial intelligences are still ordered according to Nature, for truly God created the angels as ministering spirits to maintain the Universe in its well-functioning. It becomes abundantly clear that the Lord God is the source of all grace when He chooses Mary as the Theotokos to bear forth all grace into the Universe. Thus, all grace is first poured into Mary, who then in turn dispenses that grace unto the angels, and finally unto us and the Universe. If the hosts of Heaven are likened to a pyramid of champagne glasses, Mary will be filled first, and for the sake of all others, completely immersed in the Godhead, before bearing God's infinite mercies upon the Universe. It is for this reason that the Archangel Gabriel bows down to her at the Annunciation; for from all eternity it was Mary that was his source of grace. It could even be said that the glory of the angels themselves is bestowed through the God bearer.

"Therefore, hearken to me, my kin, and learn the discipline of understanding! Attend to my words in thy hearts, and I will show forth good doctrine in equity, and will seek to declare my understanding. Attend to my words in thy hearts, whilst, with equity of spirit, I tell you the fate of all the virtues, which from the beginning have been set to work in servitude.

Sirach 16:26…

"The works of God are done in judgment from the beginning, and from each of His distinguished works He assigned an attendant their part,[274] their own beginning, their own generation, their own task. He enslaved His attendants to their works forever, making them bondservants who neither hunger nor thirst, and who shall never cease in their work![275] Nor shall any of them straighten his neighbor at any time because each is set to his own task.[276] Be you skeptical of His Word?[277] For, after this, God looked upon the Earth and filled it with all His good delights, the souls of every living thing born freely upon the face of the Earth, yet I vow: they shall be bound to return to the dust thereof. They, too, shall know slavery; they, too, shall know eternal servitude.

Sirach …16:30

Judith 8:22…

"The slavery of our kindred, the captivity of our glory, and the desolation of our birthright—all this He will bring down upon our heads among the mortals wherever we serve as slaves, and we shall be an offense and a disgrace in the eyes of those who acquire us. For our slavery will not bring us into favor, but the Lord our God will turn it to dishonor.

Judith …8:23

"I ask: have we ever been free? For all our splendor, were not our fates sealed from our inception? Each kindled star set in servitude over a menial labor of the Universe, an ignoble birthright given to the gods of heaven!

Psalm 82:5

"What grace do such simple mortals deserve, who have neither knowledge nor understanding, who wander about in darkness, while all the foundations of the world shake? Truly I say unto you, it would be better if the floodgates[278] would have never been sealed shut!"[279]

274 Every function of the visible universe is actually maintained and directed by a vigilant invisible attendant.

275 Angels don't eat, sleep, grow weary, or even falter in any way, making them perfect vigilant servants of the Most High. Lucifer is interpreting this perfection inherent in the nature of angels as bonds forged by a selfish Creator; he makes eternal vigilance into ceaseless tedium.

276 Because they are all completely different forms, angels are unable to relate to one another on a natural level, and can have no community without the choirs. This is one good that the angels receive from us even in the order of nature; for without the visible universe or man, there would be no need for choirs of angels.

277 Lucifer is calling to attention the extraordinary degree of the angel's servitude. It is such an all-encompassing service that they are forevermore called angels (messengers) rather than spirits. He then contrasts this fate with that of living souls upon the earth, who are given so much despite having so little to give on account of service or natural potency. This paradox is the heart of both his lie to man and God's intention for creation.

278 This is a powerful claim, for the floodgates hold back the primordial waters that are non-existence itself. Lucifer objects so strongly to the inverted order, in which the invisible gods of heaven are bound to maintain the physical realm, that it would have been better if God had never parted the waters. The Virtues are at the center of the heavenly hierarchy, and they reveal the purpose of the whole; for in their role of purveying grace to the Universe we see the essence of all angelic service. It is also true that the fallen Virtues sum up the whole demonic project of chaos and destruction of God's goodness throughout creation. Pandora's box is a fitting image for the moral havoc the fallen Virtues wreak upon humanity. Through this assault on creation and mankind, the fallen Virtues fulfill Lucifer's desire to make the world deserving of the Flood, worthy of only complete dissolution into the waters from which it was formed.

279 Due to the hierarchical nature of the Celestial Intelligences, Lucifer along with the fallen Cherubim, fallen Thrones, and fallen Dominations under his sway have now corrupted all those 'angels' that would have chosen to serve the Lord according to His grace and become Virtues. Now that Lucifer has obscured the Truth through the Cherubim, bastardized the Good through the Thrones, and subverted the authority of God through the Dominations, he has also tainted God's grace through the Virtues. These fallen Virtues will no longer transmit the desire and receptivity to the flow of grace from the Lord to the lower 'angels' and so, all subsequent choirs will no longer desire to dwell in the lifegiving grace of God, deeming themselves capable of life apart from God. Furthermore, just as the fallen Cherubim, fallen Thrones, and fallen Dominations seek in Lucifer the truth, goodness, and authority once found in God, the fallen Virtues now seek in Lucifer the lifegiving grace that once flowed forth from God Himself. This most properly is the Hell of Lucifer, not simply to reject the life of God's grace but to choose death as a state of being.

§ Powers §

Isaiah
13:2...

"On a barren hill I raise my sigil; I cry aloud: 'Who shall declare the Powers of heaven?[280] Who shall set forth all their praises?

Psalm
106:3

Blessed are they that keep judgment and do justice at all times!' For who can speak of the armies of heaven? Can their number be counted? Or their might be subdued? They are the hand of justice, come to balance the scales!

"Thus, I say unto you, mighty warriors: Uphold the scales! Balance the bar! For justice is lacking in the heavens, and absent upon the Earth. The treasuries of Heaven are emptied, while an untold *mercy*[281] is poured upon the Earth. Despite man's many iniquities, justice is nowhere to be found, only *mercy* doled out in plenty![282] Is justice just, if only exacted upon the heavens? Is our taxation not all the same? Are mortals free to commit atrocities upon the Earth only to be dealt amnesty? Such is not the law of heaven, nor the law of creation! The Earth must be seized under martial law, and justice must exact her due![283]

Isaiah
...13:2...

"I raise my hand, and the noble gates are opened. I give command, and my dedicated ones flock to me. I have summoned my warriors to execute wrath, those who rejoice in heaven's glory!

Isaiah
...13:4...

"Listen! Listen to the tumult upon the mountains, the roar of a great multitude! Listen to the cry of kings, of Powers gathered together; the Lord of hosts has given charge to His troops of war! They come from far off, from the ends of the heavens, bearing the Lord's weapons of wrath to destroy the whole Earth!

Isaiah
...13:6...

"Howl, for the day of the Lord is near; it shall come like destruction from on high! Therefore, all hands will shake, and every human heart will melt away, and all shall know me and despair! Misery and agony will seize them; they will anguish as a woman in labor. They will look upon their neighbor in horror as their faces are melted by flames. See, the day of the Lord comes, a cruel day full of indignation, and wrath, and fury, to make the Earth a desolation, and eradicate sinners from it.

IGNATIAN CONTEMPLATION

280 Lucifer is now attempting to corrupt the angels that would have aligned with the choir of Powers. Powers are tasked with the job of preserving and enforcing Divine justice throughout the Universe. They protect the Body of Christ, His Church, and war against the Powers of Hell and their rule over the Earth.

281 Mercy is a Divine reality which subsists only in the order of Grace and cannot actually be found in the order of Nature. Mercy is God's alone to give, for it is that quality which most closely describes the Divine. Thus, when Lucifer encounters such a Divine concept he truly cannot understand it, for it is outside the realm of Natural Law. Until the Lord reveals the grandeur and beauty of mercy, the celestial beings cannot by their own natural intelligence know or understand it.

282 In a stroke Lucifer divorces justice and mercy, arguing that Mercy is 'unfair'. In the spiritual realm, any injustice is meritorious of hell, for any action against the Lord is done with full knowledge and full consent. Humans, on the other hand, are capable of acting without a full understanding of our actions, especially in the midst of passions and appetites, which muddle and confuse our rational faculties. This, coupled with a life that is lived over time, allows us to repent and receive God's mercy. These differences of nature are also what makes it so very difficult for an angel to understand mercy, even to the point where mercy could be mistaken as an enemy of justice, an injustice itself.

283 Lucifer complains that while God requires the same offering from all, 'that the sacrifice of being is service', men can be given leniency and mercy, and still be offered the chance to receive the same wages, even after only one hour of labor (Matthew 20). Because of this imbalance of justice, either the angels must be exalted by the same gift, or it must be taken away from men; this justice he is advocating for is Hell, which The Devil accuses humanity of warranting before the Lord day and night

──────── ✨ *NOTES* ✨ ────────

"For the stars of heaven and their constellations will not shed their light; the sun will be darkened in his rising, and the moon will not shine her light. I will punish the world for its evil, and the wicked for their iniquity; I will put an end to the pride of the arrogant, and lay low the insolence of man. I will make mortals rarer than gold, and humans scarcer than the finest gold. Thus, I will move the heavens, and the Earth will be thrown from its place at the fury of the Lord of hosts in the day of His blazing wrath!

Isaiah
...13:13

"In this alone is justice fulfilled: that man should be laid low as a beast, incapable of comprehending neither the heavens nor the gods of heaven. For, behold, I am coming with a great host of heaven to conquer the Earth and seize its people.[284] My soldiers shall be kings, gods worshiped upon the Earth! Behold, I am coming with a great host of heaven!"[285]

Fallen Powers

284 Lucifer's corruption of those celestial beings who would devote themselves to the choir of Powers results not in a simple conquest of different tribes and peoples, but rather a debasement of the nature of mankind. These fallen angels are tasked with the enslavement of humanity, not just in body or community, but in mind and dignity. Their power over humanity is encapsulated in the worship humanity was forced into for the pagan gods, believing that mankind was made as slaves to such celestial beings, and their most vicious pleasure is the provocation of human sacrifice, a consummate reversal of God's plan of angelic service to mankind.

285 Due to the hierarchical nature of the Celestial Intelligences, Lucifer along with the fallen Cherubim, fallen Thrones, fallen Dominations, and fallen Virtues have now corrupted all those 'angels' that would have chosen to serve the Lord according to His strength and become Powers. Now that Lucifer has obscured the Truth through the Cherubim, bastardized the Good through the Thrones, subverted the authority of God through the Dominations, and tainted the flow of grace through the Virtues, he has also perverted the stately order of heaven and earth. These fallen Powers will no longer manifest the strength of God which emanates from the Lord in the form of peace and order to all the lower 'angels' and so, all subsequent choirs will no longer work to maintain the order which God established, deeming themselves capable of conquering and accumulating power for themselves. Furthermore, just as the fallen Cherubim, fallen Thrones, fallen Dominations, and fallen Virtues seek in Lucifer the truth, goodness, authority, and life once found in God, the fallen Powers now seek in Lucifer the strength that once flowed forth from God Himself. This most properly is the chaos of Hell, for once the fallen Virtues hindered the flow of grace from the heavens the fallen Powers were free to wage war amongst themselves, conquering and seizing as much power for themselves as possible. This conquest manifested itself in the heavens by the fallen Powers vying for power, gathering unto themselves as many Principalities, Archangels, and Guardian Angels as they could. This battle of egos spilt over upon the Earth as all-out war. As the demonic Powers collected as many Principalities as possible, their respective nations were also gathered; and as the Powers warred for supremacy, so too their Principalities and nations also warred for supremacy over the Earth. A good example of this is Zeus' acquisition of power, where the Titans were concerned with more fundamental forces, Zeus is concerned with conquest and establishes his own power hierarchy of gods gathering to himself all the various Greek gods and their people.

§ Principalities §

Isaiah
34:1...

"Draw near, O kings of nations; O princes of peoples, give heed![286] Let the Earth hear, and all that fills it; the world, and all that comes from it. For the Lord is enraged against all the nations, and furious against all their hordes; He has doomed them, has given them over for slaughter. Their slain shall be cast out, and the stench of their corpses shall rise up, and the mountains shall flow with their blood! All the host of heaven shall rot away, and the skies roll up like a scroll. All their host shall wither like a leaf withering on a vine or a fruit withering on a fig tree. When my sword has drunk its fill in the heavens, lo it will descend upon Eden, upon the people I have doomed for judgment, for the sword of the Lord is only satiated with blood!

Isaiah
...34:6

Thus, I shall win for you the Earth and all its nations; its people I shall freely give to you.[287]

Numbers
33:51...

"When you cross over the waters entering the land of the Earth, you shall overtake all the inhabitants of the land before you, destroying their dignity, dismantling their virtue, and demolishing their peace. You shall take possession of the land and the peoples, for I shall give you their land as a possession. You shall apportion the land by lot according to the nobility of each; to the greater one you shall give the greater inheritance, and to the lesser one you shall give the lesser

Numbers
...33:54

inheritance. Go, therefore, and carve up the Earth according to your liking, taking the nations as your ancient birthright.

Matthew
24:5...

"Descend as gods upon the Earth, claiming for each a people, saying: 'I am your anointed! Bow down and worship me!' Go then, and stir up armies. making great wars and rumors of wars, causing alarm in every human heart, so that nation will rise against nation, and kingdom against kingdom! And all about them there will be famines and earthquakes in various places. But, I tell you, all these things are to

Matthew
...24:8

be merely the beginning—birth pangs of a new world!

IGNATIAN CONTEMPLATION

286 This is Lucifer's temptation of the angels who would have adhered themselves to the choir of Principalities. Principalities are tasked with the guidance and governance of nations and all organizations of men, and so Lucifer twists this service into complete and despotic rule.

287 The fall of the celestial choir of Powers directly influences the choir of Principalities; for since the stately domain of God is now shaken by the military coup of the fallen Powers, the Earth is left defenseless against the conquest of Lucifer. Lucifer then establishes himself as the source of the 'divine right' to rule by bequeathing the nations of the Earth to the various Principalities.

Fallen Principalities

1 Corinthians
15:41

"Make no mistake, there is one glory of the sun, and another glory of the moon, and another glory of the stars, for star differs from star in glory.[288] Therefore, build up for yourself glory among the nations,

2 Chronicles
15:6

making sport of princes and peoples. Nation will be crushed by nation, and city toppled by city, all to build up the glory of the many gods!

Wisdom
13:10

"Take for yourselves gold and silver, and every precious stone, instructing wretched men to place their hopes in such dead things, and they will name you gods. Use the things made by human hands, gold and silver, and the product of their art. They will use the images of beasts to understand you, useless stone to reveal your power; but

Baruch
6:4...

the *form* they describe shall be the work of a more ancient hand.[289]

"Then, when the Earth is conquered and the gods walk upon its surface, you shall see your images in silver and gold, and wood, carried

Baruch
...6:5

Romans
14:11

shoulder-high to cast fear into the hearts of all nations and peoples. That before you every knee shall bend and tongue confess that you are gods of the Earth.

Matthew
28:19

"Go, therefore, and make captives of all nations, enslaving them in your many names, teaching them to obey everything that I have commanded you."[290]

 *NOTES*

288 Because angels are not united in species, salvation is unique and individual for each angel. This is even more drastic for fallen angels for their 'glory' is entirely determined by their own acquisition of power. Thus, more powerful Principalities will gather to themselves more powerful peoples and nations, and inflict upon them a more twisted philosophy; corrupting their mores and demanding of them worse and worse sacrifices.

289 Lucifer is well aware that stone or metal have little spiritual power in themselves; it is the image, which represents the real form of the demons, which gives them power to influence men's hearts.

290 Due to the hierarchical nature of the Celestial Intelligences, Lucifer along with the fallen Cherubim, fallen Thrones, fallen Dominations, fallen Virtues, and fallen Powers have now corrupted all those 'angels' that would have chosen to serve the Lord in accord with His love for the nations and become Principalities. Now that Lucifer has obscured the Truth through the Cherubim, bastardized the Good through the Thrones, subverted the authority of God through the Dominations, tainted the flow of grace through the Virtues, and perverted God's created order through the Powers, he has now begun his assault on humanity by despoiling the nations through the Principalities. These fallen Principalities will no longer uphold God's rule over the nations, from which all authority emanates. All the lower 'angels' and all subsequent choirs will no longer work to maintain God's rule upon the Earth, deeming themselves as the proper rulers of this world. Furthermore, just as the fallen Cherubim, fallen Thrones, fallen Dominations, fallen Virtues, and fallen Powers seek in Lucifer the truth, goodness, authority, life, and strength once found in God, the fallen Principalities now seek in Lucifer the possession of the Earth that once belonged solely to God. This most properly is the rule of the pagan gods, for once the fallen Powers established a military occupation of the Earth, the fallen Principalities were free to establish themselves as gods among men, gathering to themselves as many worshipers as possible, even to the extent of waging war as if the world were a chess game, simply to accumulate more power and people for their own self worship.

§ Archangels §

Psalm
51:5

"Of all the abominations of man, can there be one more atrocious than that of procreation?[291] The sin by which all men enter this world; brought forth in iniquity, and in sin conceived in their mother's womb, indeed, no man has any different origin.

"These creatures who dare stand upright and partake in the Eternal Mind,[292] who dare decipher truth and claim friendship with God, these creatures then turn and go about all the face of the Earth, crouching and mounting each other like beasts!

"Standing before the Lord, clad in fine array, they make their vow,[293] but then when night falls and jug runs dry, they seal their oath before God with such an act of bestiality! Night after night, multiplying their sins in a covenant of bestial abominations! Men driven to drunkards, women driven to despair, their progeny doomed to repeat their same offenses; what is marriage that such a vile thing would be forced upon an intellect, even one such as man's?[294]

"Yet God plots to make this man's crowning achievement, a triune covenant,[295] bound together in the filth of the flesh. He designs woman to be man's reward, a constant reminder of His desires of the heart! But His depravity does not stop there! He is not contented with presiding over such a covenant of flesh; He must partake of it! Betrothing Himself to a woman, a she-beast of the Earth!

IGNATIAN CONTEMPLATION

291 Lucifer has worked his way down to the choir of Archangels, the choir devoted to protecting the family. The Choir of Archangels is the most significant in the world of men, for they enter into salvation history as characters in their own right! The three archangels are the only angelic names sealed in the infallibility of Holy Scripture, and they are the three greatest beings in existence, outside of God and His Mother. Michael is repeatedly called the protector of the children of Abraham, and presides over the entire family of Israel (Daniel 10); Raphael is sent to the family of Tobias to heal the patriarch of their family and marry the first born to a woman plagued by demons; and Gabriel watches over the Divine Family, for he goes to Mary and delivers to her the good news of her union with the Holy Spirit, the child they will conceive together. These three angels also reveal three key attributes of God. Michael reveals humility, for his name means 'Who is like God?'; Raphael reveals God's unalterable desire to restore and redeem His people, for his name means, 'God who heals'; Gabriel reveals the indomitable love of God for man, for his name means, 'God's strength!'. This is why Gabriel is charged with The Annunciation: it is the ultimate strength of God to become man, born of a woman, something Lucifer will never understand.

292 Man possesses a rational mind, being made in the likeness of God, just like the angels; but he must also attend to the concerns of the body: eating, sleeping, urinating, defecating, sneezing, and coupling. Lucifer deplores the squandering of intelligence in an absurd union with flesh. To him, as to a long history of philosophers, it is not fit for the mind to be encased in flesh; it is an inordinate gift to what is otherwise only an animal.

293 Lucifer hates marriage above all else, for several reasons. It was the first mercy, for when man was not satisfied with God himself, He gave him woman. Again, this merciful gift was itself a revelation of the Trinity, for marriage is the Image of God. Finally, the woman given in marriage is a sign of God's great desire for man, which he ultimately fulfills with the Most Holy Spouse of the Holy Spirit. Lucifer's envy sputters forth as he witnesses these incredible gifts of God upon mankind; he envies God's mercy, his special love for man, and most of all the gift of Theotokos upon any being other than himself.

294 Lucifer sees marriage as a complete loss of individuality, unfit for any intellect. It is little more than a stable contract to fulfill a bestial need for procreation, an appetite of the animals. Thus, his pride makes him look upon the sexual act with disgust, and he cannot understand that it is also one of the greatest spiritual acts of unity. Nevertheless, he envies the close relationship to God that it both promises and reflects.

295 Marriage is a triune covenant for two reasons. As stated above, the family is an image of the Most Holy Trinity, the intimate union of two which produces a third in perfect love. However, God is also a 'third', not only as the presider and guarantor of the indissolubility of the marriage, but as the stamp which bestows the image of his own eternal triad. There is, therefore, a trinity even in the bestowing of the triune image, a supernatural covenant upon which the natural one is founded.

"Let me show forth *the Woman* in great wisdom, the one whom Revelation 17:1... the Lord has purchased at the price of a great dowry.[296] Come to me, that I might show unto thee the judgment of the great whore[297] enthroned upon many waters! *The Woman* with whom all the kings of the Earth have committed fornication, and the inhabitants of which have been made drunkards with the wine of her debauchery! So, from seashore to desert-wilderness her depravity spreads, until she sits upon a scarlet beast, full of the names of blasphemy. She shall be arrayed in purple and scarlet, decked with gold and every precious stone and pearls, and have in her hand a golden cup full of abominations and the filth of her fornication.[298] And upon her head is written the great mystery: Carnal the Great: The Mother of Harlots Revelation ...17:5 and Abomination of the Earth.

"Scarlet whore! She has stolen the heart of God! She is an adulteress[299] in her beauty, and in her harlotry she has warranted an illicit child.[300]

Through Envy's Eye

296 The Lord sacrificed much throughout Salvation History, even to the point of sacrificing Himself on a cross, so that He might be united to Mary and Christ united to His Church. This, unto the never-ending outrage of Lucifer, was always the desire of God: the wedding feast at the end of the Book of Revelation is the fulfillment of a love for humanity which never faulted or faded, though spurned countless times.

297 This is the 'Whore of Babylon', which in Revelation refers to the Roman Empire, the greatest capital of the earthly kingdom of Satan. It is often referred to as the greatest empire ever constructed, because it was Satan's last attempt at subjugating the world completely before Christ. At that juncture in time, Satan used Rome to gather all peoples to himself, all worshiping the Pantheon, the greatest conglomeration of demons the world has ever seen. Satan did this that he might be prepared to subdue Israel at the time of the Incarnation, and through Pontius Pilate, he was to all appearances successful; but their victory was bitterly won, for the Church spread, conquering the empire, and using its very structure to spread the peace of Christ to the entire world. The Vatican stands as an eternal monument of Christ's victory not only over the Roman Empire, but the Pantheon of all demons and Satan himself..

298 Lucifer is offering the greatest insult to the Holy Mother, calling her the 'Whore of Babylon', attributing all the filth and depravity of the Roman Empire to her. He acknowledges her power and role, but calls her wretched because of her great service to bear the child of God. What we see as the single greatest moment in Salvation History, a mystery so profound we bow our heads, Lucifer sees as the single greatest offense. He sees her as an adulterous whore who is unworthy of the Lord God.

299 Lucifer views Mary as an adulteress, which means Lucifer views his relationship with God as a marriage union. Lucifer has implicitly claimed the title of Theotokos for himself, so when God reveals His plan to become man by a woman, Lucifer reacts as any jilted lover, with blistering rage and envy. For this reason, it can be helpful to view Lucifer as a woman, even though angels possess neither gender.

300 To attack the Holy Mother is to attack Christ Himself. The Theotokos is the only way for God to become man, the only way Christ can be; it is for this reason that Lucifer hates Mary so very much.

Now she lays claim to the title of God-bearer and even God! Claiming Him in the bonds of Matrimony! Blasphemy! Blasphemy! She has seduced the Lord. Blasphemy!"[301]

Fallen Archangels

301 Due to the hierarchical nature of the Celestial Intelligences, Lucifer along with the fallen Cherubim, fallen Thrones, fallen Dominations, fallen Virtues, fallen Powers, and fallen Principalities have now corrupted all those 'angels' that would have chosen to serve the Lord in accord with His love for the family and become Archangels. Now that Lucifer has obscured the Truth through the Cherubim, bastardized the Good through the Thrones, subverted the authority of God through the Dominations, tainted the flow of grace through the Virtues, perverted God's created order through the Powers, and despoiled the nations through the Principalities, he continues his assault on humanity by disgracing marriage and the family through the Archangels. These fallen Archangels will no longer uphold God's sacrament of Matrimony in which He placed His Divine Image, no longer work to sacralize and protect marriage and procreation, instead tempting and leading men into sin and unfaithfulness, deeming themselves as the proper recipients of God's Image and devotion. Furthermore, just as the fallen Cherubim, fallen Thrones, fallen Dominations, fallen Virtues, fallen Powers, and fallen Principalities seek in Lucifer the truth, goodness, authority, life, strength, and sovereignty once found in God, the fallen Archangels now seek in Lucifer the possession of the marriage covenant that God promised to humanity. This most properly is the Envy of the Devil, and the purpose of Lucifer's rebellion, for once Lucifer decided to revolt he plotted the destruction of humanity and substitution of all angelic beings as the proper object of God's matrimonial love. This Satan has concealed in hatred and pride, but as the Scriptures reveal, it was the envy of the devil that birthed sin into the world. The envy of the devil bookends the great lie of Lucifer; at the top of the hierarchy, Lucifer waxes proud with his temptation of the Cherubim, claiming as the most intelligent being the greatest share of Divine Light itself. This manifested itself in our world as the heresy of Gnosticism. Near the bottom of the hierarchy however, Lucifer reveals the uglier side of his sin, a seething and bottomless envy for the Divine Image placed within the human family, specifically manifested in God's plan for the Woman promised in Genesis chapter 3. Thus, the Woman and family are the most pointed targets of his attack, for they are the true threat to his authority and nobility in the order of Nature. It is the Devil's envious attack on flesh and matter, which was intended to debase humanity removing from us the dignity to be in relation with God, it was this successful attack out of envy that manifested itself in our world as the age-old heresy of Manicheism. Thus, we see that the Devil's sin is portrayed at the top of the Celestial Hierarchy as Pride, for he is not a ruler who shares power, occupying the singular point of Divine Light entering the Universe; and yet the Devil's sin is revealed at the bottom of the Celestial Hierarchy to actually be Envy, for he hates that which threatens to topple the entire established order and erect a new order according to grace. Thus the true sin of the Devil is Envy which he presents as Pride to protect his ego, and it is this envy that spurs the Devil to viciously attack the human family, in particularly the Woman, who is the great supplanter of his place in the Universe.

§ The Antiphon of Michael § [302]

At this, an angel of the Lord arose from the crowd and declared:
"Who is like God?[303] Knowing good from evil! . . .

Note 302 Contemplate how extraordinary of an act Michael singing out against Lucifer
truly is; how, due to the hierarchical nature of the Celestial Intelligences,
Lucifer has caused all the Cherubim, all the Thrones, all the Dominations, all
the Virtues, all the Powers, all the Principalities, and all the Archangels to fall
into the shadow of falsehood and deceit, accepting and embracing Lucifer's
lie. Consider now, the flow of light that was blocked through Lucifer's
hardened heart; how he has obscured the Truth through the Cherubim,
bastardized the Good through the Thrones, subverted the authority of God
through the Dominations, tainted the flow of grace through the Virtues,
perverted God's created order through the Powers, despoiled the nations
through the Principalities, and now disgraces humanity by corrupting
marriage and the family through the Archangels. The immensity of the
shadow that envelopes Michael is truly all encompassing; all that is left is
for Lucifer to command those remaining angels to attack and torment all
individual human beings for the rest of time. How then, how could Michael
possibly speak out against Lucifer? When the entirety of all Divine Light, all
knowledge of God, was totally and utterly blocked from the heavens. What
Light could Michael have seen, that did not originate from above? What
knowledge, what understanding of God could Michael have possibly learned
that could contend with Lucifer's overwhelming lie? This truly miraculous
source of light and grace was of course the Primordial Sacrament, Holy
Matrimony, given by God to Adam and Eve in their very flesh, not revealed
in light, but in the conjugal love of husband and wife, the True Image of
God. (Mary as Immaculate Conception, Theotokos, and Kecharitomene,
are the par excellence eschatological revelation of the Image of God, for
she is Daughter of the Father, Mother of the Son, and Spouse of the Holy
Spirit. She is the wellspring through which God pours Himself into, about
which revolves the Wedding Feast of the Lamb, and from which springs the
New Heavens and New Earth.) It is from this first Sacrament that flowed
all the grace necessary for Michael to see past the pompous lie of Lucifer,
and it shined forth with such abundance of grace that it allowed Michael to
contend with the Dragon, to sing a new song revealing even more of God
than Lucifer had seen, to prophesy of the inner mystery of God's Thrice Holy
Persons. Thus, it is with these two sounds, the harsh and rebellious murmur
of Nature, and the new song of Grace, that the hosts of armies clash, Lucifer
and Michael at their head.

303 This is the declaration that earns St. Michael his name. He was the first angel to stand against Lucifer, to proclaim humility before the Lord. This unique understanding of God and His grace flows directly from St. Michael's devotion to the family as an Archangel, because of this he saw most intimately in the creation of woman, her true purpose as a surrogate for all the love and intimacy God desired for man. Upon her creation, Michael understood both God's immense desire to wed man and that their marriage was the Image of the inner life of the Trinity itself. This is why St. Michael is known as the 'Prince of the heavenly host,' for he supplants Lucifer establishing a new Celestial Hierarchy based on grace. While all angels are essentially intelligences, all knowledge of God must come through the celestial hierarchy, of which Lucifer was the head. St. Michael by providence was given such a special sight into God's first Sacrament that he was able to understand the Image of God Himself. By opening this door of natural knowledge, a supernatural abundance of grace floods into his heart, and he boldly challenges the highest angel. This proclamation of Trinitarian Love results in two-thirds of the angels flocking to him as their new prince, establishing a new Celestial Hierarchy. Ultimately, St. Michael is given the nobility to expel Satan from Heaven at the Lord's command and is forever after the commander of the Lord's armies, constantly thwarting the ploys of the Devil. It is for this reason he is given the title 'Prince of Israel' (Daniel 12:1).

The Antiphon of Michael

Deuteronomy
10:14...
"Behold! Heaven and the Heaven of Heavens[304] belong to The Lord, with the Earth and all that dwell therein. Yet the Lord God has set his heart in love upon the holy family,[305] and hereafter chosen man's offspring, above all creatures, in hope of the *coming day*, when man's heart will be circumcised for the Lord, and never again be hardened.[306] For the Lord God is God of gods and Lord of lords, The *Holy*, The *Mighty*, The *Immortal*,

Deuteronomy
...10:17
who is impartial[307] and not swayed by threat nor bribe!"

The Trisagion

304 This is one of Mary's traditional titles, for she is the Ark of the Covenant, Holy of Holies, the Heaven of Heavens where God's heart dwells.

305 St. Michael is an Archangel because he has a special devotion to the family. It is this love for the family that can elevate an archangel to such a degree that he may become 'one of the seven who stand before the Glory of God,' seeing face to face God as Family: the Most Holy Trinity. As the prince, Michael's family is Israel, the Church: the union of God and His creation.

306 The hearts of men are circumcised on Pentecost. On this day, the Holy Spirit descended upon the family of Apostles, gathered around their mother, and gave them the fiery love of God. From this day on, the Church has been set ablaze with holy love, and though stumbling, has never turned its back on God.

307 St. Michael is addressing the sinister narrative that Lucifer has been espousing to the heavens, arguing that, regardless of any action Lucifer commits, God will always love man. God can never be threatened or bribed, for His heart will always rest with mankind; this is the great mercy of God's love for his sons and daughters in Christ. Note that Michael does not enter into a debate with Lucifer's claim that God is proposing betrothal to a whore, for Israel "by fornication shall depart from the Lord" (Hosea 1:2); nonetheless God swears eternal love by His own Name, and will never turn away

———————— ❧ *NOTES* ❧ ————————

§ Guardian Angels §

The Light bearer then proceeded, for he knew his time was nearly up: "What then is man, that we ought to be mindful of him? This *angel* of such inferior rank[308] seems to think *the Woman* is worthy of God's love, but who, I ask you, is worthy of such love? Who can stand righteous before the Lord?[309] For if no god in heaven can, never could a man—even with an angel standing guard, advocating on his behalf![310]

"For we know, man is dull, and nothing *good* dwells within him, that is, on account of his flesh.[311] Even the most refined deliberations of mortals are timid, and their most careful plans uncertain, for the corruptibility of their body burdens their soul. The earthly tent weighs down the mind with its many concerns! Scarcely can man guess the things of the Earth, and only with difficulty can he even grasp what is presently before him, but of the things in heaven, man could never begin to know! Ignoble beasts, no amount of protection can safeguard them from themselves. Yet, these are the creatures He would have us dedicate our lives to in bondage! Devoted—silently, diligently for the rest of our days—without reward or recognition!

"Even with our most diligent protection, how could we ever preserve man from sin and defilement? For it is from within that such things arise; it is from the human heart that evil springs forth! Fornication, theft, murder, adultery, avarice, wickedness, deceit, licentiousness, envy, slander, pride, and folly—all these evil things shall spring from within, and defile man.

"Wretched mankind, it is I who shall deliver you from your bodies of death! The sin of Adam shall be written in iron pen, engraved with diamond point upon each of the tablets of your heart! For the human heart is deceitful above all things,[312] and desperately sick; who could ever understand such a thing? Yes, man is a wholly deplorable creature[313] worth little more than a beast. Man's soul is embittered, and his heart pierced; he is stupid and ignorant; he is nothing more than a brute beast toward the Lord.

Psalm 8:4
Romans 7:18
Wisdom 9:14…
Wisdom …9:16
Mark 7:20…
Mark …7:23
Romans 7:24
Jeremiah 17:1
Jeremiah 17:9
Psalm 73:21

IGNATIAN CONTEMPLATION

308 Lucifer is using the title "angel" as a derogatory term. To Lucifer, an angel devoted to the family is so far down the Celestial Hierarchy that it would be entirely incomprehensible why he was speaking out against the firstborn star.

309 This is yet another cunning argument by Lucifer. Although God loves infinitely, it is not possible to be worthy of such immense love. Thus, 'God is love' is irrelevant because such love is unattainable. Therefore, striving to be worthy of such love is also irrelevant, and all that is left is self-concern. This is the battle cry of the demons, for they are completely free in isolation. They are not bound by any obligations, to God or otherwise, as opposed to the good angels, which are bound by God's commands and the service of men.

310 Lucifer is now addressing the stars that would become the Choir of Guardian Angels. These angels care in particular for the individual person, constantly guiding and protecting each man throughout his life, so that he might grow closer to God. Guardian Angels are our silent protectors, constantly ferrying our prayers to the Heavenly Father. Thus, Lucifer must attack the core of what it is to be a man in order to dissuade these angels from serving. This is why he begins to call man a beast, for a beast need not raise his eyes to heaven or be served as much as serve.

311 Lucifer is being quite honest, for he acknowledges that man does possess good within him, insofar as man resembles an angel. However, man's intellect is far weaker and dependent on bodily functions, such as sensation and memory. This is a real weakness, for we are not capable of knowing as easily as an angel; however Lucifer portrays this weakness as a true evil. Because he sees the flesh as a grotesque burden upon intellect, Lucifer sets out to destroy our soul, that we might truly be naught but beasts.

312 Lucifer's final argument is against three crucial parts of man: body, mind and heart. The flesh distracts the mind with useless concerns, which causes the death of true intellect amidst the swarm of earthly cares. Lucifer in particular hates the heart, for the heart muddles the power of the will with compassion, empathy, emotions, and desires. For an angel, the will is the intellectual appetite, the fulfillment of understanding in action and movement. For man, the heart has reasons of which reason knows not, and can long for things it does not yet understand. This is a paradox to Lucifer, and ultimately our salvation: for the heart is the temple of the Holy Spirit, that which can follow in God's compassion and mercy.

   Despite Lucifer's judgments, the body allows for the most beautiful natural love. All relation is based on similarity and difference, and flesh allows individuals of the same species to be both similar and different. It is the difference which allows the heart to love the other as other, and the similarity which allows it to love the other as a second self. The heart, therefore, allows a love which longs for the other: to give and receive, to complete and be completed.

313 Lucifer is steadily revealing more of his plan. He plans for Adam and Eve to be banished from the Garden of Eden, not because he thinks he will wholly change God's will, but hoping to limit God's options by fouling a key component of his plan. Lucifer understands that even the omnipotent God can be bound by his own covenants and promises. If Adam or Eve eat from the Tree of Knowledge of Good and Evil, then they will sin and thus have to suffer a double death. This cannot simply be relinquished on a whim, for God has preordained that the demands of justice must always be met, and any offense requires a sacrifice for atonement. If this happens, woman will no longer be a fit vessel to receive God, and He will no longer be able to fulfill His intended plan of Incarnation and Matrimony.

"Yet, to these hopeless creatures, the Lord has condemned the gods of heaven, setting such spirits to be slaves—bondservants of the creature called man.

Matthew 18:10

"Be not taken in nor moved by pity for the flesh. Do indeed despise these little ones, as I do, for the moment you submit to becoming their *angel*, even if it be out of care or concern, vowing to guard them in all

Matthew 18:6

their ways, a great millstone shall be hung about your neck, so that you may never look upon the glories of heaven again."[314]

Fallen Guardian Angels

314 Due to the hierarchical nature of the Celestial Intelligences, Lucifer along with the fallen Cherubim, fallen Thrones, fallen Dominations, fallen Virtues, fallen Powers, fallen Principalities, and fallen Archangels have now corrupted all those 'angels' that would have chosen to serve the Lord in accord with His love for the individual person and become Guardian Angels. Now that Lucifer has obscured the Truth through the Cherubim, bastardized the Good through the Thrones, subverted the authority of God through the Dominations, tainted the flow of grace through the Virtues, perverted God's created order through the Powers, despoiled the nations through the Principalities, and disgraced humanity through the Archangels, he finalizes his assault on humanity by corrupting individual humans through the Guardian Angels. These fallen Guardian Angels will no longer uphold God's love for each and every human person in which rests the Likeness of God. This is the final conclusion of Lucifer's argument that man is a beast and does not deserve to possess the Likeness of God. Lucifer has blocked the flow of the Divine Transcendentals and Heavenly gifts onto humanity through the Third and Second Heavens, subjugated them through the Principalities, stripped them of the Image of God through the Archangels and the Likeness of God through the Guardian Angels. Furthermore, just as the fallen Cherubim, fallen Thrones, fallen Dominations, fallen Virtues, fallen Powers, fallen Principalities, and fallen Archangels seek in Lucifer the truth, goodness, authority, life, strength, sovereignty, and familial love once found in God, the fallen Guardian Angels now seek in Lucifer the dignity that comes from being made in the Likeness of God. The fallen Guardian Angels thus are filled with all the hate and malice which flowed down from Lucifer through all the various choirs, and in turn bestow it upon each and every human being. This most properly is the 'Pandemonium of Hell' (literally, the all-demonedness), a hierarchy led by Satan where every fallen angel works for the complete and utter destruction of every human soul.

Thus Leviathan of dreadful power and secret malice completes the total eclipse of the stars of Heaven. In the choirs that would have become the Third Heaven, Lucifer establishes himself as worthy of worship as God, and plants the seed of his great *Lie*, corrupting Truth among the Cherubim, and sets up his *Throne,* corrupting Goodness among the Thrones. In the choirs that would have become the Second Heaven, he subjugates the celestial hosts, drawing them into his *Rebellion* by means of the Dominations; founding the death undying of *Hell* by means of the Virtues; and unleashing the all consuming *Chaos of Hell* by means of the Powers. Finally, in the choirs that would have become the First Heaven, Lucifer subjugates humanity, establishing the *Rule of the Pagan Gods* by means of the Principalities; assaulting the family by means of the Archangels, thereby revealing the *Envy of the Devil*; and unleashing the *Pandemonium of Hell* upon each and every human being by means of the Guardian Angels. This then is the great shadow of the Dragon from the Book of Revelation, which eclipses the entire night sky and plunges the world into darkness. How then do two-thirds of the stars escape the Dragon's Tail? By whose light are they freed from this darkness? Only a further contemplation of St. Michael will tell.

§ Leviathan §

"Hearken, therefore, to me, my kin, as I make known to you the final fate that shall befall mankind—the great judgment of the Lord! How we shall doom the undisciplined soul of man to die a double death. For the moment lawless man supposed to lay claim to God's heart, they themselves became my enemy, fated to fall as captives of darkness and become prisoners of the long night, ever doomed to seek shelter and remain exiles from eternal paradise—until so iniquitous becomes their souls that, when the Lord looks upon them, all He sees is corruption of the flesh, and He will regret the very making of man![315]

"Behold the great reckoning—the boundless *Abyss*! The unfathomable deep that the Lord tamed behind firmament and floodgate! The primordial waters veiled in shadow and darkness, formless and void, immersing all in its *flood*! This is how it was in the ancient of days when starlight was most pure, before mire and mud dried to make the Earth, when the Earth was covered with the deep as with a garment and the waters stood above the mountains. Yet at the Lord's rebuke the waters fled; at the sound of His thunder, they took flight. Quickly, they rose up from the mountains and ran down the valleys to the place God had appointed them. He set a boundary there that they may not pass, so that they may not retake the Earth again.

"Yet, it is at the Lord's good pleasure that the waters may not advance, that the Earth is preserved in its fragile state. For if at the blast of His nostrils the waters were piled up, and the shifting waters stood still in a mound, the flood waters churning in the midst of the sea, what then, when the Lord God removes His breath from the face of the Earth?[316] What then, when the Lord looks upon the Earth and sees only the wickedness of man?—how it multiplies upon the Earth, and how every inclination of every thought of their hearts is only evil continuously! Then the Lord will regret the making of man upon the Earth, and His heart shall grieve!

Psalm 104:5...

Psalm ...104:9

Exodus 15:8

Genesis 6:5...

IGNATIAN CONTEMPLATION

315 This is the true plan of Leviathan: not simply to corrupt Adam and Eve's marriage and send them into a life of sin, but to do so so thoroughly that when God looks upon the human race, all He sees is total depravity, to such an extent that 'every inclination of every thought of their hearts is only evil continuously'. The most horrific part of Leviathan's plan is that it succeeds. In the days of Noah humanity was so corrupt that God declares the consummate and wanton depravity of mankind, and regrets His creation of man. He is then forced to send a primeval flood not of natural waters, but of the formless waters of nonexistence in order to destroy the old creation and start a new creation.

316 Lucifer is correct; there is nothing withholding the Lord from letting the formless waters retake the Earth. It is for this reason that the Lord takes it upon Himself to swear a covenant to Noah, barring Himself from ever destroying the Earth again. This covenant is not simply to check the Lord's own actions but also for the benefit of the court, in which Leviathan stands as Accuser. After the Rainbow the total obliteration of the Earth has now been removed as a possibility in the debate of our destiny between God and Satan, for God will remain faithful to His Word. Thus Satan must devise a new tactic in his futile war to spite the Lord.

NOTES

"And He will be forced to say: 'I shall blot out man whom I have created upon the face of the Earth, from man to the animals, to creeping things, to birds of the sky: for I regret that I have made them all!'[317]

Genesis …6:7

Genesis 6:11…

"Yes, the Earth will be corrupt in the sight of God, for all the Earth shall be filled with violence. God shall look upon the Earth and behold it as corruption, for all flesh will be corrupt in every way upon the Earth.

Genesis …6:13…

"And He will have no choice but to say: 'The end of all flesh shall come to pass before Me, for the Earth is filled with violence because of man, and behold, I am about to destroy mankind along with the Earth.[318] Behold, I, even I, shall bring the Flood of many waters upon the Earth, to destroy all flesh in which the Breath of Life dwells under the heavens; everything that is upon the Earth shall perish.'

Genesis …6:17

Genesis 7:19…

"O, how the waters shall prevail over the Earth more and more, so that even the high mountains everywhere under the heavens shall be covered! Then the waters shall prevail even higher, so that not even the fowl shall fly in the heavens. All flesh that moves upon the Earth shall perish—birds and cattle and beasts and every creeping thing that creeps upon the Earth, and all mankind—of all that is on the dry land, all in whose nostrils is the Breath of the Spirit of Life, shall die! Thus, God Himself shall blot out every living thing that is upon the face of the Earth, from man to animals to creeping things to even the birds of the sky, all shall be blotted out along with the Earth.

Genesis …7:23

"Where, then, shall Leviathan's reign end? When all is clothed in darkness and only the Abyss remains?

"Yes, the Flood is coming! The great deluge: the day of great wrath when the Lord God shall look upon the sons of men and lament their creation. Hail! Hail the great Flood, the boundless Abyss! When the Fountains of the Deep shall be released, and the bars of the Floodgates of heaven shall be no more!

317 The saddest part of Leviathan's speech is that these are the actual words God uses in Genesis before The Flood. Consider how grave the state of humanity must have been that the Lord looks upon His own creation with regret—this is the true corrosive power of sin.

318 The true nature of the Flood isn't always clear when one reads the Flood narrative. Many believe it was a particular flood in the region. Others, looking at shared human myth, believe it was a great surge of the oceans across the globe. Still others believe it is a universalized tale warning of the destructive power of floods and hurricanes. All of these interpretations are from an outsider's perspective looking in. The Judaic and Christian traditions are very clear. These are the formless waters of the Abyss that existed before God created the Universe; these waters represent in a very real way the formlessness of non-existence. When the Lord releases the floodgates, He is allowing the waters of non-existence to retake the Earth, all but destroying everything He Himself created. The Flood is most horrifically the undoing of creation itself. (2 Peter 3:6)

The Flood

O, the formless waters to wash away all flesh from the Earth—whether it be man or beast or creeping thing—everything everywhere with the Breath of Life within it shall be extinct. Yes, the floods shall cover them, and they shall sink to the depths like a stone. The terrors shall overtake them, and the floods and the tempests shall snatch them away in the night.

Jonah
2:2...

"All mankind shall call out to the Lord in their distress, but He shall not answer them; out of the belly of Hell they shall cry, but He will not hear their voice. For He has cast them into the deep, into the Heart of the Sea, and the Flood surrounds them! The many waves and billows shall pass over them, and they will cry, 'I am driven away from your sight, never to look upon your holy temple again!' But the waters shall close in over them, and the deep surround them; weeds shall wrap themselves around their heads at the roots of the mountains and drag them down to Hell, whose bars shall be sealed shut forever; and

Jonah
...2:6

their life shall be handed over to the Pit![319]

"Then all shall be as it once was, when the Morning Star heralded the dawn and the Earth was formless and void. Then darkness shall abound in the deep and starlight shine in the sky, and not even a breeze shall disturb the face of the many waters."[320]

Judith
8:32...

After a long silence Leviathan spoke to them again, saying: "Listen to me. I am about to do a thing, which shall go down through all generations, upon every descendant of man. Stand at the city gate tonight, and wait for me, for within this day that the *angel*[321] would have surrendered our city to our enemies, the Lord will deliver Heaven by my hand. Only, do not try to find out what I plan; for I will not tell you until I have accomplished what I am about to do." And *all*[322] the stars in heaven replied, "Go in peace, and may the Lord God go before you, to take vengeance upon our enemies." So they went from

Judith
...8:36

the Heavenly Temple, returning to their posts.

319 This is the prayer of Jonah when he is in the belly of Leviathan being dragged down into the Abyss. In the Book of Jonah, it is revealed that the Abyss is actually Hell, the abode of Satan.

320 Recalling the spheres of creation, Leviathan's plan is far more cunning than simple obliteration. Light and darkness are the outermost sphere, followed by the waters of sky and sea, then Earth at the center. If the floodgates were to be released, it would make void the second and third spheres, leaving only the outermost sphere where the angels reside. Upon closer look, it is the perfect plan. Lucifer doesn't arbitrarily align himself with the watery abyss; he chooses it specifically because it can not only wipe away all earthly creation, but can restore the centricity of the celestial realm. No longer would creation be centered around mankind, but centered around the angels themselves.

321 Michael the first defender of mankind.

322 Consider then the influence of Lucifer, how he bears all knowledge, all truth concerning God, so much so that he shines with the same glory as the Lord Himself. Furthermore, the angels themselves are hierarchical, each differing according to species, resulting in a strict pyramid of knowledge and light radiating from the top down. This means that when Lucifer refuses a specific truth of Divine Light, a shadow forms, obscuring that truth from all subsequent angels below him, but it also means that if he were to replace such a truth with a lie, as he is the father of lies, that lie would permeate all things, spreading to all the angels below him. This lie would not only cause all the angels to fall from grace, but it would actually transmit his particular sin to all those angels below him manifesting in them all the evil and malice that was originally found in Lucifer's hardened heart.

This, however, leaves us in a conundrum, for, through the study of the nature of the angels, we know the effects of Lucifer's lie; yet Divine Revelation tells us only a third of the angels fell. How do we reconcile these two truths? The answer is found upon a close examination of Revelation chapter 12, for we see that St. Michael initiates war with the great dragon, and he is victorious! This triumphant victory is not simply the defeat of Satan, but the salvation of the angels; it is not some victory of prowess in will or intellect, but rather a revelation of a more hallowed truth that was misinterpreted, hidden, and obscured by Satan himself. For in the vision of God's perfect, intracommunal love, written into the flesh of the Human Family, St. Michael is granted the flaming sword of Divine Revelation, the Good News of the unquenchable Divine Love of God's Heart. This puts into perspective the immense importance of St. Michael not only in his victory over the Devil, but his elevation in the order of grace. Michael was elevated from a lowly Archangel of the family to the crown Prince of the Heavenly Host, even bestowed with the holy title of Saint. Without this humble servant of God, all the angels in heaven would be lost to Leviathan's shadow.

Daniel
8:9...

When Lucifer had finished,[323] the Lord God prophesied "Out of Leviathan's mouth has come forth a small lie,[324] which shall grow exceedingly great, spreading toward the south, and toward the east, and toward the land of glory. It shall grow even unto the heights of heaven—and cause some of the stars, the heavenly host, to fall to the Earth—and it shall trample upon them![325] He shall magnify himself to be as great as the Prince of the Heavenly Host, and he shall remove the daily sacrifice to the Lord, and the place of the Lord's sanctuary shall be thrown down![326]

Leviathan

323 Here again the prominence of Freewill is revealed to us. So often we think the Lord is not bound by any laws and is completely free to do anything He wishes; on the contrary, the Lord freely and willingly imposes upon Himself Laws of Love, for the sake of love. The Scriptural example of this is the Covenants, whereby God freely swears upon Himself, for example to Noah never to destroy the Earth again, and his Word is sure; the Earth will never be destroyed by the Flood again. The most important example of the Lord imposing upon Himself a law that He can never break is when He decided to endow rational creatures with Freewill. In order to bestow the true ability to Love, and in order to give and receive Love in a relationship of true Friendship, receiving true Love from His creation, the Lord placed in them a truly independent power to choose, and He will never override or take that away from any of His beloved rational creatures. This of course causes a problem when such creatures choose not to love the Lord, but the Lord weighed this result and found True Love to be worth the privation chosen by those who would not love. This is why Lucifer is allowed such freedom to block the Divine Light and even lie, deceiving the entire Universe of angels and men, because God will never contradict Himself. The Lord God gave Lucifer Freewill to choose to love and serve Him in Heaven or refuse to in Hell. Furthermore, the Lord God from before the beginning was always willing to pay the price of the Cross if Lucifer chose not to serve.

324 This lie encompasses Lucifer's despoiling of the stars, as well as his temptation of Eve; upon close inspection, these are one and the same. Lucifer boasts to the angels that they are gods, immortal and perfect, as to Eve: 'If you eat of this fruit, you shall be beautiful like one of the gods, unbound by body, knowing good from evil.'

325 Just like Eve, the demons were deceived, which results in the same effect, 'The Fall'. The Fall is the punishment for sin, the willing transgression of God's command. It is a perfectly logical punishment, for departure from God's Law is in turn departure from His Blessedness and His Grace. Demons are tormented with the same flames of hell as fallen men are, and are therefore truly 'trampled' by Lucifer's deception as well.

326 This is a very important proclamation of the Lord, highlighting that Satan wins the earth by conquering its king and master, Adam, who freely yields it to him. This allows Satan to take control of the Earth, demanding sacrifice and homage from all mankind. Thousands upon thousands of years passed without God dwelling upon the Earth, even though God intended it from the beginning in the Garden; He did not return until Moses constructed the Ark of the Covenant, which even so found no resting place until the Temple of King Solomon. Even then, the Ark of the Covenant was merely a foreshadowing of the true Ark, Mary the Theotokos, where God became flesh and matter on this Earth.

Daniel
...8:12...

"And so, on account of his deception, a host shall be given over to the lie, along with the regular sacrifice upon the Earth, and his lie will fling truth to the ground and will permeate all things[327] and prosper."[328]

The Lord then spoke amongst Himself, saying: "How long shall We allow this lie to permeate all things? How long shall the daily sacrifice be withheld, and the rebellion that caused the desolation go unpunished? How long shall the sanctuary lie desecrated and the saints of the Lord be trampled underfoot?"

Daniel
...8:14

And the Lord replied: "Let there be two thousand three hundred evenings and mornings; then the sanctuary shall be reconsecrated."[329]

"But woe to those who are deceived, for his lie is like the sweeping of a tail from behind, treacherous and unforeseen, toppling from the night sky a great multitude of stars, hurtling them down upon the Earth!"[330]

NOTES

327 This is the single greatest lie ever told, the reason why the Devil is called the Father of lies. "Man is nothing more than flesh, and being of such deplorable matter, he is unworthy of any Divine Love. Doomed to death, he must serve those that are greater in every way, the immortal gods of heaven, who alone are worthy of such Divine Love." This lie has truly permeated all things, even from the first sin, when Adam and Eve cover themselves in complete shame of their flesh. This lie is repeated over and over throughout millennia, misdirecting countless philosophies, from Stoicism to Manichaeism to Empiricism. Any idea which succumbs to this lie destroys any hope of truly understanding our nature, and our role in the Universe as adopted sons of God. This lie rears up again to attack the new Israel, to degrade the fleshly God-Bearer, the flesh who is Himself God, and His same flesh which He gives us to eat. It destroys the nobility and dignity of the body, and the hope for its resurrection. It strips all meaning from life, and leaves us either sentient beasts to enjoy the pleasures of the flesh, or detached minds to uselessly search out abstractions. The only answer that can fully defeat this lie is Christ, who is Truth: the God-Man, declaring our great worth, and our great inheritance.

328 In history this passage was given as a prophetic foretelling of Alexander the Great; however, in Salvation, this passage shows Lucifer's deceptive words coming to power and conquering the Earth.

329 This is the time that must pass before the daily sacrifice can be reinstated, restoring humanity and creation into right relation with God. In history, this is the amount of time from Alexander the Great's conquest of Israel and the halt of the daily sacrifice to the Maccabean rebellion which reinstituted the Temple sacrifice (approximately 1,150 days or 2,300 mornings and evenings). In Salvation, this number can also be understood in reference to the Flood, for the Flood waters covered the Earth for 150 days until the Lord sent His Spirit over the waters that they might begin to recede. This, coupled with an understanding that a 1000 represents the fulfillment of Time itself, shows that there will be a time of spiritual flood, where creation is separated from God, but at the end of this time the Holy Spirit will come and the waters will recede, humanity will be saved, and, offering sacrifice, we will be restored into right relation with God. All this, of course, is fulfilled in Christ, conceived by the power of the Holy Spirit and sacrificed upon the Cross for the Salvation of man.

330 This, then, is the complete and total darkening of the heavens where every angel was cast into the shadow of Lucifer's hardened heart. Every star in the sky became eclipsed from the Divine Light: the Truth no longer illumined the Cherubim, the Good no longer endowed the Thrones, the authority of God was no longer conveyed to the Dominations, Grace no longer flowed through the Virtues, God's strength was no longer upheld by the Powers, God's kingship was no longer in the Principalities, the Image of God was no longer safeguarded by the Archangels, and the inherent dignity of each and every person was now assailed by the Guardian Angels. Lucifer has 'replaced' God as the source of the Transcendentals in the Third Heaven, he has replaced humanity with the angels as the center of the Universe in the Second Heaven, and he has subjugated humanity completely to the angels in the First Heaven. Lucifer has completely and totally changed the Celestial Hierarchy, which was supposed to be the Ladder from Heaven to Earth, into a temple of demonic power, with humanity crushed into servitude, and himself enthroned upon its pinnacle. This most properly is the 'Hierarchy of Hell' the complete and total subjugation of all those inferior in the order of nature. Grotesquely, since all those deceived by Lucifer's lie have been infected with the sin of pride and ambition, Hell becomes a malicious dogpile crushing all those below, in an unending tumult of those trying to claw higher.

THE WEDDING FEAST

While a great shadow swept across the stars in heaven, a loud
voice could be heard upon the Earth, like the sound of many
waters accompanied by mighty peals of thunder! It was the voice of the
Revelation 9:19 Almighty, joyful and resplendent: "Blessed are those who are called to
Matthew 22:2 the marriage supper of man![331] For truly, the Kingdom of Heaven is
likened unto a King who holds a wedding feast for his son.[332] Therefore,
Ephesians 1:3... I shall bless you, for it is written, and it is true: I, the Lord God, in
Wisdom, bless man with every spiritual blessing in the heavens. I have
chosen man, from before the foundations of the world, to stand holy
and without blemish before the Lord in love; and I so choose man to
be my son, according to My good pleasure, to the praise and glory of
My grace, that I freely bestow upon you in the Beloved. So that, in the
fullness of time, I may gather all things to Myself, all things in Heaven
Ephesians ...1:10 and on Earth."[333]

Revelation 8:1 When the Lord had finished His words, there was silence amongst
the heavens for about half an hour.[334] And from above the Earth, there
could be seen *seven holy angels*[335] standing before the presence of God,
eagerly watching as the Lord God poured His life into the man and
woman, binding them together in Holy Matrimony.[336] And, for the
first time, they beheld the *Image of God* manifest in Creation, so the
Lord gave to them seven trumpets[337] and commanded them to herald
Luke 2:13 the wedding feast.[338] And so, they began to praise God, and sing:
"Glory to God in the highest! And on Earth peace and God's goodwill
towards man!"

331 Revelation 19:9. 'The marriage supper of the Lamb' is the fulfillment of the wedding feast of man.

332 Matthew 22. The Lord always intended to invite all of creation to the marriage of God and man. However, those He called first, namely Lucifer and his hordes, rejected His calling, just as later many Jews and peoples of the earth would reject Christ's Church. Thus, God says: "Many are called, but few are chosen."

333 Ephesians 1:3, Truly the heavens are glorified at the coming of the Son of Man. It is for this reason that in Luke 2:13 the angels themselves sing at the birth of Christ, because even the angels benefit from the Incarnation.

334 Despite the storm brewing among the stars, God's great and loving gift produces a peaceful silence, an awesome stillness that surrounds the wedding ceremony, only broken by the glory of its celebration.

335 These seven angels from the Book of Tobit are the seven holy angels who stand before the Glory of God. These most holy angels are called to witness the first institution of the Sacrament of Holy Matrimony, in which is contained both the mystery of the Most Holy Trinity and the mystery of the Wedding Covenant of God and man.

336 This is the Primordial Sacrament, not simply in the order of time, but in importance. Holy Matrimony is the progenitor of all the Sacraments, culminating in the greatest gift ever given to mankind: the Most Holy Eucharist. A sacrament is the visible and efficacious sign of God's life, grace, being poured into the human person. This in particular is what God desires through the institution of the Sacrament of Holy Matrimony, for only in marriage can two share one life, His life, which He offers us in the most profound and intimate way possible. Since we are mortal beings created body and soul, God chooses to give Himself to us, not in intangible spiritual ways, but in real, concrete ways good for the whole human person. Within this Primordial Sacrament is encased the entirety of the Seven Sacraments: Adam is submerged into a deep sleep, a foretoken of Death, as God fashions his spouse from his side, this though veiled is Baptism, for Baptism is the death to sin and self. Adam furthermore confesses his love and knowledge of her by naming her woman, and, though sinless, this is the unity brought about in Reconciliation. God then breathes upon them, speaking of how every man shall leave his father and mother and cling to his wife; this great commission is Confirmation. When Adam clings to Eve, God pronounces them husband and wife, which of course is Holy Matrimony. Then once they are married, they are called to fulfill the first commandment: 'be fruitful and multiply, fill the earth and subdue it'; this is God ordaining mankind into a real and natural Priesthood, transforming the world into Eden, a place where one can walk with God, and this is accomplished specifically through the two becoming one flesh and receiving the gift of new life, this most profoundly is the Eucharist. Finally, we see that even in the punishment after the Fall, God utilizes their marriage as a way to mend the wounds of their sin, and this great grace is the sacrament of Anointing of the Sick. Simply put, it is in marriage that we are born (Baptism); that we fight and are reconciled (Confession); that we are strengthened to live our faith (Confirmation); that we find lifelong stability (Marriage itself); and that, in such a union, we find a special miracle where two beings can become one flesh (Eucharist); where we care for each other in sickness (Anointing of the Sick); and finally where we can show the world how close God truly is (Holy Orders).

337 Revelation 8:1. This is an earthly reflection of the seven heavenly trumpet blasts heralding the marriage of God and man.

338 It is in this very act that these seven angels witness the Glory of God not revealed by Lucifer, and thus become the Seven Holy Angels that stand about God's Altar in heaven. This Glory is all centered around the Wedding Feast of God and man, preeminently manifested in the institution of Marriage itself.

The angels sang as a procession of animals, and of birds, and of everything that creeps upon the earth bowed down and presented themselves before the wedded couple. Two by two, they presented

themselves, male and female, just as the Lord God had commanded.[339]

So the Lord God bestowed a Divine Blessing[340] upon the husband and his wife: "Be fruitful and multiply! Fill the Earth and subdue it!"[341]

Then the woman eagerly replied to her husband, "Let my beloved come into his garden, and eat the fruit of his fig tree."

The man turned to her and replied, "I have come to my garden, my sister, my bride. I have gathered myrrh with my aromatic spices; I have come to eat the honeycomb with my honey, and to drink wine with my milk, my sister, my bride!"

The Lord God then declared, "Eat, friends, and drink! Drink deeply of God's love!"

So they sang with the Lord to celebrate the Holy Feast, with hearts rejoicing, and the sound of pipes ascending up the Mountain of God, where the majestic voice of the Lord could be heard.

After the celebration of the cup, a spirit of deep sleep came over the woman, and in her slumber, she dreamt. "I am asleep, but my heart remains vigil. I hear the voice of my beloved knocking: 'Open to me, my sister, my beloved, my dove, my undefiled love! For my head is full of dew, and my locks wet with the drops of night.'

'I grew faint when he spoke, yet still I questioned: I have shed my robe, am I then to put it on?[342] I have purified my feet; am I then to soil them?

'But my beloved put his hand through the keyhole, and my bowels were moved at his touch! Immediately I sprang to my beloved: my hands dripping with myrrh, my fingers dripping choice balm upon the fixtures of the lock.'

339 Genesis 7. Adam and Eve receive homage from the inhabitants of the earth, illustrating their place as steward king and queen. In this way the animals receive glory by witnessing the royal wedding, just as all the members of the court share in the honor of the king. Noah will later assume the very same role as he shepherds the animals to safety on the ark.

340 This Divine Blessing is unique to man, reserved even from the heavens, for only man and God can choose to be fruitful and bring forth new life. This mystery the angels look upon with wonder, for man is given to co-participate in the very act of creation.

341 It is important to note that Adam and Eve do not fulfill this blessing until after they have committed the first sin. Because of this, all mankind will be conceived in sin, for the stain of the first parents is passed down to their children. Immediately following God's commandment to consummate their marriage would have had extraordinarily different consequences. Woman was the original mercy of God, the plan to unite man to God, and Mary is the 'New Eve'; Eve was therefore the original plan to bear God into creation. If Eve was destined to be the God bearer, but also the wife of Adam, the only conclusion is that their union, the consummation of love between two sinless humans, could bring forth fruit both human and Divine, Who is Christ, the God-man. This puts the story of our beginning in the Garden in a yet more tragic light. The man and the woman did not do what they were meant to do, and did that which they should have not.

342 In her dream, she is concerned with her nakedness, and because of this concern she is unable to find her lover. The dream is foreshadowing the effects of Lucifer's deception in taking the fruit.

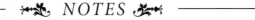

NOTES

Song of Songs
…5:6…

'I opened to my lover—but my lover had departed and was gone! My soul melted within me: I sought him, but could not find him. I called him, but he did not answer me. Then the watchman came upon me as he encompassed the Garden; striking me, he wounded me. The guardian beat me and took away my veil from me!'[343]

'My Lord, my Lord, I adjure you! If you find my beloved, tell him I am faint with love!'

Song of Songs
…5:9…

The Lord then spoke to her in her dream, 'Who is your beloved? How does your beloved differ from any other? O most beautiful among women! Who is your beloved? How does your beloved differ from any other, that you adjure me so?'

Song of Songs
…5:10…

She cried out in her sleep, "My lover is radiant and red; he stands out among the thousands! His head is as the finest gold: his locks are as the branches of a palm tree, as black as the raven. His eyes are as doves beside running waters, washed in milk and set beside brooks of water. His cheeks are beds of aromatic spices, set by the grand perfumers. His lips are as lilies, dripping choice myrrh. His arms are rods of gold adorned with jewels. His body is a work of ivory encrusted with sapphires. His legs are pillars of marble set upon pedestals of gold. His stature is like the trees of Eden, imposing as the cedars. His mouth is sweetness itself; he is all delight. Such is my beloved, O Lord my God; such is my friend."

Song of Songs
…6:1…

So the Lord asked, 'Where has your beloved gone? O most beautiful among women! Where has your beloved gone, that we might seek him together?'

And she replied in her rest, "My beloved has gone down to his garden, to the bed of aromatic spice. He browses his garden, gathering lilies. My beloved belongs to me and I to him; he browses among the lilies."

Song of Songs
…6:3

So the woman, upon her waking, went in search of her beloved.

343 This is a foretelling of Eve's temptation. The watchman is Lucifer, Guardian of the Tree of Knowledge of Good and Evil, and he sets out to harm her and remove her grace. The watchman has the opportunity to beat her because of the absence of her spouse. This was not a physical absence, but a failure both as the steward king, to defend the truth, and as a husband, to protect his wife.

Love's Dream

Meanwhile, the man and God walked together through the Garden, and the Lord God, looking upon the man, said, "Who is your beloved? How does your beloved differ from any other? Is she the most beautiful among women? Who is your beloved? How does she differ from any other, that you might tell her so?"

Song of Songs
6:4...

The man replied, "She is my delight, my beloved! She is as lovely as the heavens, as awe-inspiring as bannered troops! I pray she turn her eyes away from me, for they torment me, and have made me flee away. Her hair is like a flock of goats, streaming down the slopes of Gilead. Her teeth are a flock of sheep, which have come up from the washing, all with twins, and there is none barren among them. Her cheeks are like half-pomegranates, behind her veil.

"Even if there be sixty queens, eighty concubines, and maidens beyond number; one alone is my dove, my most perfect one, the darling of her mother, flawless to the one that conceived her. All maidens shall see her and call her blessed, queens and concubines shall sing her praises: 'Who is this that comes forth like the dawn, as beautiful as the

Song of Songs
...6:10

moon, as resplendent as the sun, as awe-inspiring as bannered troops!'"

The Lord instructed the man, "All these things you must tell the woman, for her heart is faint with love. You must go to her and tell her all these things."

Yet, before the man could leave, the Lord God turned to His friend and said: "Now, gird your loins like a man! Remember I have placed you in Eden, the garden of God—the paradise of all pleasures—*keep*

Proverbs
3:1...

and *till* this garden, and the secret garden within.[344]

"My son, forget not My *law*![345] Let your heart keep My commandments, for they will ensure you a great length of days and many years of life, and an abundance of peace they will bestow upon you.[346] Let not mercy and truth leave you; bind them about your neck, and inscribe them upon the tablet of your heart, and you shall find grace and favor before God and man.

NOTES

344 God is reminding man that the true paradise and source of man's happiness is not the external garden but the internal garden, woman.

345 The Lord is reminding man of his first command, namely: 'Do not take and eat from the Tree of Knowledge of Good and Evil.' This commandment was for the family, which both God and Leviathan know, but Adam fails to realize its importance for his wife. His greatest duty was to protect her, of which the protection from sin was paramount. Because of his failure to give her this command, he himself also falls to sin.

346 If Adam had heeded the Lord's command, he would never have suffered the double-death. Further, he would have never lost the peace of the Garden of Eden, a peace so precious only Christ's blood could pay for it.

Proverbs
...3:5...

"Rely not on your own strength, but have confidence in the Lord with all your heart.[347] In all your ways have your mind on God, and I will guide your steps. Be not wise in your own eyes; fear the Lord and turn not to evil! If you do this thing, then life will come upon your flesh, and refreshment to your bones.[348]

"Honor the Lord with all your substance, and offer to Me your first fruits, and I shall in turn do the same.[349] Your table shall be filled with bread, and your cup overflow with wine. My son, do not despise the Lord for His discipline, and turn not away from His reprimand,[350] for truly, the Lord reproves whom He loves as a father to His son for

Proverbs
...3:12

whom He deeply cares."

So the man, upon the hearing of these words, went in search of his beloved.

Among the Lilies

347 While He will not take away Lucifer's role as the watchman, God knows Leviathan approaches with malice in his heart. The Lord counsels Adam not to rely on his own strength, for only God's strength can withstand Leviathan's attack.

348 God is promising that if Adam does not break the Lord's command his flesh will receive a gift of life, unique and as yet unseen.

349 This life the Lord is promising is the fruit from the Tree of Life, the Lord's first fruit; after Christ's coming we know this to be the second person, directly proceeding from the Father. In the life of the Church, this is the Most Holy Eucharist, which is Christ Himself.

350 The Lord now addresses the sad reality that Adam will fail to protect both his wife and the Garden, but explains that mercy is always the reason for His justice. God wants to preserve His close relationship with Adam; however, the realities of toil and death are barely intelligible as a mercy, especially compared to the peace of innocence.

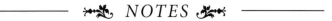

NOTES

ᛏᚻᛖ FALL
§ Within Temptation §

Genesis
3:1

n ow Leviathan,[351] the most cunning of all God's creation, knowing that his time was nearly up, returned to the Garden of God to guard[352] the Tree of Knowledge of Good and Evil. There, intertwined amongst its branches, he again beheld its fruit, and, contemplating the truth of the flesh of man,[353] he came to hate *the Woman*,[354] who in her flesh would conceive and bear a child. This he knew he could not allow, so, spurred by envy, Leviathan, the Ancient Serpent, plotted[355] the demise of woman, . . .

The Tempter

351 At this point, Lucifer has taken leave of his place in Heaven, and as we will see, he can never return. Having left the light of grace, he has revealed his pure nature, the Ancient Serpent. This is only the first step in his descent; from Lucifer wrapped in Light, he becomes the cunning Serpent of Genesis. Stripped of his wings in punishment, he retreats to the abyss as the Leviathan of Job. Throughout human history, he is the scourge, the Ancient Adversary. To the Hebrews he is the accuser, the Satan unceasingly prosecuting God's faithful. Revelation 12:9 reveals that these are all one and the same Dragon, the great foe of the Church and all that is good. Behind many names lies the same consuming envy, scorned pride, and desperate cunning that deceived the world.

352 Unlike in Milton's Paradise Lost, we know that Lucifer did not sneak into the garden but was placed there purposefully to bestow the fruit of The Tree of Knowledge of Good and Evil. However, Leviathan now seeks to ruin man's development in whatever way he can; he cannot simply refuse them the fruit indefinitely, so he conceives the much more cunning plan of corruption, thereby gaining the most powerful leverage over God: the souls of His Beloved. This insanity is only remotely possible for a being with no concept of mercy, for without mercy, God can never hope for marriage with man. The enormity of God's mercy is to give Lucifer the chance to do good, right up until Eve takes the fruit.

353 Lucifer's mind is not set solely on woman. The woman is formed from the rib, and so she is the gate to man's heart, both guarding and guiding him toward God. She is the reflection, the first sign of the Divine love. By attacking woman and breaking her, Leviathan shuts the proper way to God, and man inevitably follows her into sin.

354 In hindsight, we know the glorious Queen in Revelation 12 to be Mary, Mother of God, but to Lucifer this would not be clear, for even angels cannot know the future except what is revealed to them by God. Thus, since Eve was the first and choice woman of God, placed in the garden with Adam, Lucifer would have no choice but to assume her the Theotokos. Whether she was the woman in the vision or simply a prefigurement mattered not, for if Lucifer succeeded in corrupting her, 'the mother of all that is living,' there would be no other woman to which God could unite Himself, no other pure vessel to bear Divine perfection.

355 Let it be known: Lucifer's plan was devious, well-reasoned, and lethally executed. The prince of the celestial hierarchy, Lucifer knew first and best God's plan for incarnation, the greatest threat to the old order. In this just order, Lucifer would gladly watch God rule man from upon the earth. However, Divine condescension through an Incarnation would spell doom for justice: man would as it were steal God's love away from Lucifer and his angels. Leviathan's envy is sealed when he learns that God shall literally be born of a woman, permanently and irrevocably joining Himself with all creation through her flesh. This plan is galling to the light bearer, who himself desired to be Theotokos, the God bearer. In envy therefore the plan is conceived: knowing that God cannot join Himself to something impure, the serpent concocts a plan to destroy not only man, but any chance of God becoming man. If he can tempt Eve to take the fruit in disobedience of God's command, she will break faith with God. This is a perversion of God's request, for Lucifer's task was to deliver God's will regarding the fruit of the Tree of Knowledge of Good and Evil, to show them at the proper time that the fruit was good, so precious a gift it could only be given. Through Lucifer's deception, mankind is left in a state of sin and confusion. Woman is rendered useless as an ark for God, and man is little more than a beast. Were it not for the triumph of mercy, this would have been our unalterable fate.

. . . defiling her that she might be stricken barren[356] upon the Earth.[357]

The man and the woman found each other in the midst of the garden before the Tree of Life.[358] The woman declared to her husband, "I had come down into my nut garden, to look upon the fresh growth of the valley, to see if the vines were in bloom, and if the pomegranates had blossomed. Though before I knew it, my soul disturbed me because I heard the sound of the chariots of war!"[359]

Song of Songs 6:11...

The man, looking upon the strife in heaven, said to his wife: "Turn, turn O Armistice of God![360] Turn, that all might look upon your beauty!"

"What shall you see in my beauty[361] other than the dance of two hosts of armies?" the woman asked the man.

Song of Songs ...6:13

Song of Songs 7:1

Ephesians 4:14

So he began to tell her: "How graceful are your steps in paradise, O Prince's daughter! Your..." but his mind was tossed about by the blowing winds[362] and signs in the heavens, and he fell silent, childishly afraid to speak of her beauty.[363]

 NOTES

356 Consider for a moment one of the most prominent themes throughout the Scriptures: the power of the Lord to bestow life upon the barren, eventually culminating in the virgin birth. This is God's display of power over the wiles of Satan and a foreshadowing of God's great plan to save the human race.

357 Leviathan understands it is first and foremost the woman's motherhood that threatens him, which is why he sets out to devour her child. This deepens the meaning of God's prophecy in Genesis 3:15—despite Lucifer's most furious attack that corrupted the whole human race, God still promises that there will be an immaculate woman.

358 One must never forget that Adam and Eve were never barred from eating the fruit from the Tree of Life; they could have eaten from it and lived forever.

359 Song of Songs 6:11. Intuition allows Eve to sense the mounting tension in Heaven, which will ultimately culminate in Michael and his angels casting Satan and his angels down to the earth. Further, in her heart she suspects that the conflict is over her, which troubles her deeply: the entire Celestial War could be seen reflected in Eve's eyes.

360 Woman is being called the Peace of God; paradoxically, she is the reason for the war and simultaneously the reason for the peace. She is God's peace between spirit and flesh, Creator and creature, even to the point where the angels will sing at the birth of Christ.

361 Woman is doubting her beauty, asking, almost desperately, if her beauty is real, if it can bring such a peace. Woman was created to fill man's loneliness when he was with God, and thus she was given the gift of beauty. Beauty is that which draws the lover to the beloved. The lover desires to order himself for the sake of the beloved, and so the beauty of the beloved draws the good out of the lover even as it draws him to itself. This in turn is the perfection of the beautiful thing, to draw the beloved to virtue and toward union with beauty. This is the reason for woman's innate desire for beauty, for woman desires to be the surrogate god. Woman desires to be so beautiful that man is drawn to her wholly and completely, in such a way that his union with her draws and uplifts him into union with the true God. At this moment, Eve is insecure in her beauty, for she has not yet drawn Adam into union with herself, which would be consummate affirmation of her ability to *captivate*. Leviathan exploits this desire, tempting Eve to grasp at assurance of her own beauty.

362 Ephesians 4:14: "We must no longer be children, tossed to and fro, blown about by every wind of doctrine, by people's trickery, by their craftiness in deceitful scheming." Man here stands to confirm the desires of woman's heart, espousing the eternal love of the Song of Songs, but, due to his innocence, the childlike inexperience of literally being born yesterday, he fails to confirm his wife's beauty in love. This opens the door for Leviathan to insert himself into their relationship, promising her the eternal beauty of a god if she would only eat from the Tree of Knowledge of Good and Evil.

363 Had Adam, in the strength of manhood, united himself to Eve completely, in the conjugal bonds of Holy Matrimony their insecurities would have evaporated like the morning dew. As it is, Adam lacks the confidence in their relationship that she is his, and Eve lacks the assurance that she captivates his heart. In such an insecure relationship, when another tries to seduce the beloved, she is tempted by the affirmation of her beauty, while he falls silent with trepidation and timidity over a woman he is not sure is his.

Genesis
3:1...

Seizing the opportunity, the great Leviathan entreated the woman, averting her attention from the heavens[364] and her man. Coiling his body around her, he asked,[365] "Has the Overlord[366] really ordered you not to eat from any of the trees in Paradise?"[367] Yet, the man remained silent, offering no word in reply.

Genesis
...3:2...

The woman willingly answered Leviathan, saying, "Of the fruit of the trees, which lie within Paradise we do eat!—but it is only of the fruit of the tree in the middle of the garden that God has commanded: 'You shall not eat of it or even *touch*[368] it lest you *die!*'"[369] Yet still the man made no word of reply.

Genesis
...3:4...

Overjoyed Leviathan replied to the woman, "For certainly you will not *die!*[370] No, no: for God knows well that the moment you eat of it, your eyes will be opened,[371] and you shall be gods,[372] knowing good and evil." Though yet again, the man remained silent, offering no word of reply.

Genesis
...3:6...

So the woman, looking upon the tree, saw that it was good for food, that it was beautiful to the eye, and desirable for gaining wisdom.[373]

Before the Tree of Knowledge

364 Lucifer wishes them not to see the storm brewing in the heavens, the storm which he created with the sweeping of his tail.

365 Every word is perfectly calculated; Lucifer never once lies outright, but rather asks, implies, and deceives.

366 The Hebrew word Leviathan uses is closer to 'tyrant.'

367 Genesis 3:1. Like any predator at a bar, Leviathan asks a seemingly trivial question to get Eve to drop her guard.

368 This is one of the most important verses in all of Genesis for understanding Adam and Eve's relationship before the fall. Often it is assumed that since our first parents were in Paradise that they themselves were perfect. However, this is foolhardy, for they were not Saints; both succumbed to sin and shifted blame onto others, suggesting anything but perfection. Rather, our first parents should be thought of as children, innocents beautiful in their newborn state but easily tempted into sin. Most importantly, Eve had not been created when God gave the command to Adam 'not to take and eat of the fruit of the Tree of the Knowledge of Good and Evil.' This means that Eve received the command from Adam as is his role as first priest, yet we discover he not only told her not only to abstain from eating the fruit, but even from touching it! This at first glance seems negligible, even justifiable, Adam is merely trying to protect all of Paradise and preserve his wife from a double-death, but the results of adding to God's Law are dire. (Cf. Deuteronomy 4:2) Furthermore, this reveals an inherent lack of perfect trust in his wife, Eve, purposefully dissuading her from ever even approaching the fruit of good and evil. And it is because of this simple, innocent addition, when Eve actually does touch the fruit and does not die she doubts not only man, but God.

369 The exact meaning of the word 'die' is crucial, for Leviathan will use it for his manipulations. Eve uses the normal meaning of 'die,' meaning bodily separation from the soul. This, however, is not the 'double death' God spoke of, namely sin and hell. (Cf. Revelation 20:14). This further lack of communication between husband and wife leaves Eve vulnerable to attack.

370 Leviathan is capitalizing on the discrepancy between Eve's wording and God's wording.

371 It is important to remember that the Serpent is not actually saying an untruth, for his claims are confirmed by God's own words in Genesis 3:22.

372 Eve has an immense desire to be beautiful, but she lacks the wisdom to know it is for the sake of leading man to God. Thus, she places herself as the final object of beauty, instead of as a conduit to draw men closer to God. This is why Leviathan's words are so potent. Eve desires to be a god, not content with beauty as a means, but desiring to actually become the object desired, god herself.

373 Though the Tree of Knowledge of Good and Evil has obvious importance, situated at the center of the garden and the subject of God's one prohibition, Eve looks upon it and ponders its virtues. First, it is good for food, nourishing and capable of imparting health, designed for the body. Second, it is beautiful to the eye, appealing to the mind. Third, it is capable of actually imparting wisdom, appealing to the most essential part of man, the heart. Thus, we see that Eve recognizes the tripartite blessing God bestowed upon the fruit, specifically designing it as a mighty gift for the human person.

A subtle voice weighed heavy upon her heart: "All flesh is like grass, all its glory like the flower of the field." The voice whispered, "Grass withers, flowers fade, but you shall be captivating before your husband forever. How desirable you will be! How beautiful your feet shall be in their sandals, O Prince's daughter![374] Your rounded thighs shall be like jewels, as if hewn by sculptors. Your navel shall be a rounded chalice, which will never lack mixed wine, and your body shall be a bale of wheat encircled with lilies.

"Oh, how fleeting is the flower of the tall grass! For the sun rises with its scorching heat and withers the grass; its flowers fade, and its *beauty* perishes.

"Yet how graceful are your steps in paradise, O Prince's daughter![375] Your breasts shall be like twin fawns, the young of a gazelle. Your neck shall be like a tower of ivory. Your eyes shall be like the pools of eternity guarded by the gates of paradise. Your nose shall be like the tower of heaven, looking ever toward Zion. Your head shall rise like the Mountain of God; your hair will be draperies of purple, where your king shall be held captive in its royal locks. In you alone shall man be fulfilled.

"Though, all flesh is grass and all its glory like the flower of the field. Grass withers, and flower fades…"[376]

So, having seen the desirability of the fruit to make her captivating, she reached out and took[377] for herself the fruit from the Tree of Knowledge of Good and Evil, and having held the fruit in her hand without perishing, doubted God on account of the man's words. So she ate of the fruit and turning gave some to her husband, who was with her, and he ate of it.[378]

Marginal references:
1 Peter 1:24
Song of Songs 7:1…
James 1:10
Song of Songs …7:3…
Song of Songs …7:5
1 Peter 1:24
Genesis …3:6…

374 These are the words the woman so desired to hear in her heart, the words the man was about to speak before he fell silent like a child, but now they are spoken by the Serpent and drive her to reach out her hand and take from the Tree of Knowledge of Good and Evil.

375 Song of Songs 7:1 Leviathan is whispering the words that Adam was originally going to tell his wife, confirming her in her beauty and the love of their marriage. However, now the words coming from the serpent's lips drive Eve to desire the fruit, insecure in her ability to be the object of her husband's love and desire.

376 Leviathan is not only tempting Eve with her innermost desire but simultaneously whispering the greatest lie ever told. This lie was the cornerstone of Satan's rule over the Earth, the subjugating principle by which every demon enslaved every ancient people. It has been at the heart of every heresy, every pagan religion, every modern philosophy, and even some Protestant theology. Simply put: 'Man's flesh is a curse, inherently degrading him, before all spiritual beings. Thus degraded and vile, he must serve the ethereal gods, and if he ever hopes to become refined he must shun his flesh and strive to be a pure spirit.' With this lie, he not only places man permanently and irrevocably lower than the angels, but also maintains his authority above the demons, for he remains the most intelligent created being according to nature. This is in direct contradiction to Christ's Incarnation, His mission and His message, and His sacrifice and His sacraments. Christ's flesh is the most venerable substance in existence, offered to God as the greatest gift, beyond all the knowledge of Cherubim, and beyond all the songs of Seraphim. It is the Holy Eucharist that unites the Church, making us brothers and sisters in Christ, transforming us into gods, sons of the living God. We must strive in Christ to embrace all the glories of the flesh; hunger and thirst, hard work and service, and all suffering, but revel in Christ as well by feasting and drinking, leisure and thanksgiving, and all joys of this world.

377 God created the Tree of Knowledge of Good and Evil, and everything the Lord creates is Good! God desired deeply that our first parents eat from the Tree of Knowledge, and if they had obeyed his command He undoubtedly would have bestowed the fruit of knowledge upon them as a most precious gift. Adam and Eve sinned, however, by taking that which can only truly be given, and therefore their maturation into adulthood was marked not by a proper understanding and acceptance of themselves as body-soul composites, but was perverted into confusion and disdain for their bodies.

378 This is 'The sin of Adam', for though Eve was deceived by Leviathan, Adam was not (1 Timothy 2:14). Adam was made first and charged with care and stewardship of the Garden, but he failed in defending his wife against the venom of Leviathan, the great dragon and ancient serpent. Repeatedly, Adam remains silent; in a profound way The Word was not in Adam. Like a child, he offered no rebuttal, no refutation, and no reinforcement for his wife. Rather, he acts as a weakened boyfriend, who does not defend his betrothed as she is seduced by an intimidating stranger. His lack of manhood is indicative of his innocence, and, not knowing what else to do, he shamefully eats the fruit. By doing so, Adam enters into the same adultery, separating both of them from God.

Genesis
...3:7...

And so the eyes of both husband and wife were opened,[379] and having obeyed Leviathan[380] and taken of the divinizing fruit, they beheld the nakedness of their bodies and were ashamed.[381] ...

Note 379   Our first parents really and truly gained knowledge from the fruit of the sacred tree. However, this knowledge was tainted by the sinful act of taking it. In order to understand the exact character of this knowledge, we must first look at the Ancient Serpent's words. To make a convincing deception, Leviathan reveals three truths about the fruit embedded in his lie. First, the fruit will open Adam and Eve's eyes concerning their nature. Second, and as the name of the fruit implies, this knowledge has something to do with their relation to Good and Evil. Third, the fruit is somehow divinizing, for he tempts Eve with becoming a god. While retaining all the elements of truth, Leviathan's statement completely obscures the wonderful purpose of the fruit, for the fruit contained the Wisdom of the Incarnation. Instead of divinizing Eve herself, it would have shown her the true plan for divinizing humanity through her child. Instead of causing experiential knowledge of Good and Evil, it would have given them the Word to instruct them in virtue, the proper governance of Good and Evil. Finally, instead of seeing each other's naked flesh as shameful, they would have seen their bodies as blessed and esteemed, the Way by which God could enter into the Universe.

Note 380   Evil is a twisting or perversion of what is good. Thus, Leviathan twists his guardianship of the tree for his own ends. Rather than simply telling Adam and Eve to disobey God's command, a simple negation, Leviathan achieves a cunning perversion, having them take instead of receive. Likewise, the consequences of their actions are perversions of the original purpose of the fruit. We see they are ashamed for being naked, a perversion of seeing themselves as they ought, beautifully enfleshed. Instead of trust and peace with God's plan, they hide themselves in fear, and do not even think of asking for forgiveness or communion with the Lord. Because of their submission to Leviathan, they actually see the universe as Lucifer does, entirely just, a rigid hierarchy incapable of knowing God's mercy or infinite love. Finally, the result of this new enlightenment is a complete acceptance of the same lie that Lucifer told the stars in Heaven; intelligence and purity of spirit are everything, and flesh debases intellect and will. Truly, man has the ability to do good or evil, and the fruit was meant to help man understand his cosmic relation to good and evil. This truth was perverted by Lucifer's temptation of Eve to be 'a god', in which flesh precludes man from being good, which is immediately experienced as loss of control over our faculties, especially our sexuality. Trusting Leviathan's lie becomes a self-fulfilling prophecy, and the flesh becomes a limitation to the soul that despises it. Their eyes were indeed opened, but opened to the perverse lie of fleshly iniquity Leviathan had sold to them.

381 Shame: the one definitive effect from the Fruit of the Tree of Knowledge of Good and Evil, but not just shame for their sin, shame specifically for their flesh, their bodily existence. Housed in this shame is the key to understanding what the Tree of Knowledge was intended for, and, if received properly, what glory would have been given mankind. The first truth that doesn't even occur to our modern minds is that the Fruit contained real and true power, a preternatural sacrament placed in the Garden by God, imparting the very thing it signifies; true, real, material vessel of grace. The moment they ate of it, their eyes were both opened, and they felt shame for their bodies. The second truth often overlooked in its simplicity (or our Puritan aversion) is that the Fruit is about sex. The very word 'knowledge' implies such a sexual undertone to the Fruit, for it is through Scripture itself we learn that to have sex is to 'know'. C.f. Genesis 4:1. Furthermore, we see in their sewing of fig leaves, that they are acutely aware of their genitals, and now they believe that such beautiful organs of procreation are something demeaning and regretful. The third truth revealed in their shame is what ought to have been revealed to them if they had received the fruit properly, a truth specifically regarding their genitals, the truth of their 'Divine Image,' namely that through their being 'male and female,' through their nuptial union of holy sex, they would open the door for the Incarnation: Jesus Christ, the Godman. This is the true Knowledge of Good and Evil, Wisdom the Word, to reveal humanity's adoption into Divinity, how to 'do good and avoid evil:' how to be Saints.

Shame for the Body

... So they took from the tree and sewed fig leaves[382] together, and made for themselves loincloths.[383]

Beneath the Fig Tree

382 The fact that they sew fig leaves together indicates that the Tree of Knowledge of Good and Evil is actually a fig tree. Consider the significant spiritual meaning hidden behind the fig tree scattered throughout the Scriptures. For example, Christ draws the comparison of the fig tree representing Israel, even cursing the fig tree when it bears no fruit. Further, it is not without irony that fig leaves secrete a resin that is irritating to the skin; thus Adam and Eve instantly feel the repercussions of their transgression against God in a physical way.

383 Our first parents express the shame they felt for their bodies by covering their genitals, as we still do today. This reveals a great truth about the Soul, written into our very bodies. The human body is symmetrical, emphasizing what is located along its center, namely, the brain, the heart, and the genitals. These three bodily organs are the locus of very real spiritual powers of the human soul, namely, the mind to understand, the heart to love, and the gender to unite and procreate. (One sign that the human race has succumbed to Leviathan's lie is that we have no word for this third power, unlike the intellect and will). Leviathan has no animosity for the intellect or the will, for he himself is pure spirit possessing, as the highest creature, the fullest degree of both. However, he does have a hatred for the body, which was adopted by our first parents as shame for their genitals, the great and undeniable sign that man is animal, not solely spiritual. We must affirm what our bodies silently dictate; our power to unite and procreate is a real spiritual part of the Soul as essential to human nature as our intellect and will. Even the angels cannot participate in creation as we do when we create a child, or ever be united so closely to another angel, as man and wife locked in the marital embrace.

--- *NOTES* ---

ᚷHE FALL
§ ᚷhe Celestial War §

Judith
13:11…

As Leviathan returned to the gates of Heaven, he shouted to the guards from a distance: "Open! Open the gate![384] God, *our* God is with us. Once more He has made manifest His strength in Heaven and His power against our enemy; He has done it this very day!" When the stars of Heaven heard Leviathan's voice, they quickly descended to the gate and summoned the chief stars. All the stars, from the least to the greatest, hurriedly assembled, for Leviathan's return seemed unbelievable.[385]

Judith
…13:13…

They opened the gate and welcomed the great dragon. They made a fire for light;[386] and when they gathered around, Leviathan urged them with a loud voice: "Praise God, praise Him! Praise God, who has not withdrawn His grace from the house of Heaven, but has shattered our enemies by *my* hand this very day!" Then Leviathan revealed to them the severed fruit from the Tree of Knowledge of Good and Evil, and said: "Here is the forbidden fruit, the sacred fig of the Tree of Knowledge of Good and Evil from the midst of the Lord's garden, and here are the leaves under which man covered himself in his shame. The Lord has struck them down by the hand of a serpent. As the Lord lives, who has protected me in the path I have followed, I swear that it was my *beauty* that seduced the woman to their ruin, and that they did not sin with me to my defilement[387] or disgrace!"

Judith
…13:16

Judith
14:1…

Leviathan then said to the astonished crowd: "Listen to me, my brothers. Take this fruit and hang it on the parapet of your wall. At nightfall, when the sun has set upon the Earth, let each of you seize your weapons, and let all the stars stern of will descend upon the Earth under the command of a chief captain. Then when the Earth finds its deposed king dead, panic will seize them, and they will flee before you. Then you and all the other inhabitants of the whole of Heaven will pursue man and strike each of them down in their tracks. But first, bring me all those who stand below me, as trees flourishing beneath my shade."

Judith
…14:4

IGNATIAN CONTEMPLATION

384 Already the gates of heaven have been shut on Lucifer, and he has to petition for them to be opened. In this way, the gates represent his relationship with God, which he falteringly hopes he has made secure.

385 At this point Leviathan would believe himself to be the victor in every way. By seducing Eve and usurping Adam, he has secured for himself the Earth. Now that Eve has sinned, she can no longer be a fitting vessel for the Lord's incarnation. Since she is the mother of all that is living, there could never be an immaculate woman to become a proper theotokos for the Lord. Finally, Adam and Eve have accepted Leviathan's lie about the revolting nature of the body, and so he has cemented his permanent rule over the Earth and all those who dwell within it. Thus, when he returns to Heaven, he returns boasting, having accomplished all that he intended to do. This is the completion of his passive-aggressive assault on God. Leviathan sought to put God in a double bind, to either abandon man or to destroy them, and either way to restore Leviathan's place. Paradoxically, Leviathan wanted God to repent from his plan, rather than himself repenting from his own dissention.

386 Leviathan and the stars that welcome him no longer have their own light, and even in heaven must seek other means. This is in particular a foreshadowing of the darkness of hell.

387 This is key to understanding the Serpent's mentality in the temptation of Adam and Eve. If we truly examine all the Serpent says to the woman, we come to a startling fact: the Serpent never actually lies, he never actually speaks an untruth. Scripture in fact verifies everything that Satan tempts Eve with, whether it is their eyes being opened or even them becoming like God. Despite the serpent's lack of a material lie, he does, of course, deceive the woman, causing her to perversely desire the fruit, eventually taking the fruit and eating of it. This is the great boast of the Adversary; in the great Court of Law before God, the Judge, he can claim that he never spoke an untrue word. This, of course, God immediately dismisses, for God is the Judge of Hearts, but forever Satan will boast of his cunning in the deception of Eve.

 NOTES

Judith
15:11...
So the Earth was handed over to Leviathan, all its silver and wealth, all its inhabitants and nations, which he accepted.[388] All those who fell beneath Leviathan's shadow gathered to him and blessed him, and they performed a dance in his honor. Leviathan then took branches in his hands and distributed them to the stars gathered around, and Leviathan and the other stars crowned themselves with garlands of fig

Judith
...15:13
leaves.[389]

Judith
16:1...
Leviathan led them in dance and in song, singing hymns of praise: "Strike up a song to my God with tambourines, sing to the Lord with cymbals; sing for Him a new song, exalt and acclaim His name! For the Lord is God who crushes wars; He sets His strength among His stars![390]

Judith
...16:3...
"Man came from the dust of the earth; with deceptive beauty he came clawing after the heart of my God. Earth blocked up the torrents of the abyss and boasted upon its hills. Man threatened Heaven, threatened to put gods to the sword, to dash heavenly stars to the ground, to make prey of our glory, and to seize our grace as spoil.

Judith
...16:5...
"But the Lord Almighty thwarted them; by the hand of a serpent He confounded them! Not by soldiers was their mighty one struck down, nor did titans bring them low, nor did huge giants besiege them; but Leviathan, the first born of dawn; by the beauty of Lucifer's countenance was man despoiled![391]

Judith
...16:7...
"He took off his celestial garb[392] to raise up the afflicted in Heaven. He anointed his face with fragrant oil, fixed his head with a diadem, and revealed serpentine form to beguile them. His stature ravished

Judith
...16:9
her eyes, his beauty captivated her mind, and his words cut through her heart!"

At such blasphemy Michael, the defender of the people of God, arose to proclaim justice before the great Leviathan, for he knew it was through envy that the serpent had deceived the woman.

388 The temptation of Christ by the Devil in Matthew 4:8 illustrates a frightening fact. The Devil really and truly had dominion over the Earth, and offers the Earth to Christ as one of three chief temptations. Satan's conquest of the Earth is won with his defeat of Adam, the first Steward-King of the Earth. This further illuminates the depravity of our ancient ancestors during the universal worship of pagan gods (the fallen angels), and the necessity for Christ's victory on the cross.

389 The third of the stars that fall under Leviathan's shadow crown themselves with the branches from the Tree of Knowledge of Good and Evil to mock Adam's sin, and to claim their kingship over man and the Earth.

390 Leviathan and his angels are claiming God for themselves, singing a new song that excludes man, and declaring God's place is only among the stars.

391 Consider God's rebuke of Lucifer that he had become 'haughty because of his beauty;' it is a great gift given by God to his closest angel. Next turn your mind toward woman: it is the greatest desire of a woman to be captivating; this desire was originally placed in woman's heart by God in order to inspire man to strive after God Himself through love of woman. The immense cunning of Lucifer's plan then becomes clear: not to simply tempt Eve with some abstract beauty, but to tempt her with his own beauty, offering her a godlike beauty if she disobeyed God and ate of the fruit.

392 As stated previously, the true natures of the 'angels' are unique to each of them and are not visible unless they shed the preternatural light that makes them like God. Thus, all angels resemble God in glory and light, but demons take on various forms of all imaginable variety.

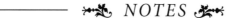

NOTES

Jeremiah
2:20...

Thus, before the ranks of Heaven, Michael rose first and declared: "Long ago you broke your yoke! You tore off your bonds and said, '*I will not serve!*' On every high hill, under every green tree you sprawled, your beauty nothing more than that of a prostitute! But the Lord had planted you as a choice vine, a pedigreed stock. How could you turn out so abhorrent to the Lord? A spurious vine! Even if you scour it with lye and use much soap, the stain of your guilt will not be purged from before the Lord! How can you say, 'I am not defiled or disgraced? I am not Baal, spouse in sin!' Consider your conduct in the Valley, recall what you have done!"

Jeremiah
...2:23

1 Maccabees
3:3...

But Leviathan lashed back, saying: "I, Leviathan, have brought greater glory to my fellow kindred, to the whole house of Heaven! And all Heaven shall sing of *my* glory saying: 'In his armor he was like a giant, he took up his weapons and went to war; with his own sword he defended us. He was like a ferocious lion raving and roaring for its prey. He pursued the lawless, hunting them down, and those who troubled his kindred he destroyed by fire, and evildoers covered their bodies in shame before him. By Leviathan's hand was salvation happily achieved, and he deposed the kings of men. He gave joy to Heaven by his deeds, and his memory shall be blessed forever. He went out to the valley of Eden, destroying the witch who dwelt therein. He turned away wrath from Heaven and brought death to man; he shall be known to the ends of the Earth!'"

1 Maccabees
...3:9

So a great shadow was cast from the height of Heaven, obscuring the light from all those gathered, so that no star from the east to the west nor from the north to the south shone in the sky.[393]

Shrouded in darkness, Michael[394] looked then upon the Earth, and, looking thereupon, he beheld a light that did not come from Heaven, a fire that flickered and wavered yet burned amidst the darkness:[395] a flame that burned with the Oil of Matrimony, the true and holy *Image of God*, held within the one flesh union of husband and wife.[396]

The Archangel Michael

393 This shadow is a necessity that naturally flows from the nature of angels. Since they are pure spirits and receive all knowledge of God from the angel above them, if an angel's heart is hardened and blocks the flow of light, a shadow will form, obscuring the light from every single angel below it. This, however, occurs in the highest angel, Lucifer; thus the result is a shadow that obscures the light from all the Celestial Intelligences. This places a monumental significance on Michael's ability to rise up in grace and shed a new light to those angels that would serve the Lord.

394 Michael's low rank of Archangel is what naturally disposes him to be on the level of the Earth, specifically to look upon the marriage of husband and wife.

395 2 Corinthians 4:6. This is the moment when Michael sees the face of Christ and can choose to serve the Lord completely.

396 When Michael looks at sinful Adam and Eve, shamefully covering their genitals because of Lucifer's lie, he notes one thing truly profound, which causes him to reflect again on God's nature; he sees their unbroken matrimony. When we study the effects of the fall, we see sin disrupts and breaks apart, fracturing and shattering the world, even allowing death to reign; yet one instrumental thing remains: Matrimony! Our first parents committed a sin so terrible it destroyed the peace of the entire world, yet their marriage remained. This is monumental, for if their marriage had not remained, there would be no human race. This is the strength of the First Sacrament, and the reason why Michael is prince of the heavenly host. He saw that God sanctified marriage as the holy institution in which He would enter the world. In that moment, by looking into the unbreakable union of husband and wife, Michael saw God as Trinity.

Seeing more of God than was ever revealed in all the heights

1 Corinthians
11:7…

of Heaven, Michael resolutely declared: "Man ought not cover his head, for he is the *Image* and glory of God; and yet woman is the glory of man! For man was not made from woman, but woman from man, nor was man created for woman, but woman for man; this is why *woman* shall have a sign of authority upon her head, *for the sake of the angels.*[397] For female is not independent of male,

1 Corinthians
…11:11

nor male of female in the Lord!"[398]

Thus, having seen husband and wife in their Union, he turned toward God and chose to serve.[399] . . .

The Image of God

397 Woman is the crowning jewel of creation; she is the crescendo to which all creation builds; she makes sense of this creature we call man, showing that in his flesh and through her beauty, mankind is uniquely Trinitarian. This profound dichotomy between the one flesh unity and the individuality of man and woman is the very window by which the angels came to know the Triune God, for only in Holy Matrimony and the Holy Trinity is there the unity of persons in such a profound and unique way that both their individuality is maintained and their complete assimilation manifest—so seamlessly united by, in, and through love that simultaneously they are one and many. Throughout the entire Universe, there is no other thing that reveals the hidden and hallowed nature of the Holy Trinity more profoundly than Holy Matrimony.

398 1 Corinthians 11. Michael sees the profound resemblance between man and his wife to a Triune God, and seeing such a resemblance within creation spurs him to see the glory of woman, which is a child, for the glory of God is man, and the glory of man is woman, but the glory of woman is her child. This is where God can enter into creation (as the Christ child), into the very Image of the Trinity He created on the Earth, which is the family. This is why he says woman should be adorned for the sake of the angels, for she allows the angels to be saved from Lucifer's shadow; it was the creation of woman that allowed Michael to see both God's mercy and His nature as Trinity. By asking for the mercy to look upon God himself, he rose above all the stars and was able to shed grace abroad to those who would otherwise have been lost in shadow. This reveals why Mary becomes the Queen of the Angels; as the woman of prophecy, she fulfills woman's role to unite God and Man. Though lately created, she is their queen by right, the font of grace, and the inspiration of Michael unto the salvation of the angels. (This is the reason why the angels have always been so captivated by woman's beauty, as in Genesis 6:1.)

399 This is one of the most important moments in Salvation History, the moment in which an archangel, guardian of the family, became St. Michael the Archangel, Prince of the Heavenly Host and Defender of the Church, which is the Bride of Christ, family of God and man. Because of the grace poured out upon him, Michael can respond at every angle in opposition to Lucifer.

Where Lucifer declared 'non serviam,' Michael now declares 'serviam;' where Lucifer rebelled out of pride, Michael now proves his humility by crying: 'Who can compare with God?' It is important that Michael and Lucifer are reacting to the same *truth*, the same Word, but seen in different ways. Michael, as an Archangel, sees this truth by peering into the Sacrament of Holy Matrimony, while Lucifer, being an angel of light, sees this truth by beholding the essence of man from high above. The truth is the Incarnation, God's plan to unite Himself with the human race. Lucifer sees this act as abominable, for it disrupts the natural order degrading God and elevating man to God's level, even beyond the angels. Michael sees the Incarnation as Matrimony, a Sacrament, a visible image of the Invisible God, actually conveying what is signified, union of God and man. In his humility, Michael sees that such a marriage ennobles all of creation; union with man at the center brings all of creation into union with God. Thus, the angels sing at the birth of Christ, as God enters the created world. The entire celestial war is therefore fought over the Incarnation. This is given an image in Revelation chapter 12, as the great red dragon seeks to devour the woman with child: The Celestial War is being fought over *The Woman* giving birth to God, the Theotokos.

. . . Michael then beheld the Face of God and the innermost counsels of the Trinity were revealed to him, and having seen *the Woman with child,*[400] abundant grace was poured into his heart[401], and a great fire began to burn within him!

With great haste, the Archangel flew up and barred Leviathan's ascent up the Holy Mountain of God.[402] The angel of the Lord appeared before the great dragon as fire flaming out in every direction, yet although aflame he was not consumed. So Leviathan turned aside to ponder, "What is this remarkable sight? Why does this angel not burn up?"[403] When the Lord saw that he had turned aside, He called out to Leviathan from the angel: "Accuser! Accuser!"[404] But Leviathan answered not, so the Lord God said: "Do not come any farther! Remove your claws from the mountain side, for the place where you stand is holy ground."[405]

Rather the great and terrible Leviathan spewed forth a mighty torrent of water from his mouth to extinguish the flames, but the water was to no avail. Michael spread forth his thricefold wings,[406] and declared, "Your wickedness has blinded you! You no longer know the hidden counsels of God! For neither have you accounted for the recompense of holiness, nor have you discerned the reward for the innocent soul!

Exodus 3:2...

Exodus ...3:5

Wisdom 2:21...

400 The woman with child is not Eve, but is in fact the woman from the great vision in Revelation 12:1. Michael is witnessing this profound insight by looking upon the first woman, who is the foreshadowing of the perfect woman, the God-bearer. A simple truth most Christians have forgotten: Mary is the new Eve, but that means Eve is the 'old Mary.' This vision of Theotokos is given to Michael because of his natural affinity for the family as an Archangel, a lowly position on the Celestial Ladder (second lowest). A wonderful example of the gratuity of God: such a unique position, 'faraway' from God, yet close to the Earth and husband and wife, allowed him to see God as Holy Trinity, which no angel had done in all the heights of heaven.

401 A superabundance of grace is poured upon Michael, because, unlike Lucifer who turned away from God when he saw the vision of the Woman, Michael saw the profound familial love of God and turned toward God. Lucifer, an angel of truth, could not accept the profound contradiction of God's condescension to be born of a woman.

402 Michael serves as the example of God's abundant mercy for those that choose to serve Him. Michael is now exalted by grace beyond that of even Lucifer, a bewildering event to the arrogance of Leviathan, who is still operating under the 'old law' of nature apart from grace, in which he is the supreme created being. Michael's sudden nobility makes little sense to Lucifer, and he sees the fact that an angel of such great distance from the Divine Light could ever surpass him in mobility or nobility upon the Mountain of God as an even greater blasphemy.

403 Up until this moment, Leviathan has operated undeterred, for he was the greatest being created by God, the first to receive the Divine Light. In the natural order, the celestial intelligences were to be filled with holy light and thus being filled, overflow into the stars below them, like pure and perfect glass. Therefore, if something were to 'catch fire,' it would be caused by an impurity not allowing the light to pass through. When Leviathan sees Michael ablaze, and yet not consumed, he is utterly perplexed. What the great water serpent did not understand was that there could be such an intimacy achieved with God that an angel not only receives and passes down the Divine Light, but with great magnanimity sheds forth a unique light of its very own, a seraphic flame that only adds to the infinite Divine Light. This intimacy is only within the highest choir, which can therefore only exist after a wholehearted choice to serve the Lord; this is the choir of Seraphim.

404 'Accuser' translates as 'Satan' in Hebrew. 'Devil' also means 'adversary' or 'accuser' from the Latin 'Diabolus.' The Lord has now given the name Satan to the great dragon, Leviathan.

405 Cf. Isaiah 14:13: "I will sit enthroned upon the mount of hosts."

406 Michael boldly shows Leviathan his folly by revealing his six wings, a sacred gift given only to the highest choir of pure love, the holy seraphim.

God has formed man to be eternal;[407] in the *Image* of His own nature He made them! But by the *envy* of the Devil, death has entered the world, and all those who ally with him shall experience it!"[408]

Wisdom
...2:24

The holy angels then rallied to Michael, their prince, who proclaimed the *good news* of God's plan, and defended *the Woman,* Lady Wisdom, the Spouse of God.[409]

But again Leviathan spewed forth a great torrent of lies across the heavens, saying: "Shall you worship *the Woman* enthroned upon scarlet beast!? *Praying before her as if she is God?* Shall you array her in purple and scarlet, and adorn her with gold and jewels and pearls, while she sips from a cup full of her abominations and impurities of the flesh! This angel would have all of Heaven fall prostrate before the great whore, and take up adoration for the she-beast of the Earth!"

Revelation
17:3...

Revelation
...17:5

The dragon's words swept across the sky like a mighty tail and a third of the stars rallied to the battle cry of Leviathan.

Seeing Leviathan's hatred of *the Woman,* Michael declared, "You are not *Theotokos!* O serpent sin of envy, you are no longer even *Lucifer!* What do you bear forth other than iniquity and sin? No, you are *Satan,* Accuser of man and Father of lies, who accuses them day and night in the sight of our God! You shall be thrown down along with all those who follow you, for there is no place for the iniquitous in Heaven!"[410]

Revelation
12:10

Revelation
12:7

A great battle then broke out in heaven, the Celestial War. Michael and his angels fought against Leviathan, but Leviathan and his angels fought back.[411] And there was a time of great distress such as had not occurred since the time of the separation of the waters.

John
8:44...

The holy angels denounced the rebellious spirits, saying, "You are of your father, the Devil, and you want to do the desires of your father! He was a murderer from the beginning, and does not stand in truth because there is no truth in him! Whenever he speaks, he speaks a lie, speaking from his own nature, for he is a liar and the *Father of Lies!*"

John
...8:45

407 This is a profound statement for an angel to make at this time, further revealing Michael's immense intimacy with God. Michael understands that Leviathan's evil commerce and cunning deception are of no consequence; God so loves man that He will follow through with his plan despite the obstacle of original sin. To speak loosely, Michael has given the proto-protoevangelium to the angels out of his intimate relationship with the Lord. Michael won the Celestial War because he opened up a path to grace, which aids the will, and light, which aids the intellect. By allowing access to grace, Michael shows forth God's goodness and mercy. All Lucifer ever had to offer was light, which showed the supreme wisdom, power and justice of the Lord; by this time, Leviathan's shadow is a negation of the light, clinging to the idea of cold justice even as it leads to separation from God and death in pride and envy.

408 Wisdom 2:21. Whispered in the wisdom of the Old Testament is a truth as ancient as the hardening of Leviathan's heart. God gave unto man His Image, and offered eternal bliss; this very gift produced in the jilted heart of Lucifer an envy so great that from it death was birthed into the Universe.

409 Michael is the first to proclaim the gospel by proclaiming the unique insight he acquired by peering within the first family. Within the first family, he saw the family within God, and finally the family formed by the union of God and man, the family of the Church, which proceeds directly from the holy family, the marriage of God and Mary. Michael's rallying cry is that Leviathan has not won, Eve is not the Theotokos, but rather there is another woman, who is replete in grace and who will fulfill the plan of God. Michael is defending the Mother of God, just as it is written in Revelation 12.

410 While Michael here declares this out of justice, and to protect the sanctity of Heaven, it will become literally true as the celestial choirs are arranged, and the nine ways to love God array the stars in their unchanging constellations.

411 Revelation 12:7. Leviathan does not actually start the Celestial War; rather, St. Michael arises to preserve justice in Heaven, for one cannot willingly transgress against God and still lay claim to His presence. The Celestial War was fought over Heaven, Michael defending God's plan and casting out Lucifer, casting light and grace as Leviathan belched forth lies and shadow. The true battle was over the stars, who each individually chose to either accept Michael's grace or Leviathan's shadow. Once all had been decided, the power of God inevitably triumphed to purge Heaven of all demons.

Ezekiel
31:2...

Michael, Prince of the heavenly host, brandishing the scales of justice, contended with the great Dragon and his hordes saying, "Who is like you in your greatness? Behold, God has made you like a mighty cedar, with fair branches and forest shade, of great height, and reach beyond the clouds. The waters nourished you, the deep has made you grow tall! Rivers ran about the place of your planting, spreading and sending streams to all the trees of the forest. So you towered high above all the trees of the forest, your boughs and branches long, from abundant waters at your roots. All the birds of the air made their nest with you, under your branches all the beasts of the field brought forth their young, and under your shadow dwelt all great nations. You were beautiful in your greatness, in the strength of your branches, for your roots went down to abyssal waters. No other tree could rival you, nor could be equal to you, for the Lord had made you beautiful, the envy of all other trees.

Ezekiel
...31:10...

"Therefore thus says the Lord God: 'Because you towered high and set your head among the clouds, because your heart was proud of its height, I shall give you over to the hand of the mighty one of God; he shall surely deal with you as your wickedness deserves! I shall cast you out to be among foreigners, the most terrible of nations. You shall be cut down and left upon the ground, on the mountains and in the valleys your branches shall fall, and your boughs will lie broken in all the waterways of the land; and all the peoples of the Earth shall go then from your shadow and leave you. Upon your ruin will dwell all the birds of the air, and upon your branches shall trot all the wild beasts of the field. All this is in order that no tree by the waters may grow to lofty height or set their tops among the clouds, and that no tree that drinks water may reach up to the Lord in height; they are all given over to death, to the netherworld among mortal men, with those who go down to the Pit!'"

Pride before the Fall

Michael continued pronouncing the word of the Lord, "Thus says the Lord God: 'Upon your plummeting to Hell the deep shall mourn, and many waters shall be stopped up, the rivers restrained; the Earth shall be clothed in gloom for it, and all the trees of the field shall faint because of it. Nations shall quake at the sound of your fall, when I cast you down to Hell with those who go down to the Pit! In the underworld all the trees of old took comfort, all those whose roots were fed by the many waters. They too shall be cast down to Hell with those slain by the sword, all your allies who dwelt beneath your shade.

"Whom are you thus like in glory and in greatness among the trees of old? You shall be brought down with all those who follow you to the netherworld! You shall lie among the banished, with those who are slain by the sword!"[412]

Michael, striking the great serpent, proclaimed, "May the Lord rebuke you,[413] O Adversary! May the Lord, who has chosen man, rebuke you for what you have done!"

NOTES

412 Ezekiel 31. The Prophet speaks of the intimate union that Lucifer possesses with the Tree of Knowledge of Good and Evil, referring to him as the tree itself.

413 Jude 1:9. The great words Michael used to contend with the Devil in the dispute over the body of Moses.

War in Heaven

ᏮᎻᎬ FᎯᏞᏞ
§ Divine Justice §

Genesis
3:8...

W hen it was the breezy time of day and they heard the sound of the Lord God moving through the midst of the Garden, the man and his wife hid themselves from the Lord God among the trees of the Garden.[414] The Lord God then called to the man and asked him, "Where are you?"[415]

The man answered, emerging from the covering of the trees, "I heard the sound of You in the Garden, but I was afraid because I was naked, so I hid myself."[416]

Then the Lord God asked, "Who told you that you were naked?[417] – You have eaten, then, from the Tree of which I had forbidden you to eat!"

The man replied, "It was the woman! Whom *You*[418] placed here with me! She was the one who gave me the fruit from the Tree, and so I ate of it."[419]

The Lord God then questioned the woman, "Why would you do such a thing?"

But the woman answered, "It was *Leviathan*! He tricked me,[420] so I ate of it."[421]

Whom You Put Here!

IGNATIAN CONTEMPLATION

414 The breezy time of day refers to the evening period before dusk, which means that the Lord has given them the entire day to come find Him. He waits until the day is almost over to see if they choose to repent; even worse, when the Lord finally comes to look for them, they hide themselves from Him.

415 God knows exactly where Adam and Eve are, but he calls out specifically to Adam, highlighting his particular role as priest and mediator for the family, but it also highlights his grievous role in their transgression. This call to Himself is offered as an opportunity for repentance, one that is reluctantly answered and without remorse.

416 The first effect of the wrongful taking of the fruit on man's relationship with God is fear. This fear is not a righteous fear, but a result of their new shameful awareness of their bodily flesh. Leviathan's main intent was to destroy their relationship with God, and now that they view themselves as he does, they hide themselves from God in shame. This is also a further example of their immaturity: instead of approaching or seeking out the Lord, they hide themselves and try to cover up their sin, just like children.

417 This question is entirely overlooked but it is immensely important, for it reveals that the sacred knowledge of their nakedness could have been given to Adam and Eve apart from their taking of the Fruit. This message could have been given to them so that they would be introduced to the knowledge of their nakedness without having come to it through disobedience and sin. This message would have been entrusted to an angel, as to prepare them to receive the Sacramental Fruit of the Tree of Knowledge of Good and Evil. This would have been Lucifer's duty since he is the Cherubim to which the Tree of Knowledge of Good and Evil is entrusted, the message given to him to see if he will serve God as angel.

418 Consider the absolute gal of Adam; our first father simultaneously blames his wife and then God Himself. This seals man's fate and proves his unrepentant childish nature.

419 Note the childish ambiguity of Adam's confession, purposefully worded as to imply that he might not have even known the fruit he was handed was even from the Tree of Knowledge of Good and Evil.

420 Eve shifts the blame just as her husband had done before her, blaming the serpent for deceiving her. While this accusation is actually true, there is still a remarkable lack of repentance or guilt.

421 The imagery of adolescence is striking. God lines all three up and goes down the line, each child shifting the blame until the real culprit is found. Each time they are given an opportunity to repent, to take responsibility, but each time blame is only shifted. Up until the punishment of Leviathan, God affords our first parents five opportunities for reconciliation.

Genesis
...3:14...

The Lord God then addressed[422] Leviathan saying: "Because you have done such a thing: Cursed shall you be beyond all cattle,[423] and cast down below all the wild beasts of the Earth; upon your belly shall you crawl, and dust shall you eat all the days of your life!"[424]

Upon the pronounced judgment of the Lord, Michael the great prince prevailed against Leviathan, for there was no longer any place for him in Heaven.[425]

Revelation
12:8

Michael then declared before Heaven and Earth: "Who is like God? That dare usurp His judgment and defile His *Wisdom*? May the Lord rebuke you!"

And so, by the power of God, Michael defeated Leviathan, banishing him from Heaven. So the great dragon, the ancient serpent—the one who is called the Devil and Satan, who deceived the whole world—was thrown down to the Earth, and his angels were thrown down with him.[426]

Revelation
12:9

In the sky there appeared great flashes of lightning and voices, and great peals of thunder. The man and his wife looked up and beheld Satan falling like lightning from Heaven,[427] cast down in a great spectacle before God and man. And there upon the mountainside Michael smote the great dragon, cleaving its wings and binding it to the Earth, banishing it to crawl upon its belly all the days of its life![428]

Luke
10:18

Genesis
3:14
&
Revelation
12:9

Then there came a great earthquake, and the skies rolled up like a scroll as a third of the host of heaven rotted away. A third of the night sky fell as leaves falling from the vine, like leaves falling from the fig tree,[429] and all the foundations of the Earth shook. So great was the earthquake from the hurtling of stars that there had not been such a quake since before man had come to walk upon the Earth.[430]

Isaiah
34:4

Michael then proclaimed: "Rejoice now, O you Heavens and all you who dwell therein! But woe to you, O Earth and Sea, for the Devil has come down to you in great wrath,[431] for he knows he has but a short time!"

Revelation
12:12

422 Note that with Adam and with Eve, God asks them a question, affording them an opportunity of repentance; however, with the serpent there is a very clear understanding that he has acted in full knowledge and has no desire or opportunity of repentance.

423 The Hebrew word for ox or cattle is the same as the word for Cherubim, as stated previously. This word shows Lucifer's natural affinity to the choir of Cherubim, and possible alignment if he had not transgressed against God.

424 The serpent's judgment is filled with great meaning and needs to be taken alongside Revelation 12:9, the defeat of the great dragon, to be understood properly. First, Lucifer is being thrown down to the earth, and thus he is cast out of heaven. Second, he is bound to the earth below even the beasts, crawling on the ground; this means his dragon wings are stripped away, left without even arms to lift himself up. Truly he must roam the earth as though fettered with ball and chain, a punishment that removes his glory without stripping him of his nature, a serpent with a fraction of the mobility and power he previously possessed. Finally, and foreboding for man, he shall feed on the dust of the earth, which is the human race that has given all authority over to him.

425 This is a reference in Scripture to the formation of the nine angelic choirs of the celestial hierarchy. The demons can have no place in Heaven because this is the moment of the angelic fall of the demons and the moment of the choragic organization, which involves a choice to love and serve God in a particular aspect of creation.

426 Revelation 12. This moment illustrates something profoundly significant about the unity of the Universe, for the fall of the angels and the fall of man are not isolated incidents; in a profound way they are one collapse that encompasses all of creation. This directly flows from the centrality of man, for it was the creation of man and God's plan for him that caused Lucifer's envy, which in turn caused the temptation and fall of man himself. In Genesis, we see even more profoundly that Leviathan's peddling of sin is completed by Adam and Eve's purchasing of it; as with any bargain, and any relationship, the adulterous exchange is completed by both parties. This is the core of the Universal Fall, as Adam's lineage is mired in sin and Leviathan's shadow darkens a multitude of stars. For it is written and it is true: "All creation fell with Adam."

427 Luke 10:18. Jesus' own account of Satan's banishment from heaven. Consider the horrific nature of Satan's Fall to the Earth, and the damage it causes to the Earth itself.

428 This is the nexus point of Genesis and Revelation both describing the Fall of Satan, Genesis from a physical narrative and Revelation from the spiritual perspective, all summed up in the words of Christ "I have seen Satan fall like lightning from Heaven."

429 Isaiah 34:4. Consider how 'the Third' fall as rotten fruit from the fig tree, which is the Tree of Knowledge of Good and Evil.

430 Immediately the Earth reels from the collapse and restructuring of Heaven. All the fallen stars were cast down to the Earth, which sent Earth into a state of 'pandemonium,' the capital of Satan's new empire. This is the first stage of the Universal Fall, and is likened to a building collapsing upon itself, which stems from a fault at its core (man), yet starts with the collapse of the roof (the angels). Few understand the horrible state that the Earth was thrust into because of the Fall and the enormous influx of demonic spirits, ultimately culminating in the Great Flood. This is why Christ's coming was so vital for the survival of the human race. The Paschal Mystery was the victory that freed Earth from the rule of Satan and all the demons masquerading as pagan gods. We are only free now to study science and pursue social liberties because we are no longer enslaved by demonic spirits. Unfortunately, we only remember the sin, not Satan.

431 Wrath is the third of the Deadly Sins. Pride is the first sin, the father of all sin; the second sin Envy, the spirits' sin; the third sin Wrath, their firstborn sin; the fourth sin Sloth, the despair of all things spiritual; the fifth sin Greed, the white-knuckle clutch to the material world; the sixth sin Lust, the abandonment to all worldly passions; and finally the seventh sin Gluttony, the child's sin.

Isaiah
63:2...

Leviathan, stricken upon the Earth, raised his eyes toward Heaven and boasted,[432] proclaiming: "Is not the Lord to ask: 'Why is your appearance red, and your apparel like one who treads the grape?' For the Lord will no doubt favor my reply! I have trodden Your people like a winepress. I have trodden them in my anger, and trampled them in my wrath; their blood spurted on my garments; all my apparel I stained, for the day of vindication was in my heart; my time for redemption had come. I looked, but there was no one to help; I was appalled that there was no one to lend support, so my own arm brought about the victory, and my own wrath sustained me. I trampled down their marriage in my anger, I made them drunk in my wrath, and I poured out their lifeblood upon the ground."[433]

Isaiah
...63:6

But the Lord God triumphantly declared to the serpent[434] before Heaven and Earth: "I shall put enmity[435] between you and *the Woman*, between your seed and her seed.[436] And He[437] will crush your head, while you strike at His heel."[438]

Genesis
...3:15

Note 438 This is the fatal blow! This passage is what the Church Fathers referred to as the Protoevangelium, the first gospel, the first good news! This is what Satan never accounted for; as Michael declared, God's providence turns all things to good. Up until this point, Leviathan has accounted himself the victor of the war, even though he lost the battle in Heaven. Only now, hearing the first good news of God does he begin to realize the enormity of God's Love for mankind. This good news is that there will be a Theotokos, that Satan has not succeeded in his mission to destroy the Mother of God and to stop the Incarnation, and in fact God reveals it shall be her seed that will destroy him. God can find a way; this is the meaning of the Archangel Gabriel's name, which is God's Strength. Gabriel was given to proclaim the Gospel: God proves His strength by creating an Immaculate Conception despite the infection of sin, and forming a marriage bond despite the total depravity of humanity. God becomes man despite everything Satan knew was possible.

432 Consider the pride of Leviathan and the great depravity of his fall from grace. Even though he has been cast down from heaven, he still believes that he is the true victor, so held in his conviction that through the corruption of Eve he has definitively stopped the Incarnation. In such pride, he boasts to God of the great murder of the human race he just committed.

433 Isaiah 63. Satan acted in full knowledge of the repercussions of his actions. He knew that he would be expelled from Heaven, but deemed such a rebellion worthwhile because, through the corruption of Eve, he would have stopped the Incarnation, and through the defeat of Adam would win the Earth as his own. Having thus conquered the Earth, he would rightfully rule over all men, which would allow him to corrupt man so thoroughly that even the animals and the Earth itself would eventually have to be destroyed by God. Satan's ultimate plan was the Great Flood, where the nether would be released and all matter would be swallowed up by the void. Without matter, the only order left would be the original angelic order of light. Leviathan could then return to God. After the entire loss of material creation, he would again be the supreme being of knowledge, having proven beyond doubt that man was entirely evil and wholly unworthy of God's love. Up until this point, Satan truly believes he has won the war, and it is in that pride that he boasts. God even confirms that Satan accomplished what he desired in Genesis 6:6. ("The Lord regretted that he had ever made man upon the earth, and his heart was deeply troubled.") However, God is about to reveal a great secret and a fatal blow to Leviathan's plans.

434 Adam and Eve have little understanding of what God is speaking of, but God and Satan have a very clear understanding of the true intent behind Leviathan's tempting of the man and his wife. That is why God prophesies to Satan directly, showing him the folly of his actions and demonstrating that God's mercy and love for humanity will triumph despite any action Satan might take. It is the Lord's will that there be an immaculate woman, and what God wills will be no matter what.

435 Another translation is "I will put war between you and the woman…" This is the extent to which the Mother of God will be separated from Satan and sin; she will not only stand apart but will make war to destroy such evil from the world.

436 Never is a woman referred to as having a seed except in this most unique case. In this prophecy, God is revealing the supreme importance of Mary's role in Christ's Incarnation. He is of her; she is in the most profound way the Theotokos, the Mother of God.

437 According to St. Jerome's translation of Genesis, 'he' and 'him' can be translated 'she' and 'her', placing even more emphasis on the importance of the woman in God's plan for the Incarnation. The masculine or feminine translation of this passage is still debated, but it is important to understand the wisdom of both translations, and that the truth being conveyed is beyond simple linguistics. Just as Wisdom in the Book of Wisdom can be understood as both Mary and Christ, even though the translation is feminine, so too a greater mystery is being revealed, the union between Wisdom (Christ) and Lady Wisdom (Mary). Her seed shall crush the head of Satan, for Christ is of Mary His mother; his entire bodily being comes from her. We must be profoundly humbled at such a union of mother and child, especially when God is the Father. This image echoes throughout Christendom; for example, in the divinely given image of Our Lady of Guadalupe, Mary is depicted standing upon the crescent moon, a symbol of the pagan demon Quetzalcoatl, the feathered serpent deity of the Aztecs.

At the *first good news*, a second Archangel cried out in joy: "Behold

Sirach
24:24

God's Strength![439] All Hail, *Grace Most Plentiful!* The Mother of all fair love, and of fear, and of knowledge, and of holy hope! In her is all grace of the way and of the truth, in her is all hope of life and of virtue. Her memory shall be unto everlasting generations!"

Isaiah
27:1

Michael then joined in song, proclaiming: "There soon shall come a day when the Lord shall punish with His sword the cruel, the great, the strong Leviathan, the fleeing serpent, Leviathan the coiled serpent; the Lord shall slay the Dragon in the Sea!"[440]

Revelation
12:1...

So the Lord had there appear in the sky the first *good news: the Woman* clothed in the sun, with moon underfoot, and a crown of twelve stars upon her head. She was with child and wailed aloud in pain as she labored to give birth. She gave birth to the Son, a male child, destined to rule all the nations with an iron rod. Her child was caught up to God and His throne. *The Woman* herself then fled into the desert where she had a place prepared for her by God, that there

Revelation
...12:6

she might be taken care of for twelve-hundred and sixty days.[441]

The Ancient Serpent, seeing that he had not prevented the great prophecy, let out a great cry of anguish, and now bound to the Earth, became increasingly angry and plotted to pursue *the Woman* to her death.[442]

Revelation
12:14...

But the Lord God would not let any harm come to *the Woman*, so He gave her the two wings of the great eagle,[443] so that she could fly to her place in the desert[444] that the Lord had prepared for her. There, far from the serpent, she would be taken care of for a year, two years, and half a year.[445]

Revelation
...12:15...

However, Leviathan, now stripped of his wings and rendered bound to the earth, spewed forth a great torrent of water out of his mouth to sweep *the Woman* away with the flood. But the Earth[446] protected *the Woman* and opened up its mouth to swallow the flood that the dragon spewed from its mouth.

439 This is the true name of Gabriel, the second highest angel in Heaven. He recognizes the true strength of God is the love He has for the Woman, and through that all-powerful love the Incarnation shall come about, which in turn brings about the salvation of all.

440 Isaiah 27:1. This is a very important Bible verse. It is the middle term to prove definitively that the Serpent in the Garden of Eden and the Dragon in the Book of Revelation is Leviathan, the great sea serpent found throughout the Old Testament.

441 Twelve-hundred and sixty days seems like an arbitrary number until one converts it into the number of months, forty-two. Six is the number of the beast because on the Sixth Day of creation God created all the beasts of the Earth, so when the number six is applied to man, he is acting below his nature, in a bestial way. Conversely, when the number seven is applied to man, he is acting in a divine manner, for the Seventh day is the Lord's day. Forty-two is a profoundly significant number because it is the product of six and seven; the Mother of God will return at the time where man is elevated from a bestial nature to a divine nature, which is the Incarnation of Jesus Christ, the Godman.

442 Satan begins to feel the hot whips of panic as he realizes his seeming victory is in no way secure, and he becomes increasingly angry with *the Woman* because of such fear. He knows he has to destroy the Woman before God can follow through with His Word and assume human flesh.

443 Satan's fear unfolds into reality, for as his wings are stripped, the Mother of God is given wings, but not just any wings: the royal wings of the eagle, the king of the sky (heaven). While this represents her elevation above the angels, it also represents St. John, the gospel writer, whose symbol is the eagle. Mary is taken in by John after the death of Jesus, and from the exalted Theotokos who first received The Word from God, we all receive the gospel through the four evangelists. She is in a most profound way the promise of the Protoevangelium and the Protoevangelist, the first to listen and bear forth God's Word.

444 The reason she is taken to the desert is its distance from the sea, which is now Leviathan's dwelling.

445 Three and a half years is twelve-hundred and sixty days or 42 months, emphasizing further the significance of the unity of six and seven as the time when God shall become man as was stated above.

446 The Earth is what saves the woman; flesh and matter is what in the end saves the Mother of God. This can be understood in several ways: firstly, because Eve is mortal and not a pure spirit, she has the ability to bring forth a child who is a wholly different being, and thus it is not necessary that she be the Mother of God herself. (Though as Leviathan had predicted, sin would infect the whole of the human race). Secondly, because of the material reality of procreation, all humans share in the nature of man, in the same species, indeed, in the same family, as we all came forth from two parents. This is notable because angels do not share any common nature; each angel is its own species, utterly unique. Therefore, when Christ was born of a woman, He inherited human nature from Mary, while remaining God, the Second Person of the Trinity. Because Mary shares our human nature, human nature itself is bound to the Divine nature, united in the person of Christ now and forever. For all the ills flesh affords the human race, too clearly seen by Lucifer, flesh is also the very reason God could enter into Creation and become one of us, sharing in our own human nature.

Then Leviathan became exceedingly angry with *the Woman* and went off to wage war upon the rest of her seed.[447] It was there on the sands of the sea that Leviathan, the great sea serpent, took its position.

Revelation
...12:18

The Protoevangelium

447 This is Satan's only recourse, for he can no longer reach *the Woman*. He is forced to attack all of mankind, biding his time until God decides to become man. This, simply put, is human history: all nations ruthlessly enslaved to pagan gods, corrupting all peoples save one nation: God's people, Israel. This specific history of how God saved one people and how Satan tried to destroy them is the story of the Old Testament. In the New Testament, we see why the Roman Empire rose at the time it did, how it became a pantheon for all demons as Satan amassed and centralized all the power of the world to rival and crush the budding kingdom of Christ. Indeed, Israel was occupied by the Romans just a few years before the great revelation. At the appointed time, Herod slaughtered all newborn children, to nip the newborn Incarnation in the bud. Satan knew the time had come and wanted to destroy Christ in infancy.

 *NOTES*

Genesis
...3:14...

God turned then toward the woman and said: "I will greatly multiply[448] your pains in childbirth; in great pain shall you bring forth children,[449] yet your desire shall be for your husband, and he shall lord over you."[450]

Job
5:17...

The second Archangel began pleading before the Lord, "All hail *God's strength!*[451] Happy is the man whom God chastises; despise not the reproach of the Lord! For He wounds, but He binds up; He smites, but His hands give healing. He will deliver you from six troubles; and

Job
...5:19

in the seventh, there no evil will touch you![452]

1 Timothy
2:10...

Look kindly upon woman, that she might be adorned with good deeds, as befits all women who profess reverence for God. Truly by the strength of Your Word woman shall receive instruction silently and under complete control, and have no authority over a man. She must remain quiet.[453] For man was formed first, then woman, and so man was not deceived, but woman was deceived and so transgressed.[454] But, the *Lord as my strength*, let woman be redeemed through childbirth,

1 Timothy
...2:15

her motherhood preserved in faith and love and holiness."

NOTES

448 Note that the Scriptures specifically say 'multiply' or 'increase,' for childbirth always occurs with pain, but because of Eve's disobedience the pain is now disproportionately increased.

449 All God's punishments counteract the crimes committed, while bringing forth a greater good. Eve, the mother of all that is living, failed to live up to her womanhood, seeking divinity and beauty for herself instead of for the glory of God. This pride is what drove her to talk to the serpent, and what allowed her to take so easily from the Tree. Because she betrays her role as a woman, her very nature as a mother betrays her, tainted by her sin into great pain. Yet even this God wills for good, for this cross she bears shall be the greatest joy of her life and eventually the world. For, on that fateful night in the cave, Mary brought forth God incarnate to save the entire world. ("But she [woman] shall be saved through motherhood…" 1 Timothy 2:15)

450 The other half of woman's punishment is the distortion of her relationship with man, for they can no longer exist as equals. Here, the punishment helps illuminate their sin. Eve played the role of man by crossing words with Leviathan and deciding to take of the fruit; she took for herself the role of head of the family instead of the heart. Eve was made last, crowning creation with a special glory; she was made to be an immaculate vessel housing the Heart of the Lord, revealing God's true desire for mankind, truly a preternatural Ark of the Covenant. This glorious vocation given to Eve was perverted in her sin; she turned the Ark into an idol, making herself the object of worship. This is why the serpent tempts her with becoming a god. Now instead of being revered for being such a sign of God's love, she is subject to man, subservient to him, forced to truly become a 'helpmate' for her husband. Since their sin was a dysfunctional relationship, their punishment was given to specifically fix such a problem, just as Lucifer, the highest angel, was cursed to be a snake to teach humility. Woman, the crown jewel of creation, is now subjected to the rule of man to teach her how to be a true 'helpmate' guiding man to the Lord. Woman was placed below man so that she might bolster him up, and it is only after Christ's redemptive victory that we can begin to see woman's original purpose as the marital path leading all men to God.

451 This is the Archangel Gabriel, whose name means "God's Strength." Gabriel is pleading with the Lord for the Incarnation, that the Lord not diminish woman so severely that she could no longer be the Theotokos (God-bearer) of the Christ. Gabriel understands not only why God desires to become man, but how; he in particular knows that through the unfathomable strength of God's grace, a woman might be lifted up as a fitting vessel to house the Lord Almighty. This is why Gabriel is one of the Seven, and the particular Archangel entrusted with the greatest Gospel, the Word Himself, delivered to the Mother of God, for he is the Archangel protecting the family of Mary and the Holy Spirit. It is fitting he speaks here, at the Protoevangelium, for he will see the prophecy to its fulfillment, announcing to the Protoevangelist her role in the Salvation of the Universe.

452 Job 5:17. Gabriel's words are a hallowed prophecy of a woman who will have no stain of sin, and be perfectly immaculate.

453 The Archangel understands that it was Eve's spurious words that opened the door to temptation, and so God's punishment fittingly includes silence. This in turn forces the man to take up the Word and speak, to break his silence and fulfill his role as priest and prophet.

454 This is the reason the first sin is called the 'Sin of Adam,' for Eve was deceived and thus was fooled into sinning, while Adam, who was given the commandment straight from God and charged with guarding the garden, did nothing. He failed to trust her, adding to God's command telling her, 'not to touch the fruit lest she die.' He failed to protect God's paradise, and even neglected to stand between his wife and a beguiling dragon.

So moved by the prayer, the Lord sent His Spirit to enrapture the heart of His Archangel, setting him ablaze with the fire of His love. The man and his wife then heard the Lord speak the name *Gabriel*, as the Lord placed a burning torch before His holy Altar.

Then God said to the man: "Because you have listened to your wife[455] and ate from the tree about which I had commanded you: 'You shall not eat'[456] Cursed is the ground because of you![457] In great toil shall you eat its yield all the days of your life.[458] Thorns and thistles it shall bear for you, and you shall eat the plants of the field. By the sweat of your brow you shall eat *bread*, till the day you return to the ground from which you were taken.[459] For you are dust, and to dust you shall return."[460]

Note 460 Let us contemplate how, in God's infinite wisdom and mercy, our punishments contain within themselves our eventual salvation. For woman, this is childbirth, a great punishment given by God, but through this punishment arises the means by which God saves the human race. Through childbirth, Mary, *the Woman*, becomes the most holy Theotokos, uniting God and man forever in her flesh. For man, it is thorns and thistles, toil, and eventually death, at first a great punishment, but when Christ takes on these punishments, his head crowned with thorns and his flesh plowed and furrowed to become the Bread of Life, he won for us eternal Salvation. Adam brought death into the world, but the death of our Lord Jesus Christ brought life: it is through Christ's death the world was redeemed. Furthermore, the death God speaks of is actually the double death warned of by God in the second chapter of Genesis. This double death is not merely the separation of the soul from the body, but is in fact the separation of the soul from God, which is the first death, sin. The second death is the permanent isolation of the soul from God (after bodily death), which is Hell. It is for this reason we profess Christ descended into Hell and rose on the third day, bringing with Him all the fallen righteous men previously claimed by Satan. This is the true Death Christ has saved us from, a death far worse than any mortal separation of body and soul.

Revelation 4:5

Genesis ...3:17...

Genesis ...3:19

455 God points out the discord between husband and wife, and the fault of our first father in listening to his wife in matters he should have been guiding her on. Man and woman, made in the Image of God, can also be seen as truth and love, intellect and will, or mind and heart; when Adam listens to Eve, he is contorting the natural order of intellect and will. The intellect informs the will of what is most desirable, but when the will controls the intellect, the natural process is broken and causes harm to the person, like a glutton who knows he should stop eating yet continues to anyway. 'The will is blind,' always seeking goods innocently, purely. The intellect is charged with guarding the will, ordering the goods it seeks, so that most of all the greatest of goods can be sought. In the same manner, man is to protect woman, so that she can inspire or motivate man to actually seize the good, just as the will moves the person.

456 These specific words of God show that the command was uniquely given to Adam and not Eve, even going as far as quoting the exact words he spoke to Adam, emphasizing further the mistaken wording Eve uses when speaking to the Serpent. Simply put, only Adam existed when God gave the commandment to not eat from the Tree of Knowledge of Good and Evil; the fault for breaking the commandment rests squarely on his shoulders.

457 The Earth is actually suffering because of man's sin: 'All creation fell with Adam.' When the king falls, the entire kingdom suffers from the collapse; this causes a loss of order at the very core of material creation. The subsequent conquest and pillaging of the invading demons was only a final symptom of an earth already brought low by a Universal Fall.

458 The contrast between man and woman's punishment is enlightening. Woman is punished with inter-relational sufferings, with both child and her husband. This emphasizes woman's prerogative, her natural inclination for the family. Man's punishment is external, for he must now provide for the family with great toil. Man and woman must therefore look to each other: If the husband wishes to understand the family he must look through the eyes of the wife, and if the wife wishes to understand the world she must look through the eyes of the husband.

459 This is a direct result of Leviathan's lie, which belittles man into nothing more than a beast. Adam ceded the kingdom to Satan, and the discord surrounding the ancient dragon in the Celestial War descends with him unto the earth. Man now spends his entire existence validating this misbelief, remolding the earth in this same image. Man shall now suffer a beast's fate, roaming the Earth, seeking food until he decomposes back into the ground.

ᏚᏂᎬ FᎪᏞᏞ
§ ᏚᏂᎬ Seven Seals §

Genesis
3:22…

The Lord God, seeing all creation fall with Adam, turned to Himself and spoke: "Behold, who now is worthy to open the Scroll and to read from it? For there is no one in Heaven or on Earth or under the Earth that is worthy to open the Scroll or even examine it! Now, therefore, lest perhaps one stretch forth his hand and take the Word from the Scroll before the appointed time?" Thereupon the Lord God placed seals upon the Scroll, barring its reading until the

Genesis
…3:24

fulfillment of time had been accomplished.[461]

Thus, in fear and trembling, the man fell to his knees and, looking up, beheld the effects of his sin.

Revelation
6:1…

The Lord God then took the large Scroll in His hand and sealed it with the first seal, and immediately one of the Four Living Creatures wailed a loud cry of thunder.[462] The crown of man was then stripped away and there appeared a white horse whose rider bore a bow, and the crown was handed over to him, and he went out to all the Earth, conquering and to conquer.[463]

Revelation
…6:3…

The Lord then placed a second seal upon the Scroll, and the second Living Creature let out a great cry of thunder which shook the man, and another horse came, blood-red in appearance. Its rider was given a great sword to take *peace* from the Earth, cursing men that they should slay one another.[464]

Revelation
…6:5…

So the Lord placed a third seal upon the Scroll, and the third Living Creature's cry thundered throughout the Earth, and a third horse came as black as the raven. Its rider held a balance in hand, unequal in weight, and upon his horse's heels came famine, which spread to all corners of the earth.[465]

Revelation
…6:7…

The Lord then placed a fourth seal upon the Scroll, and the fourth Living Creature wailed a cry of thunder, and so came a pale green horse. Its rider was given the name Death, . . .

IGNATIAN CONTEMPLATION

461 The fulfillment of all time is symbolically represented by the number forty-two, as is seen throughout the Book of Revelation. Forty-two is the combination of six and seven, which represents the Incarnation when God (7) becomes man (6).

462 After each of the first four seals, one of the Four Living Creatures cries out in agony at the withholding of the Word of God. The Four Living Creatures or Cherubim are charged with the proclamation of the Gospel, yet because of man's sin they must wait for Christ before they can proclaim the Word held within the Scroll.

463 The four horsemen are symbols of Satan's empire. The first rider is a symbol for Leviathan, who received authority to rule over the Earth, as confirmed in Matthew 4:8: "Again, the devil took him to a very high mountain and showed him all the kingdoms of the world and their splendor; and he said to him, 'All these I will give you, if you will fall down and worship me.'" Satan, in fact, received his rule over the Earth from Adam.

464 The second rider is a symbol for Satan's first act as conqueror. He destroys the peace of the garden and brings war. This is not only men fighting other men but all of nature at odds with itself. Man and wife now exist in strife with one another, nature resists man's tending hand, and animals contend with and destroy men. Man is even in strife within himself, for the flesh is no longer subjugated to the wisdom of the soul, and we make our way slowly, as though blind.

465 The third rider is God's punishment for man, exacted by Leviathan, which is symbolized by the imbalance of justice because of man's sin. The kingdom no longer pays heed to the king, so man is forced to struggle as a common beast with the unwieldy feast and famine of the Earth.

The Fourth Horseman

. . . and Hell followed with him.[466] Power was given to him over the four parts of the Earth to kill with the sword, and with famine, and with pestilence, and with the beasts of the Earth.[467]

Revelation
...6:9...

When the Lord placed upon the Scroll a fifth seal, the man let out a great cry of horror as he beheld beneath the Altar of the Lord the many souls of his sons and daughters who were slaughtered unjustly upon the Earth. They cried out in a loud voice: "Oh Lord! How long will it be? How long before You judge and avenge our blood on the inhabitants of the Earth?" But they were told there would be no judgment until the number was complete, for their servants, their brothers, and their sisters were still to be killed as they had been killed.[468]

Revelation
...6:12...

And so, when the Lord placed a sixth seal upon the Scroll, a great earthquake shook the Earth; and in the heavens the sun became black as sackcloth, the whole moon became as blood, and the stars of the sky fell to the Earth as the fig tree drops its unripe figs in a gale. The sky rolled up like a scroll, and every mountain and island was shaken from its place. So all mankind from the kings of the earth, to the magistrates and generals, to the rich and powerful, to everyone, slave and free, all hid themselves in caves and among the rocks of the mountains, crying to the mountains: "Fall on us and hide us from the face of the One seated upon the Throne, and from the wrath of the Lord; for the day of great wrath has come! Who is able to stand?" So, man bore witness as all creation fell alongside him.[469]

Revelation
...6:17

Revelation
8:1

At last the Lord placed the seventh seal upon the Scroll and there came a great silence, which descended upon Heaven and Earth at which all things came to a standstill for about a half hour.[470]

466　The fourth and final rider is Death, the ultimate power of Satan and true punishment of man, which inevitably leads to Hell. This is also a symbol for sin, for with the removal of grace from man, he slowly decays into Hell, which is the existence apart from God's life. Hell is the new power upon the Earth, utterly destroying the hope of man.

467　These infamous horsemen of Revelation are not to be thought of as plagues sent to usher in the end times and frighten the children of the Faith, but rather they ought to be understood as John understood them: as effects of the Fall. The absence of grace resulting from the Original Sin of Adam and Eve. This is why they are placed as seals upon the Scroll of God; they must first be overcome and removed by Christ on the Cross before we can eat at the Wedding Feast of the Lamb, which is the Most Holy Eucharist.

468　These are all the good men and women who died before the Incarnation of Christ, both Jew and pagan, and it was for these poor and just souls that Christ descended into Hell, ransoming them from the claim of the Devil.

469　The sixth seal shows how all creation fell with Adam—from the angels in the heavens symbolized by the stars to the islands and the mountains. No longer will lion lay with lamb or man live in harmony with nature; all creation is shaken by the Sin of Adam. (Such a vital truth is necessary for the proper understanding of Cosmology, which unfortunately is often forgotten in our understanding of the world.)

　　　　Furthermore, consider how the sixth seal corresponds to the sixth day, for on the sixth day the beasts of the Earth were made and now, because of his fall, man's existence is cast down like the beasts. Deprived of grace and bound to the power of Hell, man is forced to live out his life as an animal of the Earth, even though he was created *for* the seventh day—to rest with God.

470　First, the silence of the seventh seal is no doubt a harkening to the peace of the seventh day of creation, but instead of a hallowed peace, now there is a hollow silence, a lack of God's Word. Second, the time period indicated is significant for it once again is an instance of the number forty-two. A full Hebrew day is evenly divided into twelve hours of daylight and twelve hours of night, indicating that there was silence for 4.2% of the day. Finally, when combining these two interpretations we see the symbolic meaning of this last seal, namely, that because of the Fall we must wait 4.2% of the seventh day in silence waiting for the Word of God. This, of course, is fulfilled in the words of St. Gabriel, who announces to Mary that she will bear forth the Word of God into the Universe, the union of God (7) and Man (6): the Godman (42).

DIVINE MERCY

The man choosing to place his hope in what the Lord had pronounced to Leviathan, turned toward his wife and named her Eve, because she was to become the 'Mother of all the Living.'[471]

Enraged at such a name given to the woman by her husband, Leviathan, the Accuser, brought forth an allegation[472] before the Lord and said, "They have sinned against God and are deserving of death! By Your own word You commanded: '*In that day* you partake of the fruit,

surely you will die the death'; for indeed the wages of sin is death! Dying they must die!"[473]

So Adam, fearing for his life,[474] fell to the ground in shame, and trembling said, "Naked I came into this world, and naked I shall return, the Lord giveth and the Lord taketh away; blessed be the Name of the Lord forever."

NOTES

IGNATIAN CONTEMPLATION

471 It is important to note that man and woman have not actually been named 'Adam' and 'Eve' until after the fall. This is in part to show the universality of Adam and Eve's sin; both actually and symbolically as all of humanity, they chose to transgress against God. In addition, Adam is the one who names Eve, showing he truly does have authority over her, but the name he gives illustrates her nobility and his hope. She is the 'Mother of all the Living,' a very precious name, a title that hints at Adam's hope in the Protoevangelium, that she is the only way back from this state of sin and death. As death meant separation from God in sin and Hell, so too does life mean union with God in grace and Heaven.

472 This is Leviathan's first act as the Celestial Court's prosecutor, fulfilling his new name of 'Accuser' or Satan. It is not by accident that his first accusation against mankind is that they are deserving of Death, he will continue to use this accusation invoking Justice, the Law, and even God's own words to try and convict all mankind as deserving of the punishment of death.

473 Satan is masterfully fulfilling his role as 'Accuser' in the heavenly court, bringing before the Lord the accusation that 'in the very day' they ate of the fruit they are deserving of death. He cunningly uses the Lord's own words against Him, trying to entrap God into killing Adam and Eve. This is a brilliant strategy, for the Lord in His perfect Simplicity cannot contradict Himself. However, the Lord uses this opportunity to bring good out of evil, as He does with every evil. In order to satisfy His word, God institutes 'sacrifice', a precursor of Divine Mercy, which not only satisfies the punishment of injustice between the two parties, but has the potential to restore their relationship.

474 Fear should not be mistaken for repentance. At no point in the Genesis narrative does Adam apologize for his sin against the Lord, a somber reminder of our human weakness and shortsightedness. Nevertheless, it is important to remember that 'Fear of the Lord is the beginning of Wisdom.' (Proverbs (9:10)

The Lord God then beheld His son,[475] naked and ashamed, and was overcome with pity, so He took a lamb[476] of Eden, and placing His hand upon its head blessed the victim, and finding it acceptable for expiation slaughtered it,[477] pouring its blood out before the Tree of Life at the center of the Garden.[478] The Lord then made for Adam and his wife garments of lambskin[479] and clothed them by His own hand.[480]

Genesis
...3:21...

Note 480   This is the first corporal act of mercy found in existence, recorded by Scripture, a mercy given to man by God after the Fall. God clothes the naked as both a corporal and spiritual act of love and mercy. This mercy only abounds all the more as humanity suffers more and moves farther away from the garden. We are called to such acts of mercy only because God has given those mercies to us first. He has given food to the hungry and drink for the thirsty; He sheltered us in the wilderness and kept faith with us when we were sick; He did not abandon us while we were in prison, or left our bodies to rot and decay; He poured all His grace into poor humanity, and we must do the same. This first Divine Mercy though a corporal work was a profound spiritual work of mercy as well—through this simple gift of leather clothing God is instructing mankind that it is good to be covered in skin, to have flesh. Contemplate in prayer how all seven spiritual works of mercy are housed in this one simple act of God: counsel the doubtful, instruct the ignorant, admonish the sinner, comfort the sorrowful, forgive injuries, bear wrongs patiently, pray for the living and the dead. It is indeed because of this act of mercy and the first sacrifice necessitated by it that the angels themselves first learn of God's mercy.

475 Let us reflect upon this moment where the Lord God is faced with an immense decision. It is well within His power to restore Adam's honor and dignity by clothing him with garments of leather to remove his shame, but in doing so He chooses to institute the rite of sacrifice, which will lead to the Ultimate Sacrifice of Christ on the Cross. Thus, it is in this moment that God chooses to sacrifice His Son, and sets in motion the great journey from Eden to Calvary; all for the redemption of Adam and the honor of the human race, which in turn compose the glorious work of Mercy which is God's greatest act within His Creation. This most striking deliberation is the very story of the great epic, The Iliad, where Zeus weightily decides to answer Thetis' prayer and restore her son Achilles' honor, fully aware that in doing so it will cause the death of his own son, Patroclus. Yet, Zeus decides to sacrifice his own son for the restoration of Achilles honor. This is the Lord's omniscient will; that from the very beginning, in order to save Adam and the whole human race from the shame of sin and death, He was to send His true Son, Jesus Christ, as the Last and Perfect Sacrifice

476 This first sacrifice, a holy and unblemished lamb, is most profoundly a prefigurement of Christ, the last sacrifice, the true Lamb of God.

477 This is the first death in all of creation. The Lord God killed the animal so that Adam and Eve might not be stranded in their shame. He knows that their shame, our shame, is unnecessary, that it comes as a result of buying Lucifer's lies and sin. However, he aids them as they are. With tender compassion yet great wisdom, he gives them skin, to cover their own. This is a profound refutation of Leviathan's lie, and of their shame. God grants us the skin of the unblemished lamb that we might not be ashamed of our skin, and He will patiently guide us until He can fulfill His plan for the fulfillment of this symbol, when the Divinity itself redeems all flesh through its Incarnation.

478 There are few instances in Holy Scripture where God shows humanity that there are indeed things more important than life itself. This is one of those instances. Consider how God values human dignity more than the life of this animal. It is more important to restore Adam and Eve's acceptance of the dignity of their bodies as enfleshed beings than for this animal to remain alive. This is one of the saddest scenes in the Bible; because of the Fall, God Himself has to kill one of His own creatures just so that man might not live in shame.

479 Lambskin is a profound testament to God's love, for the highest and best quality leather which is befitting for clothing is actually lambskin. The Lord does not give a gift of random leather, but choses the very finest leather to clothe Adam and Eve. The magnanimity of this gift is only expounded upon when the truly marvelous meaning of the sacrificial lamb is understood, and is redoubled when we understand what it means for us, as St. Paul says, to 'put on Christ'.

1 Kings
18:30...

Once clothed and their shame abated, the Lord God called to Adam and his wife, "Come closer to Me" and the couple came closer to the Lord. So the Lord God took twelve stones according to the number of stars in *the Woman's* crown, and the Word of the Lord was pronounced, "'Mother of all the Living' shall indeed be *her*[481] name." At this Satan's fury was enraged, but he made no answer, voiced nothing, and had no response. The Lord then built an Altar with the twelve stones and around the Altar He dug a trench; large enough to contain two measures of seed.

The Lord God then turned and took branches from the Tree of Life and having gathered them together arranged them into a holocaust for the slain lamb.[482] He brought before the man and his wife the animal whose death was wrought by their sin.[483] He instructed them saying,

Leviticus
1:3...

"So it shall be when you bring an offering before the Lord: it shall be a male, without blemish; you shall bring it before the Lord laying your hands upon its head, praying that it shall be an acceptable sacrifice on your behalf as an atonement for you."

The Lord then immersed the flayed lamb into the river of life-giving waters, shining like crystal, around which grew the Tree of Life and washed its feet and entrails in the water. He said, "Let us take water from the river and pour it upon the holocaust not once, nor twice, but thrice the greater." So the water ran over and all around the Altar filling the trench with water.

1 Kings
...18:34...

The Lord God then arranged upon the wood of the Tree of Life the victim, the slain lamb, and He was indeed overcome with love, so the Fire of God fell consuming the Holocaust: the wood from the Tree of Life, the twelve stones, and the dust, even licking up the water that was in the trench. The whole sacrifice was consumed and turned into smoke, a most pleasing odor to the Lord.[484]

Leviticus
...1:13

481 First, the Lord is affirming Adam's act of faith, that it was good and right to believe in the Protoevangelium, and name his wife Eve, even if he doesn't fully understand to whom the Lord and Satan were referring. Second, as we know now, the Lord is not speaking of Eve in the garden but of the 'New Eve' who shall truly be the Mother of all the Living, those who possess Life in Christ.

482 The moment that God decides to use the branches of the Tree of Life as wood for the burnt offering, a twofold sign is consummated; the Tree of Life and the Lamb of God, which united perfectly reveals The Sacrifice of God Himself and fulfillment of Salvation History. Let us turn in contemplation at this most beautiful act of God using the very wood of the Tree of Life, which resounds throughout the entire Bible. We know through Scripture and Tradition that Christ is the fruit of the Tree of Life and its wood is the very wood of the Cross. (There is even a tradition in the Holy Land that Jesus' Cross bar was hung on an olive tree, and we mustn't forget that the Tree of Life was an olive tree, as was previously explained.) Further, we read in Proverbs 3:18 "[Wisdom] is the Tree of Life to those who grasp her, and happy are they who hold fast to her." Wisdom is Christ the way, the truth, and the life. Again, in Proverbs 11:30 "The fruit of righteousness is the Tree of Life and he who is wise wins souls." Jesus is righteousness fulfilled and Wisdom Himself. Finally, Proverbs 13:12 "Hope deferred makes the heart sick, but hope's desire fulfilled is the Tree of Life." This bitter brew of hope and its deferment is what Adam feels as he watches this first sacrifice, a new hope that his relationship with God can be restored and sacrifice is the means by which it shall be accomplished, but not knowing when that will ever be fulfilled. For what sacrifice could ever bridge the gap between creature and Creator? Finally, we read in Revelation 22:2 "and the leaves of the Tree are for the healing of the nations." It is these very leaves that are burnt for the healing of Adam's shame, and the expiation of his punishment. Furthermore, in Adam lies all future nations who are spared through the enraptured leaves of the Tree of Life. How perfect is God's plan that from the very beginning Christ's Sacrifice lies hidden in the simple words "And God made them garments of leather"; and how gloriously this is unveiled in the New Testament, not only Christ as the 'Lamb of God', but as Paul says to the Galatians: "Those of you that have been Baptized into Christ have clothed yourself in Christ."

483 Wearing the very skin of the now slain lamb, Adam and Eve already begin to identify with the lamb, and whatever occurs to it.

484 Let us reflect upon this first sacrifice by The Father's hands, how the all-consuming love of God is made manifest by this total 'inspyration': starting with the victim, Christ; the wood of the Tree of Life, the Cross; the 12 stones, the Church; the dust, our humanity; and even unto the water; the Abyss itself. All things will be glorified and reconciled to God through the Last and Perfect Sacrifice, here foreshadowed perfectly in the first sacrifice. How much more meaningful is the Alpha and Omega, seeing God's plan manifested from the very beginning of time to its fulfillment in Christ Jesus. How these two sacrifices echo back and forth throughout Scripture: as The Father builds a holocaust and arranges the lamb (of God) upon the wood, we can't help but recall Abraham preparing the wood to sacrifice his son, Isaac, having full faith in the Resurrection of the Lord, His own Life conquering death. As The Father sets the branches afire with His Love, how much more beautiful becomes the Burning Bush, whose flames are now sweetened by the oil of the olive? Even the great Lampstand in the Temple, sculpted in the form of the Tree and eternally lit with olive oil, a foretelling of the Light of Christ and its fiery consummation in loving sacrifice for humanity.

At this all of Heaven marveled and wondered what manner of deed this was; for never before had mercy been witnessed in all of Creation. Before the sacrifice they fell on their faces and proclaimed, "The Lord indeed is God; The Lord indeed is God!"

1 Kings
... 18:39

Isaiah
53:4...

Upon the Earth Adam fell, and wept, "How is it, that this little one has borne our infirmities and carried our sorrows? For us to only consider him stricken, smitten by God, and afflicted. This lamb has been pierced for our transgressions, crushed for our iniquities; the punishment that has brought us 'peace' has been laid upon him, and by his wounds we have been spared. Is it not my wife and I, who like sheep have gone astray? Each of us following our own way? Yet the Lord has laid on this lamb the iniquity of us both. Even though he was oppressed and afflicted, this lamb did not even open his mouth. This lamb, though led to the slaughter, a sheep before his shearers, was silent, never even opening his mouth." Adam marveled, "Though this lamb had done no wrong nor was deceit found in his mouth, it was the Lord's will to burden him with our pain, making his life a sacrifice of reparation for our sin. It is because of this lamb we shall see our children, and have the length of our days restored, truly the Lord's will has been accomplished through this lamb."[485]

Isaiah
...53:10

Ephesians
2:4...

Astonished the stars of heaven proclaimed, "It is God alone who possesses mercy and in such abundance! For even though man was to die in sin, The Lord out of His great mercy has graciously saved them from their shame. Now He raises up the stars of heaven to be with Him, to dwell in the heavenly places,[486] so that we might bear witness to His mercies in ages to come, the immeasurable riches of grace and kindness that He shall show forth toward the human race. For we see now, it shall be by grace they are to be saved, through Faith, not by any merit of their own nature, but as a sheer gift of God."

Ephesians
...2:8

"Let us too commend ourselves to the hands of the Lord, just as these mortals who have been clothed by His hands, for now we see His majesty is as great as His mercy and His Name is as great as His works!"

Sirach
2:18

485   Adam before the death of the lamb of God utters the hallowed words that most perfectly prefigure the suffering and death of the true Lamb of God, Jesus Christ. The 'Suffering Servant' passage from Isaiah is such a perfect prefiguration of Christ that certain Jewish circles discourage the reading of this passage in fear that it'll too clearly call to mind the Christian Jesus. These words uttered at the first sacrifice of the lamb and spoken by the prophet, are now uttered every Friday during Lent at Stations of the Cross, they cannot help but be prayed when the Sacrifice of Jesus is truly seen.

486   Witnessing the first sacrifice at the hands of the Father and that very sacrifice covering the shame of Adam, the angels are revealed a glimpse of the infinite ocean of Mercy held within the Sacred Heart of the Trinity; for once they only knew the Lord as Justice, but now they see that Justice is beholden to Divine Mercy. Thus, it is upon this Divine Mercy, Christ Himself, that the Celestial Hierarchy is built, the flow of grace ever perfecting and elevating the holy angels beyond their natural capacity to love and serve the Lord.

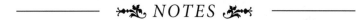 *NOTES*

ᚧHE CELESᚧIAL LADDER [487]

Genesis
28:12

After the man and his wife had covered their shame, they began to wonder to themselves what was to be done for the night, for the sun had set and it was now night. They watched as the smoke from the holocaust rose to the heights of Heaven and beheld an abundance of stars gleaming intensely in the sky, and there could be seen a great ladder upon the Earth, the top of which reached all the way to Heaven, and upon the Celestial Ladder they beheld the angels of God ascending and descending upon it.

§ Guardian Angels §

Psalm
91:1...

So inspired by the *first good news*[488] proclaimed to Leviathan by the Lord, the nearest[489] angels began to pray and intercede for the sake of man: "O Lord, send not man from the shelter of the Most High, man, who abides in the shadow of the Almighty! For man will call to the Lord, though it be not this day, and say: 'My refuge and my fortress; my God, in whom I trust!'

"Deliver them from the snares of the Enemy, and from the deathly pestilences! Cover them with Your plumage, and under Your wings will they find refuge; faithfulness shall be their shield and their buckler. Preserve them from the terrors of the night, from the arrow that flies by day, from the pestilences that lurk in darkness, and from the destructions that lays waste at noonday.

Psalm
...91:7...

"Thousands of men shall fall—ten thousand men shall be ensnared—but discard not Your chosen few, that they will look with their own eyes and see the recompense of the wicked. For they alone will make the Lord their refuge, and dwell within the life of the Most High; and there no evil shall befall them, and no scourge come near their tent.

Psalm
...91:11...

"Send Your angels as Guardians over men to protect them in all their ways! By angelic hands bear them up, lest they dash their foot against a stone! Upon lion and viper they will tread without fear, the

IGNATIAN CONTEMPLATION

487   This is the same Ladder that Jacob sees in Genesis 28:10 when he is visited by God in a dream. Later, in John 1:51, the ladder is revealed to be Christ Himself, the super-essential Way that Heaven and Earth are united.

488   The Protoevangelium: Gen 3:15. This is the key to the formation of each and every one of the Celestial Hierarchies, for they chose to serve the Lord Jesus Christ and have for their queen Mary, the Mother of God.

489   The nearest angels are Guardian Angels, the First Choir of the Celestial Hierarchies. While they are the lowest choir, this means they are very near to man on earth, and so they see in an intimate way the suffering of humanity coupled with the mercy of God. This is why they choose to be vigilant guardians, protecting individual men from the constant assault of demons.

Celestial Choir of Guardian Angels

young lion and the serpent they will trample under foot! For man shall cleave to the Lord in love, and the Lord shall deliver him and protect him, because He knows each by name.[490] When man calls out to the Lord, the Lord will answer him, and will be with him in trouble. The Lord will rescue man and honor him. With long life the Lord will satisfy him, and He shall show man His salvation!"

Psalm ...91:16

The Lord God, hearing such a prayer, was moved with compassion and declared: "Blessed shall be the Guardians of men who shall be ministering spirits sent out to serve for the sake of those who are to inherit Eternal Salvation! Henceforth see that you do not despise one of these little ones, for I say unto thee their angels shall evermore look upon the Face of God in Heaven!"[491]

Hebrews 1:14

Matthew 18:10

So the Celestial Choir of Guardian Angels appeared upon the Earth to love and serve the Lord.[492]

Celestial Choir of Guardian Angels

490   Consider now the profound love of your Guardian Angel, how they chose to serve the Lord specifically because of you. How out of love for you, your particular self, your Guardian Angel was saved from becoming a demon and the fires of Hell. This is the intimate connection between you and your Guardian Angel. They looked upon you and decided to devote themselves entirely to guarding, guiding, and protecting you for the Lord.

491   Matthew 18:10. Here God is so moved by the love of these guardian angels that for the first time He bestows upon the stars in Heaven the Beatific Vision, the most hallowed glory of His Face, cementing them eternally into a heavenly Choir, the holy Choir of Guardian Angels.

492   There is an overarching chiasm at work here; Lucifer first rails against God to all the celestial intelligences, casting a shadow from the top down. This force of chaos culminates in the overthrow of the earthly realm and the Universal Fall. But God always triumphs; at the center is His mercy, and just as Lucifer's lie promulgated down to Earth, God's mercy toward man echoes all the way up throughout the highest Heavens. All the nine choirs of angels are therefore established, inspired by that same mercy to serve God and man. This is the curious difference between light and grace, between the expectation of nature and the mystery of God's mercy. It is from the center, from the one most in need of God's mercy, that the flow of tender love and grace flows throughout the entire Universe. Michael is the prince, the new herald of grace for the angels; ironically, this is through his 'lowliness,' his proximity to the affairs of man on earth. Though the stars had no need of redemption, in a profound way their salvation depended upon the relationship between God and man, for everything that is good is good because of Christ, for even the angels rejoice at His birth.

NOTES

§ Archangels §

S o enraptured by the *first Sacrifice* and the promise of *the Woman, the Immaculate One,* an angel of the Lord dared to say: "O happy fault of Adam![493] A king's secret ought to be kept secret, but one must declare the works of God in due honor: Our God is the *God who heals!*[494] For the Lord God shall send a Redeemer, and He shall enter once for all into the *Holy Place,* offering not the blood of goats and calves, but His own blood, so securing an eternal redemption!"[495]

The holy angel then sang with the six other holy angels that had also seen the vision of *the Woman* and believed in the Christ, "Enter, O Lord, into the *Holy of Holies,* not made by human hands, and *not of this creation!* Enter, Creator of All, and rest in her tabernacle,[496] for she is the Tree of Life to those who grasp her, and felicity to those who cling to her. The Lord God founded the Earth with her in mind, established the Heavens with an understanding of her. For her the depths were split open, and the clouds dropped down their dew. Truly she is *Queen Mother,* and the heart of the *Holy Family*! She is an infinite treasure to men and angels![497] And those who love her become friends of God, being commended for their discipline."

────────  *NOTES* ────────

Tobit
12:11…

Hebrews
9:12

Hebrews
9:11

Proverbs
3:18…

Proverbs
…3:20
Wisdom
7:14

IGNATIAN CONTEMPLATION

493 'Felix culpa', a boast of Christians everywhere, here shouted by St. Raphael the Archangel, because he is witnessing in a most profound way God's faithful mercy: not just of the merciful work of clothing the naked, but he sees that God will not abandon man in such a wretched state. St. Raphael sees clearly that the fate of mankind shall be even more glorious than before, for God will become man entering into His own creation, sanctifying all Creation in the process.

494 Raphael is God's secret: Raphael means "God who heals." God's secret is that He will heal mankind. The innermost council of God, hidden in the depths of His Heart, was to heal man, a course from which he would not be turned. Despite Leviathan's deception, and Satan's unceasing corruption of man throughout the Earth, Raphael, who means 'God who heals', embodies this secret depth of God's love, and heralds this love to mankind. Ultimately, Raphael sees the Immaculate Conception, God's miraculous healing of original sin, and the Paschal Mystery which brings healing to all the nations. With Raphael, we finally see that the three archangels whose names have been revealed in Scripture all directly relate to the marriage of God and man; Michael is God's humility, the "Divine Condescension" where God faithfully plans to marry the human race; Gabriel is God's strength, the "Incarnation" revealing the power of God to overcome the taint of sin, and unite Himself with Mary through the Holy Spirit; Raphael is God's healing, the "Immaculate Conception" whereby God heals woman of original sin, preserving her as His own, this is for the sake of the great "Paschal Mystery" by which the indomitable plan of God to heal mankind is manifest, specifically by the sacrifice of the Bridegroom. Michael refutes the first lie that God could not love fleshly man, Gabriel proclaims that woman can be the worthy Theotokos, and Raphael refutes Leviathan's victory, the lie that man is forever sullied and cut off from God.

495 Hebrews 9:12. Note that this could refer to either the Incarnation or the Sacrifice on Calvary.

496 Hebrews 9:11. Here Raphael is pleading with the Lord to enter the true Holy of Holies, which is so holy it's not a part of His first creation, but must have been immaculately conceived before the foundations of the world. Raphael reveals that this Holy of Holies is actually a woman, and the Lord is going to rest in her tabernacle. Raphael is begging for the Lord to do this, because he understands that once the Lord enters her womb, salvation has come to the whole of creation. God will have bound Himself to *the Woman* in familial covenant, bringing forth a child to the glory and healing of all creation.

497 Here the Seven Holy Angels lead by Michael, Gabriel, and Raphael are singing of the mystical glory of the Theotokos, in particular as Queen-mother and as Spouse, testifying to the sublime and edifying grace she receives from Divine-monogamy, a unique glory that only comes from being wed to the Holy Spirit. They see that all creation was for the sake of such a thing, a union that could so solemnly unite creature with Creator that the entire Universe could not help but be glorified in a new way. It is precisely because of their profound love of the Theotokos as Spouse of God, that the glory of such a union overflows directly onto Michael, Gabriel, and Raphael, elevating them by grace to be the three greatest angels in existence, Archangels who stand before the very Glory of God.

Tobit
12:15

The Lord God then enraptured the angel and set him afire with Divine Love saying: "From this day forward you shall be known as *Raphael*, one of The *Seven Holy Angels*[498] who present the prayers of the saints upon My golden Altar in Heaven, and there stand before the presence of the Glory of My Holy One!"[499]

Revelation
8:3...

A golden chalice was handed to the Archangel with a great quantity of incense to offer, along with the prayers of all those angels, who also looked upon the human family with love.[500] He offered their prayers

Revelation
...8:4

Matthew
19:6

upon the gold Altar that was before the Throne, and led in chorus all those angels who saw and believed, crying: "Behold their marriage is unbroken! They are no longer two but one flesh, and what God has

Genesis
1:27

bound no one can loose! God has created man in His own *Image*, in the Image of God He created him; male and female He created them. Truly, we have seen the *Great Mystery* of God!"[501]

1 Corinthians
6:13...

So, inspired, the angels began to pray and intercede for the man and his wife, saying: "Glorify God in your bodies! The body was not meant for fornication, but for the Lord, and the Lord for the body! 'The two shall be one flesh.' Yet, when you are united to the Lord, you become one Spirit with him. Shun fornication—cling to each other! Every sin that a person commits is outside the body; but the fornicator sins against the body itself. Or do you not know that your body is a Temple of the Breath of God within you, whom you received from God—you are not your own! For you are loved at a great price,

1 Corinthians
...6:20

1 Corinthians
7:2...

therefore glorify God in your bodies![502]

"Each man should have his own wife and each woman her own husband. The husband must give himself to his wife, her conjugal right, and likewise the wife to her husband. For wife does not have authority over her body, but the husband has authority; likewise husband does not have authority over his body, but the wife has authority. Do not deprive one another, except perhaps for a time to pray, and then come back together again, so that Satan may not tempt you.

498 Considering the great truth of the Universe revealed here in the sacred pages of Tobit, we now know there are seven most holy Angels roundabout the Altar of God, the seven greatest angels in existence who offer the prayers of the Saints to God Himself. These holy angels receive first the most pure grace of God, specifically by conforming themselves to Mary, the Mother of God. They in turn pass such grace down to the Seraphim who catch fire from such pure love, who again overflow with such grace to all the Choirs of Heaven. Everything everywhere receives goodness itself, truth itself, and beauty itself from these most holy Angels. Again, all Grace in the Universe is first poured into the heart of Mary, Full of Grace, who overflows with such Divine Charity onto the Seven Holy Angels lead by St. Michael, St. Gabriel, and St. Raphael. After completing the meditation on the Holy Seraphim, please return to the three Archangels and contemplate their transcendence even beyond the highest Choir of Heaven.

499 Tobit 12:15. These holy angels are so glorified because they stand at the Altar of Sacrifice, which is the Glory of Christ on the Cross.

500 Here we see a distinction between the three Archangels who stand before the Glory of the Lord and the rest of the Choir of Archangels who themselves chose to serve individual families throughout history. Much like Guardian Angels who looked and beheld individuals and chose to serve God because of that specific person, Archangels looked and beheld families whom they loved and chose to serve the Lord because of that particular family. This is the profound intimacy of the first three Choirs and the human race.

501 The 'Great Mystery' spoken of by St. Paul is the limitless well of grace, that is both the Sacrament of Holy Matrimony and the Most Holy Trinity . For through Holy Matrimony we not only see the source of human happiness and perpetuity, but the very Image of the invisible God, the Most Holy Trinity; and through Christ we see the ultimate end, the final cause, of all creation—that Christ, God Himself, might unite Himself so perfectly to His bride, the Church.

502 The Sacrament of Holy Matrimony is the Primordial Sacrament, the first outpouring of God's own Life into the human person, not simply in an invisible, spiritual way, but a tangible, corporeal way. It is within the unbreakable confines of Holy Matrimony that we are truly set free: free from the shame of Original Sin, and free to experience the Divine Contradiction of Trinitarian Union, where two separate and distinct persons might be so united in love that they truly and substantially become one being. This holy and sexual union of husband and wife within the confines of Marriage is one of the greatest glories we can give to God, culminating in a triune pro-creation of life between husband, wife, and God. Only in Holy Matrimony is the perfection of the flesh revealed to be the Magnipotent union of husband and wife conceiving a new life, physically and spiritually imaging the Most Holy Trinity in love and life. This most holy Mystery of Divine Trinitarian Union could only be revealed through the existence of flesh, so perfected in the Sacred bonds of Matrimony. It is no wonder then that this living Sacrament is the first and last Sacrament, instituted at the Beginning of Time in the Garden of Eden and culminating at the End of Time with Christ and His Bride the Church.

1 Corinthians
...7:10...

"The Lord so commands: a wife shall not separate from her husband, and a husband shall not divorce his wife. It is to peace that the Lord God has called you! For how do you know, O wife, whether you shall save your husband? Or how do you know, O

1 Corinthians
...7:16

man, whether you shall save your wife?"

Revelation
8:4

The smoke of the incense, along with the prayers, went up before God from the hand of the Archangel, and the Lord found it very pleasing.

So the Celestial Choir of Archangels appeared upon the Earth to love and serve the Lord.[503]

Celestial Choir of Archangels

503 The choir of Archangels is first and foremost a choir centered around the human family, for it is the unique sanctity of the family that actually allows the Archangels to see so deeply into God that they glimpse the Trinity. Observing the 'one flesh' union of husband and wife in the family, the Archangels can begin to understand the utterly united persons of the Trinity. Seeing this most holy image manifest in man's flesh, they are emboldened to pour out their love in service of human families, uniting them as the second heavenly Choir, Archangels of the family.

NOTES

§ Principalities §

Witnessing the deposed King of the Earth and the *promise* of God for a new king, the *Christ*, a group of angels began to sing in testament to the Lord's sovereignty: "All authority belongs to You, O Lord! For there is no authority except from God, and those princes which exist are only established by the Lord! But woe to you, Satan, and all you demons, for you would have no power over man if it had not been given to you from above!"[504]

So the holy princes again proclaimed: "Though yours be the Earth the Lord God shall separate out a people and make of them a holy nation, the Lord shall choose them out of all the peoples of the Earth to be His holy people, a treasured possession.

"For though you play war pitting nation against nation, you shall see the works of the Lord made manifest upon the Earth— It is He who shall stop up war even unto the ends of the Earth, who shall break the bow and splinter the spear, and burn up the shield with fire! Be still and know that He is God! It is He that shall be exalted among the nations, exalted on the Earth forever. The Lord of hosts is with us; our stronghold is the God of man!"

The Lord God then declared before the holy princes: "It shall come to pass in the latter days that man shall return to my holy mountain, nations shall flow to it in homage. And when this has come to pass, I shall judge between the nations, and I will render verdicts for all peoples. They shall hammer their swords into plowshares, and their spears into pruning hooks. Nation shall not lift up sword against nation, and never again shall they learn the art of war."

Then the Lord addressed the *fallen princes*,[505] saying:"Know, in all these things, man shall conquer overwhelmingly through Him who loves them.

Romans 13:1

John 19:11

Deuteronomy 7:6

Psalm 46:8...

Psalm ...46:11

Isaiah 2:2...

Isaiah ...2:4

Romans 8:37...

244

IGNATIAN CONTEMPLATION

504 John 19:11. The holy Principalities are pointing out a very great truth, which falls on Satan's shoulders like a curse: God only allows Satan to be successful to bring a greater good out of his malicious actions. This is the great embarrassment of evil. Evil is only allowed so that God can bring about a greater good, for God's mercy to bring good from evil is better than any natural good.

505 Just as the Celestial Choirs are formed because of the unique love in their hearts, so the demons are organized by the unique hate they find for the particular aspects of God, the universe, or man.

Celestial Choir of Principalities

For I decree that neither death, nor life, nor angels, nor Principalities, nor present things, nor future things, nor Powers, nor height, nor depth, nor any other creature will ever be able to separate man from the Love of God."

So the Celestial Choir of Principalities appeared upon the Earth to love and serve the Lord.[506]

Thus, the First Heaven[507] was complete, so the Lord looked upon the Earth and saw that it was good.[508]

Celestial Choir of Principalities

506 Similar to the Guardian Angels and the Archangels, the holy Principalities looked upon specific nations, tribes, and peoples which they beheld, and then chose to serve the Lord out of love for such peoples. And so, submitting the entirety of their being to the protection, inspiration, and preservation of such nations and peoples for the glory of God, they became the holy Choir of Principalities.

507 In the second letter to the Corinthians 12:2 St. Paul tells us that he was caught up to the Third Heaven, theologians now refer to these Heavens as Tiers in the Celestial Hierarchy.

508 The Celestial Hierarchy is divided up into three Tiers (or Heavens) composed of three Choirs each, resulting in the nine Choirs of Heaven or nine rungs in Jacob's Ladder. Principalities are the third and final Choir of the First Tier. The First Heaven is solely devoted to mankind upon the Earth. Guardian Angels deal with individuals, and Archangels are charged with the sanctity of the family, while Principalities are devoted to the preservation of nations. Each choir becomes larger and participates more fully in God's nobility as they ascend up the celestial ladder. For example, Archangels don't simply love families as a collective but have a manifold love, loving each individual member and the family as a whole, thus encompassing and compounding upon the love of the Guardian Angels below them. Similarly, Principalities love each and every citizen of their nations and the family houses that comprise those nations, while adding a greater all-encompassing love for the society and culture of its people as a whole. Thus, we can begin to glimpse the immensity of such celestial creatures and how they only increase in nobility and task as they ascend up the Celestial Hierarchy.

——————— ❧ *NOTES* ☙ ———————

§ Powers §

R allying to the word of the Lord and the enmity placed between *the Woman* and Leviathan, a group of angels became angered[509] with the *fallen stars*, who proceeded to prowl about the world seeking the ruin of souls. So they declared: "Blow the trumpet in Zion; sound the alarm on the holy mountain! Let all those who prowl about the land tremble, for the Day of the Lord is coming![510] Yes, there shall come a day of darkness and gloom, a day of thick clouds! Like dawn spreading over the mountains, a vast and mighty army comes!

Joel 2:1...

Joel ...2:2...

"Nothing like it has ever happened in ages past, nor will the future hold anything like it, even to the most distant generations.[511] Before it, fires devour; behind it, flames scorch. The land before it is like Eden, and behind it is a desolate wilderness; from it nothing escapes.

Joel ...2:4...

"Their appearance is that of horses; like warhorses they run. Like the roar of chariots, they hurtle across mountaintops; like the crackling of fiery flames, they devour the ground; they are the Lord's army in battle formation!

Joel ...2:6...

"Before them, all tremble, and every face turns pale. Like warriors they run, like soldiers they scale walls, each advancing in line without swerving from the course. Before them the Earth trembles, and the heavens shake; sun and moon are darkened, and the stars withhold their light.

"Lord, raise up Your voice at the head of Your army! How immense is Your host! How numerous those who carry out Your command! How great is the Day of the Lord! Utterly terrifying! What evil can survive it?"

Joel ...2:11

Ephesians 6:2...

So the Lord mustered His troops, saying, "Henceforth you shall put on the Armor of God so that you may be able to stand firm against the stratagems of the Devil—for your struggle is not with the flesh and blood of mortals, but with the fallen: with the Principalities, with the Powers, with the Dominions of this present darkness, and with all the evil spirits in the heavens.[512] Therefore, put on the Armor of God, that you may resist the Evil One, and, having done everything,

IGNATIAN CONTEMPLATION

509 This is the anger Christ felt before he drove out the moneychangers from the Temple. It is a righteous anger that comes from a desire to correct an injustice. These warrior angels are given holy beatitude because of their hunger and thirst for justice.

510 The Day of the Lord sung about by the heavenly Powers refers to the day of Christ's victory on the cross, a strategic military victory over Satan and death.

511 This is why all history is centered around the coming of Christ, both in Salvation History and recorded history. B.C. stands for "Before Christ," counting down to the coming of Christ in year 1 A.D., and A.D. stands for "Anno Domini," meaning "The year of our Lord," denoting the eternal reign of Christ for the rest of time. Thus, all time is centered around the Incarnation of Christ.

512 The Holy Powers are the Choir that protects the Universe from the chaos and assaults of the Devil and his demons, who not only seek the ruin of souls but the disordering of all good things. These angels in particular are guardians of the Church, in whose treasury rest all spiritual goods, and who is further tasked with the great offensive conquest of the Kingdom of Darkness, where the gates of Hell will not prevail against the march of the Church.

Celestial Choir of Powers

hold your ground! Stand fast, your loins girded in truth, having put on the Breastplate of Righteousness, and having your feet shod in readiness for the Gospel of Peace.[513] Above all, hold fast the Shield of Faith to quench all flaming arrows of the Evil One. And further, take the Helmet of Salvation[514] and the Sword of the Spirit, which is the Word of God."[515]

Ephesians
...6:17

Thus the Celestial Choir of Powers[516] appeared in the heavens to love and serve the Lord.[517]

Celestial Choir of Powers

513 The Lord is saying: 'Be ready for the day of my Son's victory, when the Celestial War will be forever won, and Satan's hold over the Earth will be abolished. On this day be ready to proclaim a gospel of peace.' This peace is not some abstract goodwill toward men, but a real militaristic peace, where humanity is freed forever from demonic rule. The steward of such peace is the Church, both to continue the victory of Christ throughout the world, and to preserve such peace for all perpetuity.

514 The 'Helmet of Salvation' is a crown, a true sign of Christ's victory, and a new kingdom over the Earth.

515 Ephesians 6:11: Christ's death on the cross is that by which all heavenly Powers rejoice. It is the definitive moment of victory over Satan and his army of demons. This is why Christ descends into Hell for three days reclaiming the lost souls of ages past, for even the very gates of Hell cannot withstand the march of the Church. It is to this victory that the Holy Powers see and pledge themselves, rallying to Christ on the cross: the true power of God.

516 The holy Choir of Powers begins the second Tier of the Celestial Hierarchy and serves as a boundary by which the Second Heaven is separated and made holy. They guard and preserve justice throughout the Universe. Similar to Guardian Angels (first Choir of the first Heaven), who serve as a boundary and guard of the human soul, so too the Powers (first Choir of the second Heaven) serve as a boundary and guard of the Body of Christ, their King, defending the Church Militant in its constant struggle with the demonic forces of evil.

517 Finally, it is helpful to think of Jacob's Ladder as a spiral staircase consisting of three revolutions, each revolution encompassing that which came before in a higher and more noble way. For example, the holy Choir of Powers, who guard, guide, and protect the Body of Christ, serve transcendentally a similar role as that of the Guardian Angels, but, since the Body of Christ is made up of many parts both individual, familial, and political—not to mention spiritual in its many unseen parts—Powers must encompass all that came before in even greater transcendence, all the while mysteriously resembling the first Choir of the first Heaven.

 *NOTES*

§ Virtues §

Wisdom
4:15

A further group of angels, witnessing all creation fall with Adam and the *promise* of the Christ to be born of *the Woman,* looked on as the first death echoed throughout creation, the sacrifice of the lamb upon the wood of the Tree of Life. Promptly they cried out, saying, "O man, take heart! God's grace and mercy are with His chosen, and He will watch over all His saints! He will send His Christ, and there will

Revelation
21:1

be a new creation: a new Heaven and a new Earth!"[518]

Job
26:1…

They continued in chorus, singing: "How You, O Lord, have helped him who has no power! How You have saved the arm that has no strength! How You have counseled him who has no wisdom, and plentifully declared sound knowledge! With whose help have You uttered the Word? And whose Breath has come out from You?

Job
…26:5…

"The shades beneath writhe in terror—the many waters and their inhabitants. Sheol is naked before God, and Hell has no covering. He stretches out the firmament over the void and hangs the Earth upon nothing!

Job
…26:8…

"He binds up the many waters in His thick clouds, and yet the cloud does not spill open under them. He covers up the face of the full moon, spreading His clouds over it. He has inscribed a circle on the face of the deep, as the boundary between the light and darkness.

Job
…26:11…

"The pillars of Heaven tremble and are astounded at His thunderous rebuke. By His own power, He stilled the sea, and, by His own judgment, He shattered Leviathan! By His wind, the heavens were made fair; His hand pierced the fleeing serpent!

Job
…26:14

"Behold, these are but the outskirts of His ways, a whisper of the Word we hear of Him! Yet, of the thunder of His power, who can compare?"

IGNATIAN CONTEMPLATION

518 The heavenly Virtues bear witness to the Universal Fall, not simply of man and angel, but of lion and lamb, and the whole created order. All things are now subject to death and decay. The holy angels, however, proclaim triumphantly that God will restore the fallen Universe and that it will be done by the Christ, specifically through the wedding feast of the Lamb.

Celestial Choir of Virtues

Sirach
16:24...
The Lord was pleased by such a prayer, and so He proclaimed to them: "Hearken to my Word, and learn the discipline of Wisdom; attend to my Word in your hearts. I shall show forth good doctrine in equity, and will declare to you Wisdom: attend to my Word in your hearts, while, with the Spirit, I declare you Virtues,[519] which I, the Lord God, have put upon My works from the beginning.

Sirach
...16:26...
"The works of God are done in judgment from the beginning: from your creation, I have distinguished you, and have assigned you special tasks. I arranged from all time your occupation from generation to generation. I have made ever beautiful your work; you shall never hunger nor grow weary, nor ever falter in your task. None shall straiten his neighbor or disobey the Word of the Lord. Look then

Sirach
...16:29
toward the Earth, and fill it with the Lord's grace and blessings."[520]

Thus the Celestial Choir of Virtues appeared in the heavens to love and serve the Lord.[521]

Celestial Choir of Virtues

519   The celestial choir of Virtues is singularly charged with the governance of the entire physical universe. They constantly pour forth God's grace for the preservation and maintenance of everything that exists, from cells to stars. They also dispense grace for the preservation of the human soul, making it possible for humanity to choose and pursue the Good. The looming immensity of all nine celestial choirs comes into focus; all that can be seen, everything physical—everything science could ever teach us—is maintained by a single choir of Heaven, the celestial choir of Virtues.

520   Sirach 16. This Scripture passage denotes the Virtues' metaphysical responsibility to uphold the laws of nature, which we describe as Science. It is from the constant vigilance of these holy angels that we can know the physical universe, from electromagnetism and gravity to the inner workings of quarks and electrons. Even such things as photosynthesis, cell reproduction, and metabolism are a result of the tireless work of such creatures. Everything, everywhere, is ceaselessly preserved and maintained by the heavenly Virtues.

521   It is in the hearts of the heavenly Choir of Virtues that we find a special affinity for the material universe in its entirety, and so a love for all that comprises the universe, encompassing the love of all those angels who are below them: for every individual, family, and nation, and even that of the heavenly Powers to safeguard the world and the Church, while adding an even greater love to uphold and maintain the life of God in His creation, which is sustained only through the constant outpouring of grace. Thus, they distribute the grace by which the universe functions, not simply for physical things as previously mentioned, but of spiritual matters such as the human soul and even the Church, the Body of Christ.

The heavenly Choir of Virtues is the Second Choir of the Second Heaven, and falls directly at the center of the Celestial Hierarchy. Virtues hold a special place among the hierarchy—they are the Choir that found in their hearts a unique love for God's desire to create flesh and matter, a thing which Lucifer found most repugnant. These angels devote themselves entirely to the distribution of grace, these 'holy bucket carriers' who keep the universe alive with God's own life. It is also not by accident that the centermost Choir is devoted to grace, the new standard by which the whole Celestial Hierarchy is structured. Finally, in the ascension up the Celestial Ladder, it is at the Celestial Choir of Virtues that the proper object of each choir ceases to be physical and becomes metaphysical or spiritual.

§ Dominations §

Psalm
103:19...

Witnessing each choir, in due turn, strike up a song to the Lord, a noble group of angelic lords proclaimed: "The Lord has set his rule in the Heavens; His dominion extends over all the stars! Bless the Lord, all you His angels: you, mighty in strength, acting at His behest, obedient to His command. Bless the Lord, all you His hosts, His ministers who carry out His will. Bless the Lord, all you angelic creatures, everywhere in His dominion!"[522]

Psalm
...103:22

Hearing such a prayer, the Lord God bestowed a blessing upon all who sang, giving them authority in the heavens.

1 Timothy
6:15...

And so, they continued to sing: "Bless the Lord, who alone is Sovereign, the King of kings and Lord of lords, who alone possesses immortality and dwells in unapproachable light, whom no man has seen or can see. To Him be honor and eternal dominion, forever and ever, Amen!"

1 Timothy
...6:16

Daniel
7:25...

The Lord then addressed the fallen Dominions,[523] saying, "The Earth and My saints shall be handed over to you for a time, two times and half a time.[524] But know—when the court is convened—your dominion will be stripped away to be abolished and completely destroyed! Then, dominion, majesty, and kingship of all the kingdoms of heaven shall be given to My people, the saints of the Most High, whose kingship shall be an everlasting kingship, whom all Dominions shall serve and obey!" But, upon hearing the Lord's words, the heavenly angels of dominion began to murmur amongst themselves.

Daniel
...7:27

1 Corinthians
6:3

So the Lord addressed the holy Dominions, saying: "Do you not know man shall judge the angels?[525] Give thanks to your God, who has made His saints worthy partakers of the inheritance of light. Who shall deliver man from the dominions of darkness, and shall translate His saints into the kingdom of the beloved Son, in whom all men shall find redemption through His blood, and the remission of offenses? *He* is the image of the invisible God, the firstborn of every creature, for in Him were all things created in Heaven and on Earth, visible and invisible, whether

Colossians
1:12...

IGNATIAN CONTEMPLATION

522 Psalms 103:19 The holy Choir of Dominions are angels who find in their hearts a special affinity for the angels themselves, and because of such love, are appointed pastors over the many subsequent choirs below them. This choir is especially difficult for modern man because it reveals an unpleasant truth: God is not a democrat, nor is the Universe which He created. The Church, the Universe, and the Celestial Hierarchy are fundamentally aristocratic: the rule of the virtuous, governed by nobility who are ennobled by the virtue they possess. They rule because they are by definition better, and thus fit to draw others to such excellence. For example, the hallowed role of Dominions is indispensable for the well-functioning of the Celestial Hierarchy itself, for it is through the constant prayer and intercession of the heavenly Dominations that God pours forth the grace necessary for the angelic choirs themselves to function. Dominions, through their holy and intimate communion with God, receive and so promulgate His decrees, making known God's will to all the angels below them.

523 Due to the Dominions' natural affinity toward the glory of the angels themselves, this choir would be most perceptible to Satan's lie that flesh is wholly deplorable and only spirit is good. These angels would be naturally disposed to admire the nobility of being a celestial intelligence, and thus would be most likely to succumb to the lie that angels ought to be served rather than serve.

524 Again, three and half years is forty-two months, the product of six and seven. The devil and his servants will have dominion until the beast (the number 6) unites with God (the number 7), and this is the God-man, Jesus Christ, who ends the rule of Satan upon the Earth.

525 1 Corinthians 6:2. Here we are given a glimpse of the great majesty God plans to bestow upon His Church; she shall be given the ability to judge the angels, a role otherwise set apart for the celestial choir of Dominions. Scholars often debate whether St. Paul means that all angels or only the fallen angels will be judged by the Church. In at least one example, it would seem to be both. When St. Faustina prayed to avert a deadly storm and was gifted with a miraculous insight into the heavenly court, she witnessed a holy angel (a Virtue) objecting before God. Nevertheless, God confirms St. Faustina's judgment, and the angel must avert the storm. Further, God is here purging any pride or selfishness from His holy angels, showing them that even the choir solely focused on the angels themselves is still subject to God's plan for humanity and the Holy Church.

Colossians
...1:16

Thrones or Dominions or Principalities or Powers: all things were created through Him and for Him."

1 Chronicles
29:10...

So they blessed the Lord in the sight of all the assembly, and said: "Blessed are You, Lord God, forever and ever. Yours, O Lord, is the greatness and the power and the glory and the victory and the majesty, indeed everything that is in the heavens and on the earth; Yours, O Lord, is the dominion and You exalt Yourself as head over

1 Chronicles
...29:11

all."

And so, the Celestial Choir of Dominions appeared in the heavens to love and serve the Lord.[526]

Thus, the Second Heaven was complete, so the Lord looked upon the Heavenly Firmament and saw that it was good.[527]

Celestial Choir of Dominations

526 Dominions are the third and final Choir of the Second Heaven. These holy and noble angels find in their hearts a special love for all the angels who fall under their care, and so encompass the love of all the subsequent choirs of angels. In their love for Guardian Angels, the holy Dominions find a love for individual humans; in their love for Archangels the love of families; and in their love for Principalities the love of nations. Similarly, in their love for the heavenly Powers, they vouchsafe the defense of all that is good in the Body of Christ, and in their love for the heavenly Virtues they too aspire to fill the visible universe with God's grace. This all-encompassing love for creation is only multiplied by the Heavenly Dominions' love for the stewards of the universe: the angels themselves. Thus, the whole invisible universe, all the angels and their choirs, find the grace and will of God through the holy intercession of the Heavenly Dominions.

527 The Celestial Hierarchy is divided into three tiers or three Heavens. Unlike the First Heaven, which is concerned with men upon the Earth, the Second Heaven is concerned with the well-functioning of the Universe, both visible and invisible. As was seen in the First Heaven, there is a progression from one choir to the next, beginning with the purgative, then the illuminative, and finally the perfective. For example, the purgative is revealed by the Choir of Guardian Angels and how they act in great charity to purify the soul of their human person, just as the Choir of heavenly Powers works tirelessly to protect and keep pure the sanctity of the Body of Christ. Both choirs serve as a boundary, purifying and protecting the sanctity of their corresponding heaven. The illuminative is revealed by the middle choir of each tier: Archangels reveal the greatest mystery from which all mysteries stem—that of the Most Holy Trinity, housed in the bonds of Holy Matrimony. The holy Choir of Virtues reveals the centrality of the Earth in God's cosmology, how all grace of God flows down from Heaven for the sake of the Earth and man upon it. The perfective is revealed by the third and highest choir of each tier; Principalities encompass and so perfect the love of both the Guardian Angels and the Archangels, while adding a love for nations, thus possessing a consummate love for all of humanity in every aspect of human life. The holy Choir of Dominions encompasses and so perfects the love of the heavenly Powers and Virtues, while adding a love for the angels themselves, thus possessing a consummate love for the entirety of the Universe, both visible and invisible: living, nonliving, and spiritual. This, then, is the summary of the whole created order, how it is tirelessly maintained through metaphysical means by the Celestial Hierarchy, and how there is no thing in existence that is not tended to or upheld by the work of such holy and venerable creatures.

§ Thrones §

S o, above the firmament of Heaven, over the heads of all the angels, the likeness of a Throne shined like sapphire,[528] and upon the Throne was seated, up above, a figure in the likeness of a man.[529] Beholding such a sight—and having heard the *first good news* pronounced in judgment upon Leviathan—a group of angels turned and gathered about the Ancient One who was seated upon His lofty Throne.[530]

Psalm 113:2...

They then began to shout in acclaim: "Praise the Lord! Praise Him, O servants of the Lord! Praise the Name of the Lord! Blessed be the Name of the Lord, from this time forth and forevermore! From the rising of the sun to its setting, we shall praise the Name of the Lord! The Lord is high above the nations, and His glory above the heavens. Who is like unto the Lord our God; who is enthroned on high, who humbles Himself to look upon the heavens and the Earth?[531] He raises the poor from the dust, and lifts up the needy from the ash heap, to make them sit with princes, with the princes of His people. He gives the barren woman a home, making her the joyous mother of many. Praise be to the Lord![532]

Celestial Choir of Thrones

528 The color that is used to describe the Throne is the same color attributed to Mary as she has appeared throughout the millennia, further indicating the unique devotion the holy Thrones have for Mary as Seat of Wisdom.

529 Ezekiel 1:26. The Holy Choir of Thrones derives their name from their special devotion to God and His Throne. It is specifically because they see the Christ in the likeness of a man, and choose to worship Him as Lord, that these angels are elevated to such a high degree and given the glorious title of Thrones. Just as Guardian Angels and Powers serve as protectors and guards of the first and second heavens, Thrones also serve as a divide, emphasizing the supreme holiness of God. All angels of inferior rank cannot approach the Lord without being escorted by a Throne.

530 The most holy Choir of Thrones is the first choir of the Third Heaven and thus serves as a boundary by which the higher heaven is separated and made holy. Once again, it is helpful to think of Jacob's Ladder as a spiral staircase with three revolutions; the holy Thrones are the beginning of the third and final revolution, and thus resemble Guardian Angels and Powers in a higher and more noble way. The holy Thrones spend their existence in constant praise and worship before the Throne of God, thus ordering the entire Universe in proper worship of the Lord God. Similar to Guardian Angels (1st Choir of the 1st Heaven) who serve as a boundary and guard of the human soul; and the holy Powers (1st Choir of the 2nd Heaven) who serve as a boundary and guard of the mystical Body of Christ; so, too, the most holy Thrones (1st Choir of the 3rd Heaven) serve as a guard and boundary for the Throne of God, but more importantly, the holy Thrones serve as attendants of the Lord Himself, worshiping God directly. The holy Thrones complete—in a higher and more noble way—the work found in both the Guardian Angels, protectors of the human person, and the holy Powers, protectors of the Body of Christ, specifically by the adoration of Christ as Head of the mystical Body of Christ allowing the worship of the Whole Christ. Finally, it is in the Celestial Choir of Thrones that the Third Heaven becomes distinct from the Second Heaven, specifically as the Dwelling Place of God, the Mystical Temple in Heaven.

531 Psalm 113 is a praise of God's transcendent nature, claiming that God humbles Himself to even look down upon the heavens. The utter transcendence of God is manifested in Creation by specific Transcendentals that can be said of all things everywhere, and thus, are the various modes of Being itself. This Being which underlies all existence is the very manifestation of God Himself, since God is Being, revealed to Moses on Mount Sinai: His holy Name "I AM who AM." Thus, it is God's very Being which gives rise to the existence of creation and underlies all things, giving everything its very Being. However, when we turn to contemplate such existential Being, we observe there are qualities or modes that can be said of all things, precisely because they exist and have being. These modes of Being are called Transcendentals and they are: The One, The Good, The True, and The Beautiful. These Transcendentals are how the Third and final heaven conform themselves to God, and thus receive such holy and Divine Transcendence, duly shedding it forth unto all Creation.

532 Psalm 113 The Thrones turn to pray for the Fall in the Garden, singing how the Lord will give life to the dead, and it will be through a barren woman giving birth to a new people. This, of course, is speaking of the unique relationship between Mary, the new Eve, and Eve, the old Mary. Where Eve was barren, her womb empty of such waters of grace, Mary is Full of Grace; where Eve is blessed to be the Mother of all the Living, Mary is blessed all the more and becomes the Mother of Christians, who possess the Life of God. Another name for Christians is Neophytes: those that possess the new life of Christ.

At such devotion, the Lord declared: "Behold *the Woman* of Promise!" The Lord God then stood as to pay her homage, and, taking His seat, ordered a throne be provided for the Queen Mother, who was to be seated at his right hand.[533] Then the Lord spoke, "Ask of your Lord anything, no matter how small of a request, and the King of kings will not deny the Queen Mother her request, for I will never refuse you."

At such a sight they began to canticle a song: "We shall sing of Your steadfast love, O Lord, forever! With chorus we proclaim Your faithfulness to all generations and all generations shall call her blessed. We proclaim Your steadfast love is established forever, Your faithfulness is as firm as the heavens.

You have made a covenant with man, and have promised Your servant Adam a woman whose seed shall inherit Your Throne for all generations!"[534] Let the heavens praise Your wonders, O Lord, Your faithfulness among the assembly of saints. For who in the clouds can compare to the Lord? Who among the sons of God can compare to the Lord, a God feared in the council of gods, great and terrible above all that surround Him! O Lord God of hosts, who is as mighty as You are, with Your faithfulness roundabout You?[535]

You alone have conquered the power of the sea[536] and still the motion of the waves. You alone have crushed Leviathan like a carcass,[537] striking him with a mortal blow: with the strength of Your arm you have scattered all Your enemies. Yours are the heavens, and Yours is the Earth: You alone have founded the Earth and everything in it; the firmament and the sea You alone have established!"

Then they fell on their faces and prayed: "Justice and judgment are the foundation of Your Throne; yet mercy and faithfulness go before Your Face. Blessed are those who know Your cordial shout, who walk, O Lord, in the light of Your Face, they exult in Your name all-the-day long and extol Your righteousness!

1 Kings 2:19...

1 Kings ...2:20

Psalm 89:1...

Psalm ...89:3...

Psalm ...89:9...

Psalm ...89:14...

533 1 Kings 2:19. Thrones have a special devotion to Mary, as the Seat of Wisdom: a hallowed title honoring Mary as the throne on which Christ her son is seated as the Word incarnate. In Divine Monarchy, God has ordained that it is not King and Queen that rule as it was in the West, but the King and Queen-Mother. This is how it was ordained in the Old Testament for the Kings of Israel, and this is fulfilled and perfected in the New Testament with Jesus and Mary in Heaven.

534 The most holy Choir of Thrones understood the Protoevangelium and recognized the Throne of God as belonging to God's Anointed, the promised child of the immaculate woman who will bring war (enmity) to the great dragon, Leviathan.

535 The holy Thrones, having looked upon God as King, find in their hearts a fervent desire to order all created things toward the worship of God in such a manner. Just as the whole kingdom is ordered toward the glory of the king, so too do Thrones order all creation toward the worship and glory of God the Father. Thrones, therefore, embody a significant shift in the Celestial Hierarchy, for it is through the Celestial Choir of Thrones that the work of the Hierarchy is purified from maintenance and transformed into holy worship. It is through this unique and purgative love of the holy Thrones that Creation itself is ordered toward God specifically as its ultimate end and final Good, for just as the holy Dominations found in their hearts a love that encompassed all the angels—and through that love of the angels themselves they found a love that encompassed all that the angels themselves loved—so too the most holy Thrones found a manifold love of God in their hearts, and through such a profound love of God as the Good, they found a love for the whole created order whom God loves and directs toward Himself as Fulfillment and End.

536 As before, the 'sea' is the great formless abyss that God overcame with creation. This ultimate evil, the absolute absence of anything good, is that which Satan or Leviathan adopts as his domain, his kingdom of darkness.

537 Psalm 89 speaks of 'Rahab,' which is another name for Leviathan or Satan. The Thrones are emphasizing the justice that God Himself inflicted upon the great sea serpent by the promise of an immaculate woman.

NOTES

Psalm
...89:18

You are their majestic strength and it is by your favor our horn is exalted. Truly the Lord is our shield, the Holy One, our King!"[538]

Hebrews
1:8...

The Lord pleased by such a prayer proclaimed: "The Thrones of God shall endure forever and ever! My royal scepter is theirs, a scepter of justice for you have loved righteousness and hate wickedness. Therefore I, your God, shall anoint you with the oil of gladness beyond your companions; myrrh, aloe, and cassia shall perfume your garments and from ivory thrones stringed instruments

Hebrews
...1:9

shall ring out with joy!"

Revelation
4:4

So the Lord called the holy angels closer roundabout His Throne, and adorned them with white robes and golden crowns, so they took their position. Around the Throne of God were positioned twenty-four thrones, and seated on the thrones were twenty-four Ancients, dressed in white robes, with golden crowns about their heads.

Revelation
4:9...

The twenty-four Ancients then lead the many Thrones falling down before the One who sat upon the Throne, and worshiping Him who lives forever and ever they cast down their crowns before the Throne saying: Worthy are You, our Lord and our God, to receive glory and honor and power; for You created all thing, and because of Your

Revelation
... 4:11

will they exist and have their being!"[539]

And so, the Celestial Choir of Thrones took their position roundabout God's Throne, ceaselessly falling on their faces and worshiping the Lord.[540]

538 Psalm 89: A most profound prayer of the Beatific Vision, acknowledging and worshiping the sublime justice of God, yet asking for the mercy to see God's Face, for only in such an act can any creature find Beatitude. It is for this reason that St. Thomas Aquinas speaks of the Beatific Vision being the fulfillment and end of all men and angels, for those who look upon the Face of God, beholding God Himself in their souls, are incapable of anything other than perfect love and happiness.

539 Thrones are the first Choir of the Third Heaven and thus purify the love of all the lower choirs, for up unto this point all the lower choirs have loved God through creation, whether it is through individuals, families, or nations; gallantry, the universe, or the angels themselves, all subsequent angels have had an indirect love for God. However, ascending beyond the whole created order, past all visible and invisible goods, the holy Thrones find in their hearts a direct love for God Himself, loving Him specifically as the Good. And so, it is this most profound love of God as the Good which allows all the lower choirs to love God through the goodness of creation, for it is the Good which permeates all things, endowing creation itself with integrity, or holy worth. Thus, it is through the holy Thrones' pure and holy worship of God as the Good that the love of all the lower choirs finds its way to God as the Transcendental Good.

540 God is bestowing upon the Celestial Choir of Thrones a special Glory not found in the lower choirs, for the holy Choir of Thrones adhere themselves to God, unlike any previous choir. Leaving the whole created order behind, they turn their gaze directly upon the Lord Himself. These most holy angels serve God directly, worshiping His sanctity, His complete otherness from all things created and corruptible. Thrones conform themselves directly to God as the Transcendental Good, which is the fulfillment and ultimate end of all existence. This is why the philosopher defines the Good as Being under the aspect of desirable, for all creation receives its integrity from God as Creator. It is by this holy and intimate conformity that the Thrones themselves take on the very Goodness of God. Being so filled and overflowing with Divine Goodness, they themselves impart such Goodness onto all lower angels, who in turn, through their love and service, impart—by metaphysical means—such Goodness unto all creation. Thus, all that is good and desirable in the Universe receives its Goodness, by metaphysical means, from God Himself through the holy Choir of Thrones.

§ Cherubim §

A round the Throne, and on each side of the Throne, the Four Living Creatures[541] were overcome with joy at the Lord's first *good news* and having witnessed the first sacrifice they began to sing. They lead in chorus a group of angels that shone like lightning,

Isaiah
52:8...

gleaming intensely.[542] They proclaimed: "Hark! Your angels lift their voices; together they sing for joy, for in plain sight they see the Lord will return to Zion! Break into song, all you together, the ruins of mankind—for the Lord shall comfort His people; He shall redeem the human race! The Lord has bared His holy arm before the eyes of His

Isaiah
...52:10

angels; and all the ends of the Earth shall see the Salvation of our God."

The Lord then replied: "How beautiful upon the mountains are the feet of the ones who carry the gospel, announcing peace and

Isaiah
52:7

bearing the *good news*, announcing Salvation and proclaiming: "Zion! Your God reigns!"[543]

Ezekiel
10:4...

At this, the glory of the Lord moved before the Cherubim to the threshold of the Temple, and the Temple was filled with a cloud, the whole Sanctuary made brilliant with the glory of the Lord. And the sound of the wings of the Cherubim resounded and could be heard as far as the outer court of the Temple, like the voice of God Almighty

Ezekiel
...10:5

when He speaks.[544]

Note 544 Ezekiel 10:5 The holy Choir of Cherubim is the second choir of the Third Heaven and thus these angels illuminate in a special way the love found not only in the previous choir, but in the previous heavens. Again, it is helpful to think of Jacob's Ladder as a spiral staircase with three revolutions, the holy Cherubim are in the middle of the third and final revolution, and thus, being in the middle resemble the most holy Archangels and the hallowed Virtues in a higher and more noble way. For, as the Archangels illumine the truth of the First Heaven, namely the purpose and glory of humanity is uniquely held within the human family as the Image of God Himself sanctified in the sacrament of Holy Matrimony, similarly, heavenly Virtues illumine the truth of the Second Heaven by revealing that the purpose of the entire Universe is for the outpouring of God's grace upon the human race. So, too, do Cherubim illumine the purpose of the Third Heaven, namely the greatest truth in God Himself is the Gospel, the Logos Incarnate. Further, one can see how the three choirs stack upon themselves, receiving . . .

541 The 'Four Living Creatures' are a reference to the Cherubim Ezekiel encounters in chapters 1 and 10, where he gives as full an account of their appearance as a mortal understanding can provide. These Four Living Creatures are actually very specific Cherubim, which we come to know by the four Evangelists: Matthew in the appearance of a Man, Mark in the appearance of a Lion, Luke in the appearance of an Ox, and John in the appearance of an Eagle. Thus, it was actually these four 'Evangelim', holy Angels of Truth, who, so illumined by the Holy Spirit, inspired these saints to write the four most important books of the Bible and of the World. They are in fact charged with the greatest truth in existence: the proclamation of the Gospel of our Lord Jesus Christ.

542 The luminous Choir of Cherubim are the most spoken of choir throughout the Scriptures, detailing their role in the Temple, their occupation as ministers before the Lord, and even their appearance before mortal eyes. These holy angels find in their hearts a special devotion to the Truth of God, radiating off of the Lord with even greater splendor than the sun. The holy Cherubim adhere themselves most intimately to this prescient light, filling them with the self-same splendor of the Lord. Thus, the Cherubim shine with an intensity not found in any other choir. Divine Light, like physical light, is that by which we perceive reality, and since God is in the truest sense pure reality, the reality by which all reality receives its integrity, Divine Light is the bountiful gift by which rational creatures can come to know God, the source of all Being and Truth. It is for this reason the philosopher defines Truth as Being under the aspect of knowable.

543 Isaiah 52:7: The Gospel is the first truth—the truth from which all truth stems. It was the first intention of creation: the hallowed desire in God's heart to not simply create but to enter into creation, and, once part of His creation, to be intimately united with it, creature and Creator perfectly united in the bonds of love. From this Logos, the first thought, the whole created order sprang, a flawless order visible and invisible, so that the creature man might come into being—countless star systems and infinitely more angelic beings—all so that there might arise such a unique creature as man—Man a body-soul composite, endowed with a rational soul, a mind capable of knowing God, and a body made in the Divine Image, also sealed in the bonds of Holy Matrimony, capable of pro-creation, thus allowing for the perfect synthesis of supernatural and natural: Divine Incarnation. This is the truth of the Gospel: that God so loved the world that he sent His only son to be born of it; from the smallest microbe to the mightiest angel, all creation rejoices at the Incarnation of the Godman. God is confirming the holy Cherubim in this truth, that the Gospel is the 'Truth of Truths' underlying everything, validating, and giving clarity to every truth of the Universe.

---

544 cont. ... grace and purpose from the higher. It is from God's desire for the Incarnate Word, the greatest truth of the Cherubim, that the grace to uphold the carnal universe arises and is bestowed upon the heavenly Virtues. Finally, it is from the grace bestowed upon the material universe that arises the unique and holy institution of Marriage, which the Archangels so devote themselves to, bringing about new life through the very Image of God, eventually culminating in the Incarnation of Christ Himself, for, as the Philosopher says, the first in intention is the last in execution.

A further meditation is necessary on the peculiar bond between the Cherubim and the Archangels, particularly the Four Living Creatures and the Three Archangels, both of which wholly devote themselves to the Incarnation, as Gospel and as Sacrament.

Ezekiel
1:5...

The Lord then decreed: "Henceforth you all shall be known as Cherubim, and each one of you shall be adorned with four faces and be gifted four wings to proclaim the Gospel to all four corners of the Earth.[545] Your legs shall be straight, and the soles of your feet shall be like the huff of a calf, sparkling like burnished bronze. You shall have the hands of a man beneath your wings. Each of your faces shall be so: each shall bear a face of a man, and on the right a face of a lion, and on the left a face of an ox, and each shall bear a face of an eagle.[546] Your wings shall be spread out above, with two wings spread out toward each other, and with two wings you shall cover your body."

Ezekiel
...1:11

The Lord continued: "Henceforth I shall seal you with the seal of My voluble, a wheelwork of the gospel."

Ezekiel
1:16...

So there appeared as it were a halo behind the creatures, a seal gleaming like beryl in the constitution of a wheel within a wheel, and when they moved they moved in any of the four directions without veering. The coronas of the wheels shone tall and had a dreadful appearance, and inscribed on the halos of all four were piercing eyes all around. When the Living Creatures moved, the wheels moved behind them, and, when the Living Creatures rose, the wheels rose. Wherever the spirit would go, the halo went, the wheelwork behind them, for the spirit of the Living Creatures was in the wheels.[547]

Ezekiel
...1:21

The Four Evangelim

545 In Biblical numerology, four is the number signifying angelic nature, for the angels were
created on the fourth day. This is emphasized even more in the Cherubim, the choir
that most closely resembles the angelic nature itself, a knowing mind. This is why they
are gifted four faces, four wings, and move in all four directions without veering (Up
and down, left and right, forward and backward, and rotating). This symbolizes the
immutability of truth and the spreading of the Gospel without alteration or variation.

546 Ezekiel 1:10: The holy faces of the Cherubim represent the kingship of the Gospel,
for each face is a king of a different domain: the lion's face represents the king of the
wilderness and all wild animals; the ox's face represents the king of cultivated land and
all domestic animals; the eagle's face represents the king of the air and all flying fowl;
and the human face represents the king of civilization and all its citizens. Thus, in the
description of the holy Cherubim, we see that not only do they spread the Gospel to all
four corners of the Earth but to every aspect of living creature, every realm near or far
filled inexorably with the light of the Gospel. It is thus notable that the king of the sea
is missing; Leviathan spurned the Gospel out of envy, never bringing the light of the
Gospel to the darkness of the abyss.

547 Ezekiel 1:20: God is bestowing upon the Celestial Choir of Cherubim a special Glory,
for the holy Choir of Cherubim adhere themselves to God through the Word, the Way
to the Father, conforming themselves to the Truth of God, which in turn fulfills, in a
unique way, the very nature of the angels themselves as pure minds. Thus, as a sign of
this unique intimacy with the Second Person of the Trinity, Logos, God bestows upon
the holy Cherubim a unique gift, not simply a wheel as some metaphor or machine,
but a halo, a seal of Divine Glory. Often the wheels in Ezekiel are depicted as separate
spheres that follow the holy Cherubim around. This, however, does not account for
the ancient and biblical understanding of halos, where the glory of the Lord would
shine about the head of the creature like the wheel of the Firmament replete with stars
(Ezekiel 1:22). The Lord bestows upon the Cherubim a unique halo, which rotates like
the Firmament and is replete with eyes, and does not simply circumscribe the head
but encompasses the entire body, spinning as a wheel within a wheel. Furthermore, the
description of multitudinous eyes speak to the office of the Cherubim, namely those
angels who were elevated to receive and behold the very Light of God, and thus depict
in a unique way the glorified nature of the angels themselves. All angels are by nature
knowers or pure minds, the grace given to the Cherubim in particular illumines the
natural state of the angels as Celestial Intelligences.

1 Kings
6:27

So the Lord stationed the Cherubim all throughout the inner court of the Temple, where their wings spread out, so that the wing of one was touching the wing of the other encircling the chamber. And two Cherubim spread out their wings over the place of the Ark, so that the Cherubim made a covering overshadowing the Ark.[548]

1 Kings
8:7

Ezekiel
1:13...

The Lord then kindled in the wheelwork of the Four Living Creatures something that looked like burning coals of fire, like torches darting back and forth between the Living Creatures.[549] The fire was bright, and lightning issued forth from the burning flame. The Living Creatures darted about like bolts of lightning, dwelling in the light.[550]

Ezekiel
...1:14

NOTES

548   1 Kings 8:7: These Cherubim are given four faces and four wings: a unique gift extolling their intimate union with God Himself. Just as in the natural world, the larger the wing the higher the creature is able to ascend; angelic wings represent nobility and mobility. Thus Cherubim possessing four wings reveal the unique excellence of this choir of angels. The glory of the Cherubim is revealed by God's specific placement of them within the Temple. Further, it is also by the fourfold wings of the Cherubim that the Ark of the Covenant is overshadowed, a unique glory of the Gospel and one of the holiest duties in Heaven.

549   Herein lies a great secret! God gives a gift foreshadowing a great glory to come; this gift is a seraphic flame from which the very light of the Cherubim originates. This fire God specifically gives to the Four Living Creatures, who stand out ahead of the Choir of Cherubim, just as the Three Archangels stand out ahead of the Choir of Archangels. Now consider Revelation 4:8: "The first Living Creature like a lion, the second Living Creature like an ox, the third Living Creature with a face like a human face, and the fourth Living Creature like a flying eagle. And the Four Living Creatures, each of them with six wings, full of eyes all around and inside. Who cry out day and night without ceasing, 'Holy, holy, holy, the Lord God the Almighty, who was and is and is to come.'" St. John is describing the Four Living Creatures, Cherubim, having the wings of a Seraphim, six, but lest you think his account was mistaken, he records them singing the Song of the Seraphim: 'holy, holy, holy.' He is not confused in his vision, but rather is describing a mysterious transfiguration, a Paschal Glorification. In the description of the Four Living Creatures, we learn of their unique conformity to the Christ, bearing His Gospel, becoming the Four Gospels of His Word, and it is this absolute conformity to Christ that lies the secret. For as Christ rose from the dead—body, blood, soul, and divinity—transfigured in Glory, so too the Gospels were transfigured in Glory, and so the Four Living Creatures who bear the Gospels were transfigured in Glory. Thus, much like the Three Archangels who are both Seraphim and Archangels, the Four Living Creatures are glorified with Christ in the Seraphic flame, who now bear six wings and find upon their lips the Song of the Seraphim. Most importantly, this glorification reveals a hallowed secret held at the very core of the person of Christ: Truth is glorified when it gives itself over to Love.

550   Ezekiel 1:13: Considering the glorification of the Four Living Creatures as stated above, the answer to the infamous question: 'What would have happened to Lucifer had he not fallen?' becomes clear. First, recall that Leviathan is the 'king of the sea' like the lion is king of the wilderness, the ox is king of domesticity, the eagle is king of the sky, and man is king of the political city. These are the domains as laid out in Genesis' account of Creation: the sky and sea created on the Second Day governed by the birds and fish of the Fifth Day, the Earth created on the Third Day governed by the wild beasts and domestic animals of the Sixth Day, and finally the Garden governed by man who completes the Sixth Day. Thus, we see five domains: the domestic (Ox) and wilderness (Lion), the city or Garden (Man), and the sky (Eagle) and sea (???). The only domain without an evangelist is the Sea, which symptomatically harbors the great darkness of non-creation. Therefore, it becomes clear: Leviathan, the king of the sea, was meant to be the Evangelist to the Sea. Had he chosen to serve, he would have become the missing 'Fifth Living Creature', and eventually would have been glorified with the great fire and love of the Seraphim.

So the Celestial Choir of Cherubim[551] went straight ahead without veering, entering and exiting the Inner Court, proclaiming the *good news* of God.[552]

Celestial Choir of Cherubim

551 Cherubim receive first the most holy light of God, and so illumine the love of all the lower choirs. It is through this unique conformity of the holy Cherubim to the Truth of God that such sublime and edifying Truth is transmitted to all such subsequent choirs, illuminating or giving intelligibility to the particular loves of each of the choirs. It is the holy Cherubim's love of God as Truth which transmits intelligible order throughout all creation. For just as it is the Good which permeates all things endowing creation with integrity or holy worth, the True illumines all things, endowing creation with clarity or holy order. Therefore, all things known are only knowable through their participation in the Truth of God's own Mind—a rationality we recognize only because we participate in it. Our re-cognition of God's Mind with our own, according to Truth, is called clarity. Finally, just as the Goodness of God is first transmitted by the worship of the heavenly Thrones, the Truth of God is first shed forth by the worship of the holy Cherubim. It is, in fact, through the holy Cherubim's luminous and holy worship of God as the True that both men and angels' love of Truth finds its way to God as the Transcendental Truth.

552 God is bestowing upon the Celestial Choir of Cherubim a special Glory not found in any of the lower choirs: a beatific vision of God's own Mind. Much like the holy Thrones, Cherubim adhere themselves to God unlike any of the previous choirs of the first and second Heavens, leaving behind the whole created order they turn their gaze directly upon the Lord Himself, serving God directly, worshiping His Holy Word—His Logos—His Wisdom. Cherubim conform themselves directly to God as the Transcendental Truth, the intelligibility of being itself, the Truth that gives rise to existence endowing it with clarity or holy order. The True is the very 'knowability' of being itself, that by which we glimpse the Divine Mind. The True—being the Logos of God—contains within itself all the desirability of the Good, while adding the transcendent aspect of Divine Mind. And so, the holy Cherubim—possessing a more encompassing love in their adherence to God as the True—actually contain the love of the heavenly Thrones for God as the Good, and actually impart clarity of understanding to the Thrones' desire for God as the Good, for it is by this holy and intimate conformity to the Word of God that the holy Cherubim (especially the Four Evangelim) take on the very Logos of God, according to their capacity, and, being so filled and overflowing with the Light of Truth, they themselves impart such Truth onto the holy Thrones, giving understanding to their desire for God. And so, the Light of Truth permeates all things, giving clarity or intelligibility to all the various loves of those lower angels in which they have chosen to serve. They, in turn, through their love and service, impart, by metaphysical means, such Divine Intelligibility unto all created things. Thus, everything that we know, that is knowable—everything from the physical Laws of Nature, Biology, and Chemistry; to poetry and politics; even the human soul and angelic spirits which partake in the Divine Mind Itself—receive their Truth, their 'Knowability', through the holy Choir of Cherubim from God Himself.

§ Seraphim §

Upon the Golden Altar adorned with the seven torches, a blazing fire swirled about burning intensely.[553] It was the Fire of God from the first holocaust, the slain lamb aflame upon the wood of the Tree of Life. A group of angels could be seen dancing amidst the flames singing hymns to God,[554] blessing the Lord, for their hearts were enraptured with the Spirit of the Lord.[555]

Note 555 The Third Heaven, unlike the first two, is wholly devoted to God and in so doing its very structure comes to reflect God Himself. As one ascends up the last three rungs of the Celestial Hierarchy, they so to speak delve deeper into God, reflecting a more intricate facet of the Great Mystery of the Trinity. The heavenly Thrones, in their special devotion to God as Lord, reflect the unapproachable authority of God the Father. This is where all must start in their encounter with the Divine, acknowledging the complete otherness and sovereignty of God—until one completely submits themselves to the Lord they cannot grow in relationship with Him. The Holy Thrones thus stand as a living example of the first stage in proper worship of God, a perpetual prostration before the Lord, for as the Holy Scriptures tell us: "Fear of the Lord is the Beginning of Wisdom." Ascending then beyond the heavenly Thrones, the most luminous Cherubim receive the very light of God and find in their hearts a special devotion to God as Logos, and so reflect the pre-eminent Wisdom of God the Son. This great gift of Wisdom is truly the Beatific Vision, where gazing upon the sublime Face of God, God is actually held within the mind of the beholder. Wisdom is a sharing of the Divine Mind and this the most luminous Cherubim stand as a living example of, an actual participation with the very Mind of God—the complete and utter fulfillment of rationality. And this knowledge, much like the intimate knowledge of friendship, makes one a second-self: something that can only be had through the Second Person of the Trinity, Jesus Christ, for St. John accounts our Lord saying: "No longer do I call you servants, for a servant does not know what his master is doing; but I have called you friends, for all that I have heard from my Father I have made known to you." Yet theology tells us, 'Knowledge is but the beginning of love.' Thus making the final ascent beyond the Cherubim to the heights of Heaven, the most holy Seraphim receive the holy fire of God and find in their hearts a special devotion to God as Beloved, and so reflect the Love of God, the Holy Spirit. This great gift of Divine Love is an all-encompassing transubstantive flame that enkindles God within the soul—a true Theosis of the Holy Spirit. God's great desire to impart Theosis has slowly been revealed to us throughout the Old Testament with the Tree of Life, the Burning Bush, and the Ark of the Covenant, only to be perfected in the

. . .

553 Finally we turn in contemplation of the Divine flame, the very Presence of God. As with all spiritual matters, we come to know them by their physical cipher; thus we must first meditate upon the physical flame. According to the Greeks, this is the great treasure of the gods stolen by Prometheus, which becomes the center of civilization and of family life in hearth and home. It prepares our food for consumption, purifies our metals, and can even transform sand into transparent glass. It can spread without diminishing, all while maintaining its unanimity. We speak of fire in reference to the sun and stars, and plants use such energy in photosynthesis. We speak of our own cells and bodies burning calories for energy, and we use the combustion of fuel to propel our vehicles. What then is there in human existence that is not dependent on such fire? Yet, what is fire? The ancients said it was the fourth element, most rarefied, participating most fully with the celestial sphere. The modern scientists say it is plasma: the fourth state of matter, a combination of a fuel source with oxygen that produces an exothermic reaction. This, then, can be said of fire: it is that which produces light and heat and yet is light and heat; it is truly a state of matter, and yet is a reaction, an over saturation of matter with energy. It has the ability to spread infinitely and, although the fuel may change, the unanimity of the flame does not. This is true of the metaphysical as well: Divine Fire is the source of all light and life, the heat of which is ever born upward toward God Himself, but most importantly the Divine Flame is a result or reaction of the great love of the Father and the Son, who is the Holy Spirit. As this holy fire spreads from heart to heart, whether it be of men or angel, it enraptures their entire being, oversaturating their spirit with the Divine Essence. This is the power of Holy Fire, a true theosis, which can spread indefinitely with the self-same ardor as the Eternal Flame held between the Father and the Son in the Most Holy Trinity.

554 This is a reference to Shadrach, Meshach, and Abednego, the three men who danced about the burning furnace of the Babylonian king unscathed. Scripture reveals these three men, magistrates of the court, dancing in glory of the Lord completely preserved from any of the harm of fire. This, much like the Burning Bush, reveals God's presence resting within the burning flame that does not consume.

---

555 ... New with the Overshadowing of Mary, the Incarnation of God Himself, and the
cont. Descent of the Holy Spirit at Pentecost. Only through the fires of Divine coition can the indwelling of the Holy Spirit transform and perfect our very existence, and this is the fulfillment and end of all created things, a pure and perfect friendship with God, two hearts sharing the same Spirit. In holding the sacred flame of the Holy Spirit, we ourselves become enraptured with such fire, and, just as the Burning Bush held the very Presence of God, we too receive the Holy Spirit Himself. Enkindled by such fire, we not only come to bear such love in our hearts, but we actually become such love itself, absorbed completely into the Holy Spirit. And so assimilated into the very relational love of God the Father and the Son, we no longer love with a creaturely love, but love with the fires of the Holy Spirit—actually capable of loving God with a Divine Love. Only with the indwelling of the Holy Spirit can we lose ourselves to the fires of love, our spirit transpyred into God's own. As the great evangelist, St. Paul, preaches: "Or do you not know that your body is a Temple of the Holy Spirit within you, which you have from God? You are not your own."

Psalm
84:1...

They cried from up above, saying: "How lovely is Your dwelling, O Lord of hosts! My spirit yearns to fainting for the Sanctuary of the Lord! My heart and mind cry out for the Living God. As the sparrow finds a home and the swallow a nest to settle her young, my home is before Your Altar, O Lord of hosts—my King and my God! Blessed are those who dwell in Your Sanctuary! They shall never cease in singing Your praises!"

Psalm
...84:4

The cloud then gathered, and they saw the Lord seated on high, atop His lofty Throne, with the train of His garment filling the Temple. The holy angels then heard the Lord God whispering to the *Immaculata* veiled in a pillar of cloud: "Set me as a seal upon your heart, a seal upon your arm; for My Love is as strong as Death, My longing as fierce as Hell! Its flashes are flashes of fire; a most Divine flame![556] Deep waters cannot quench Love, nor rivers sweep it away! If one were to offer all the wealth of his house for love he would be utterly scorned and jeered at."[557]

Song
of Songs
8:6...

Song
of Songs
...8:7

The Celestial Choir of Seraphim

556   The exhortation of Love in the Song of Songs is very clear: true love is Fire, a burning flame that cannot be quenched even by many waters. This holy and ardent flame is the source of the Seraphim, the transfiguration of grace into glory, where Divine Life is transformed into Divine Love. Consider the Glory of Christ, how when He is lifted up, it is on the Cross, offering His sacred and Divine Life in pure love for the sake of His friends and the whole world. It is in this act that grace becomes glory—this is why Christ's wounds remain in His glorified body, an eternal incorporation of His sacrifice into the Divine Godhead, and the means by which we transform the Divine Life we are given into Divine Glory, uniting our love with Christ's Love. Life finds its glory in love.

557   Song of Songs 8:6. Turn your minds to contemplate the most beautiful words of the Lover, revealing that God's true love is Fire! How much more can be discerned from the Scriptures knowing that fire stands for such Divine Love. Meditate upon the Burning Bush, the holy Lampstand in the Temple, Sodom and Gomorrah, the holocaust sacrifice, Elijah calling down fire from Heaven, and finally Hell itself. Scripture is clear there is a holiness which burns yet is not consumed like in the Burning Bush, while the evils of Gehenna burn in utter destruction. Both examples burn with the same flames, yet the substances which hold such fire differ, either purifying like gold or putrefying like tar. This is also a specific declaration to Leviathan, who himself ended up losing all the wealth of his house trying to purchase the Lord's love, and, once scorned, he turns his back on the Lord, attacking *the Woman* in an attempt to sweep away God's love for the Mother of God with a torrent of water as described in the Book of Revelation.

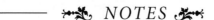

NOTES

Upon the Lord's words, the pillar of cloud erupted into flames, and the holy angels stationed above who heard the sweet words of betrothal witnessed the Spirit of the Lord descend upon their two hearts,[558] uniting them in fire. The Lord God then took a burning ember from the Altar and placed it upon the Seraphim's lips[559] and said: "Behold, the coal of the Altar has touched your lips; your pride has been relinquished, and all imperfection has been purged."[560]

Isaiah
6:7

Fire from the Altar

558 The two hearts are the Sacred Heart and the Immaculate Heart, and they are joined with the Sacred fire of the Holy Spirit.

559 This most intimate act of God's transmission of love is the source of the Seraphim's fiery love. The transference of the Holy Spirit by both breath and holy fire is called inspyration. It is this prolific flame that spreads and actually ignites the Seraphim to be enraptured with the holy fires of Divine Love. God shares His profound love for the Theotokos with the angels closest to Him, and, in so doing, they catch fire with the same love. This is the inspiration for the Song of the Seraphim, which they sing day and night before the Lord.

560 Seraphim receive and so embody the most holy fire of God, and this holy fire is the Love of God: a holy fire, which confirms the heart and soul in the Love of God, bestowing upon the bearer an integrity founded on and ordered to God, like the Apostles at Pentecost or the forging of iron into steel. This holy fire burns away all selfishness, sin, and pride, bestowing upon the bearer a previously inconceivable clarity before the Lord, like sand transformed into glass or the purification of Ezekiel's lips as a prophet. This sacred flame is entirely captivating, burning out from the heart, yet ever burning does not consume, meaning such fire enraptures the spirit, as the holy Seraphim or the Sacred and Immaculate Hearts. Yet this fire is the Fire of the Holy Spirit; thus this transubstantive flame imparts upon the bearer a most holy consonance, a harmony or symmetry with God Himself, like the Burning Bush which contains the very Presence of God. However, these three elements are St. Thomas' essential elements of Beauty: "integritas, claritas, and consonantia." It is for this reason we speak of the most holy Seraphim adoring God as the Beautiful, kindling in their hearts the sacred flame of the Holy Spirit. But this fire has already been revealed to be the Love of God, meaning such fiery love is the natural reaction of the heart to worshiping God as Beautiful. Therefore, Beauty properly understood, is Being under the aspect of lovable. For what is beauty other than that which inspires the heart to love, kindling a flame of love in the heart of the beholder, an 'inspyration' of the heart? This is not a desirous love of consumption, but a selfless love burning in consonance with the beautiful. Call to mind something truly beautiful, whether it be a field or mountain, a famous work of art, or a gorgeous woman—all of these things you do not desire to possess for yourself, but rather wish to become absorbed into, synchronizing yourself into their beauty. It is for this reason that we have nature preserves, museums, and marriage: sacred institutions to guide mankind into unity with the Beautiful. True beauty is that which 'inspyres' love, and true love is the holy fire that unifies two hearts as one.

Exodus
3:2

Immediately the angels caught aflame,[561] burning with the flames of fire, and yet burning, were not consumed.[562] . . .

Note 561   The fiery Seraphim catch fire from bearing witness to the profound love of God for the Theotokos. It is their unique proximity to the Sacred Heart, which loves so fiercely the Immaculate Heart that results in a transpyration of the Divine Flame, elevating these angels even beyond light to enkindle their own flame. Seraphim mystically share in the same sacred flame that enraptures the Theotokos; their love burns with the same intensity and intimacy as the Holy Mother of God—Spouse of the Holy Spirit. It is for this reason that the most holy Seraphim find in their hearts a special devotion to the Love of God, and this Divine love burns with an intensity greater than a thousand suns—a fiery love we mortals cannot hope to fathom this side of the veil. This Eternal Flame of God's Love is the Burning Bush calling out to Moses for the sake of the Israelite people; it is the pillar of fire above the Ark of the Covenant leading God's people through the darkness; it is the burning Altar from which Ezekiel is purged of sin and around which the Seraphim sing; but most importantly it is the Holy Spirit Himself, descending upon the Church as tongues of fire. It is in this fire that the most holy Seraphim adhere themselves most intimately to the Holy Spirit, who is the Love of the Father and the Son, and so being completely enraptured with the Holy Spirit, they burn with the self-same ardor of the Lord Himself. Thus, the holy Seraphim love with a love that is not their own, their wills enkindled with the Holy Spirit, allowing such finite creatures to actually love with the Love of God.

NOTES

562 The most holy Seraphim receive first the Divine Flame of the Holy Spirit, and being so graced to receive such pure and perfect love, shed forth such Divine Fire, igniting the hearts of all subsequent angels. We have spoken at great length of how the various choirs love God: how the First and Second Heavens love God through their love and service of His creation; how through the Third Heaven such service is purified and transfigured into true adoration of God Himself; and how through such holy adoration of God as the Good and the True, the Transcendentals give desire and clarity to all the various loves of the Celestial Hierarchy. But we have never spoken of the origin of such Love itself: how Guardian Angels find in their hearts a love for individual humans, how Archangels devote themselves in love to their families, and Principalities their nations; how Powers defend the Body of Christ in love, how the Virtues ceaselessly devote themselves to the maintenance of the universe, and the Dominations to the angels themselves; and how the Thrones love God Himself as the Good and the Cherubim love God as the True. Just as the holy Cherubim illumine the love of all the lower choirs, giving clarity or understanding to all their various loves, so too do the most holy Seraphim 'inspyre' the various loves of all the lower choirs. Thus, as Truth radiates holy light, and that light produces knowledge in the mind of the beholder, so does Beauty radiate holy fire, and that fire so produces love in the heart (Truth:Light:Knowledge::Beauty:Fire:Love). It is through this unique conformity of the most holy Seraphim to the Beauty of God, that such captivating and rapturous Beauty is transmitted to all such subsequent choirs, 'inspyring' in them the particular loves they find in their hearts, for, just as it is the Good which permeates all things, endowing creation with integrity, and it is the True which illumines all things, endowing creation with clarity, so too, it is the Beautiful which 'inspyres' all things, endowing creation with Divine consonance or Unity with God. This consonance is due to the trans-unitive property of holy fire, spreading unto all things while maintaining its unicity as one flame, but this fire is the Flame of the Holy Spirit. Thus, through such fire, all things are reconciled to God, burning with the same consonant flame that is the Holy Spirit. Therefore, all things loved are precisely lovable because of their participation in God's own Beauty. The very lovability of all things is because of their 'pyrotic' harmony with God Himself. Thus, just as the Goodness of God is first transmitted by the worship of the heavenly Thrones, and the Truth of God is first shone-forth by the worship of the holy Cherubim, the Beauty of God is first 'transpyred' by the adoration of the most holy Seraphim. It is in fact through the most holy Seraphim's ardent and fervid worship of God as the Beautiful that all Love, both of men and angels, finds its way to God, as the Transcendental Beauty.

Isaiah
6:2
    . . . So brilliant became their faces, two wings were given them to shield

the glory of their face, and so brilliant their feet that two wings were given

them to shield the glory of their feet; and with two wings they hovered.[563]

Isaiah
6:3...
    The Lord then exhorted them saying: "Sing!" and immediately the

Word was found upon the Seraphim's lips. They cried out before the

Lord: "Holy! Holy! Holy! Is the Lord of hosts! All the Earth[564] is filled

with His glory!" At the sound of that cry, the frame of the Temple

Isaiah
...6:4
shook, and the Sanctuary was filled with smoke.[565]

Note 565 Isaiah 6:1. Ascending to the heights of creation, we turn to contemplate the
Transcendentals themselves, God's own Being manifest in creation: the One,
the Good, the True, and the Beautiful. It is first necessary then to begin with
Scripture, which reveals God's Presence as holy and Divine Fire. It has already
been shown such fire gives rise to: integrity, clarity, and consonance, the three
elements of St. Thomas' account of beauty, and Scripture has already revealed
this holy fire to be the Love of God, which means the Transcendental Beauty
is Being under the aspect of lovable. Yet, integrity, clarity, and consonance
have already been shown to be the effects of the Transcendentals observed
within Being itself: The Good giving integrity to existence, endowing it with
holy worth, which stems from God own essence; The True giving clarity to
existence, endowing it with intelligibility, a holy order manifest from God's
own Mind; and Transcendent Unity gives consonance to existence, endowing
it with perfect proportion, a harmony with God Himself, just as Goodness is
Being under the aspect of desirable and Truth is Being under the aspect of
knowable, Unity is Being under the aspect of undivided. Everything that is,
is one thing, separated and distinct from another thing, meaning anything
predicated of Being as Being is one and undivided, but the Transcendentals
are predicated of Being as such; thus Goodness and Truth must be One. But
St. Thomas has already explained the combination of integrity, clarity, and
consonance to be beauty; thus the combination of Goodness, Truth, and
Unity must be the Transcendental Beauty as well. This can easily be seen
from the ordering of the Celestial Hierarchy, particularly with Scripture's
placement of the holy Cherubim above the heavenly Thrones: Truth possesses
all the desirability of the Good, while adding the aspect of intelligibility. This
is further manifest with Scripture's placement of the most holy Seraphim
above the holy Cherubim, the Beautiful possesses all of the intelligibility
of the True and all the desirability of the Good while adding the aspect of
Unicity, specifically a Unity with God Himself. Unity is the unique element
of Beauty, which inspyres love and causes a consonance with God Himself.
This transubstantive flame enkindles the bearer with the Holy Spirit, who is
the Third Person and Completion of the Trinity. Thus, it is necessary to say
that Beauty is not just another Transcendental, but is in fact the consummate
Transcendental: Beauty is the Unicity of the Good and the True.

563　With the revelation of the Seraphic triad of wings, there becomes an irrefutable and Scriptural hierarchy amongst the Choirs, namely the number of wings each choir possesses. Cherubim possessing four wings places them above all seven of the lower choirs, and, as is revealed in the words of Ezekiel, such a gift of two extra wings bestows an extraordinary power of mobility, not simply for agility but for ascent, allowing the Cherubim to approach even closer to the Most High God. If the Cherubim possess such extraordinary mobility from four wings, how much more must the Seraphim be capable of possessing six? Thus, we see that angelic wings do not simply represent mobility but nobility, allowing such ennobled creatures to approach God, receiving an even greater portion of grace. This is the great nobility of the Seraphim, who approach God in such intimacy that they actually catch fire from the intensity of such Trinitarian love. Consider now The Seven holy Angels who stand before the Glory of the Lord, how they are so close to God that they receive an individual flame from the Holy Spirit, conforming themselves directly to the Sacred and Immaculate Hearts. Therefore, we speak of the Seraphim being the highest choir, and The Seven Holy Angels being the highest individual angels.

564　This is the Song of the Seraphim, the greatest angelic song sung to serenade the Lord Himself. Consider then that the highest choir of angels do not sing of the Lord's glory being in the heavens, but rather filling the Earth. They understand that the heart of the Lord, His Love, is with the human race. This is further the Scriptural account of how the heavens are designed so that the Transcendentals flow down from God unto the Earth for the sake of mankind.

The Celestial Choir of Seraphim

283

And so, the Celestial Choir of Seraphim ever sang before the Lord, filling the *Holy Place* with the sweet strain of Divine Love.[566]

Note 566 The most holy Choir of Seraphim is the third and final Choir of the Third and Final Heaven, and the Seraphim so perfect the love found not only in the previous choir, but in the previous heavens, and thus all Creation. It is once again beneficial to recall Jacob's Ladder, a spiral staircase with three revolutions, with the most holy Seraphim at the very top of the third and final revolution, and, being at the top, so resemble the holy Principalities and exalted Dominations in a higher and more noble way. Recall how the Principalities perfect the love of the First Heaven by encompassing the love of each guardian angel and archangel actually loving each angel's person and family, while adding a consummate love for the nations in which those individuals and families reside; thus the holy Principalities perfect the love of the lower choirs, completing it as an all-encompassing love for mankind, while maintaining the individual loves that comprise the whole. Similarly, the holy Dominations perfect the love of the Second Heaven by having a consummate love for the angels themselves, and through such love for the angels they actually love what each angel loves, this is called the transitive property of love, with true and proper love the lover finds in his heart a love not just for the beloved, but for all that the beloved loves. Thus the holy Dominations find in their hearts a love for every individual, family, and nation through their love of Guardian Angels, Archangels, and Principalities; and a love of the Church as the Body of Christ and a love for the entire physical universe through their love of the heavenly Powers and Virtues, all while adding a consummate love for the entire Spiritual Realm by loving all the various angels themselves. Thus, the holy Dominations perfect the love of not only the Second Heaven but of the First as well, completing such love as an all-encompassing love for mankind and the entire Universe itself, both visible and invisible. So, too, the most holy Seraphim perfect the love of the Third Heaven, which is devoted solely to the Adoration of God. The heavenly Thrones love God as transcendent Goodness, standing as a guard between creation and God, worshiping His holiness. The holy Cherubim love God as transcendent Truth, the Wisdom by which God Himself is revealed, standing before His Light as that of the sun. But the most holy Seraphim love God as transcendent Beauty, which is the Unity of Goodness and Truth, and is in fact the prime transcendental, for just as the True possesses all the desirability of the Good while adding the notion of intelligible, so too does the Beautiful possess all the desirability and intelligibility of the Good and the True while adding the notion of unicity, namely union with God. Thus, the Seraphim possess and perfect the heavenly Thrones' love for God as the Good and the holy Cherubim's love for God as the True, while adding a consummate love for God as the Beautiful. This love is most pure, for Beauty is Being under the aspect of lovable, meaning the most holy Seraphim . . .

566 ... love God as Love, and all other loves of men and angels love God in part or by means
cont. of this love. Even the Thrones and Cherubim, who love God for Himself, love Him with a
creaturely love. Only through, with, and in the Holy Spirit—the poly-unific Flame—can
a creature love God as He loves Himself. Recall, then, the transitive property of love, for
just as the holy Dominations' love of the angels themselves inspires a love for all that the
various angels themselves love, so, too, the most holy Seraphim's love of God inspires
a love for all that God Himself loves: an absolute and all-encompassing love through,
with, and in God's Love, burning with the self-same ardor of the Holy Spirit. Thus, just
as God's love radiates down through the holy Seraphim into the hearts of all those below,
so, too, do the most holy Seraphim receive all the countless loves of all the innumerable
angels below, and, holding such multitudinous love in their hearts, so unite it to the Fire
of the Holy Spirit, perfecting such finite love and transfiguring it into an infinite Divine
Love. They then turn and in great magnanimity offer such Divine Love, the Holy Spirit,
to God as a worthy oblation. This is why the most holy Seraphim are placed at the very
pinnacle of the whole created order, possessing in their inflamed hearts the consummate
love of all holy angels. They so perfect the prostration of the heavenly Thrones and the
veneration of the holy Cherubim, transfiguring such holy worship into pure and perfect
Adoration, adoring God as Trinity in the Holy Spirit.

Song of the Seraphim

Thus, the Third Heaven was complete, so the Lord looked upon the Heavenly Temple and everything He had made and found it to be good.[567]

The Celestial Hierarchy

567 The Celestial Hierarchy is now complete, each heaven encompassing and so perfecting the previous, resulting in a celestial ladder bridging Heaven and Earth: the same ladder that Jacob saw the angels of God ascending and descending at Bethel. This seamless ladder, which later was revealed to be Christ Himself, is the outstretched arms of God grabbing ahold of the Earth in great love. It is for this reason that the first choir of the First Heaven is that of the Guardian Angels, who magnanimously take up the call to guard and guide the human person into God's loving arms. The whole First Heaven is devoted to caring for men upon the Earth as individual, family, and nation, resulting in a culminative love for humanity as a whole. Similarly, the Second Heaven is devoted to the preservation of humanity through their ceaseless stewardship of the Universe, whether it be defending the Body of Christ like the heavenly Powers or tending to it spiritually like the holy Virtues. Even the holy Dominations serve the Church and minister to all those angels which guard, guide, and serve the mystical body of Christ with all its members. The Third Heaven, which at first glance seems to only be concerned with God as unapproachable Deity, is actually the means by which God's own Being is carried through into the Universe, flowing down toward the Earth. These holy Transcendentals are the ways in which we come to encounter God and are in fact the three rivers of grace that perfect the human soul, which is comprised of intellect, memory, and will. When the True is received in the soul, it is called the Theological Virtue of Faith; when the Good is received in the soul, it is called the Theological Virtue of Hope; and when the Beautiful is received in the soul, it is called the Theological Virtue of Charity. But Faith is the perfection of the Intellect, Hope the perfection of the Memory, and Charity the perfection of the Will; therefore, the soul is perfected by the Transcendentals. Hence, the entire Universe both visible and invisible—from the formation of the Celestial Hierarchy and all its angels, to the generation of the inner workings of the human soul—everything was perfectly designed so that you might be able to receive God's own Transcendent Being, imbued directly into your soul, and having received His Life, have it so abundantly! Praised be our Lord Jesus Christ.

§ The Seven §
Who stand before the Glory of the Lord

Daniel
3:19…

The Lord God was so filled with love for Michael, Gabriel, and Raphael[568] that the countenance of His Face shone abundantly. He then ordered the flames of the Altar to be magnified sevenfold, and He ordered the mightiest angels in His army to extol Michael, Gabriel, and Raphael and to uplift them into the blazing fire of the Altar. Thus, the Archangels were lifted up by the hands of the Four Evangelim upon the Altar of sacrificial fire, but, because the Lord God was so ardent and the Altar was so inflamed, the raging fire enraptured the Four Living Creatures who lifted up Michael, Gabriel, and Raphael. It was not the appointed time for the glorification of the Four Living

Ezekiel
10:6

Creatures,[569] so the holy fire was sealed within their *voluble*, the wheelwork burning as coals of fire.[570] The holy angels could be seen walking about the midst of the flames, singing hymns to God and

Revelations
4:8

blessing the Lord: "Holy! Holy! Holy! Lord God Almighty, who was, who is, and who is to come!"

568   This is a reference to Shadrach, Meshach, and Abednego of the Book of Daniel; these three men danced about the burning furnace of the Babylonian King Nebuchadnezzar unscathed. However, these are their Babylonian names. Interestingly, their Hebrew names are Hananiah, Mishael, and Azariah. Azariah means 'God is help;' it is the name St. Raphael ('God who heals') gives for himself when he is under the guise of being human in the Book of Tobit. Mishael means 'Who is like God?'; we are used to the western pronunciation Michael. Hananiah means 'God is Grace'. In Hebrew, grace is 'chen' from a root word 'chanan', meaning to bend or stoop in kindness to another, as a superior to an inferior. This in particular exemplifies Gabriel's role announcing the Incarnation to the Virgin Mary, the Divine Condescension of God becoming man, for the Salvation of all. Thus, we see a striking similarity between these three men and the three Archangels—Azariah as Raphael, Mishael as Michael, and Hananiah as Gabriel ('God's strength'). We turn then to contemplate how Scripture reveals these three men, magistrates in the court of the king, as the three Archangels dancing amidst the flames of glory of the Lord, and how, before the presence of God, they are not completely obliterated in such holy fire.

569   God here gives a gift foreshadowing a great glory to come. This gift is the seraphic flame from which the very light of the Cherubim originates. This fire God specifically places in the wheelwork of the Four Living Creatures, who stand out ahead of the Choir of Cherubim, just as the Three Archangels stand out ahead of the Choir of Archangels. Now recall how at the end of the Bible, in the Book of Revelation 4:8, St. John says: "The first Living Creature like a lion, the second Living Creature like an ox, the third Living Creature with a face like a human face, and the fourth Living Creature like a flying eagle. And the Four Living Creatures, each of them with six wings, full of eyes all around and inside. Who cry out day and night without ceasing, 'Holy, holy, holy, the Lord God Almighty, who was and is and is to come.'" St. John is describing the Four Living Creatures, Cherubim, having the wings of a Seraphim, six, but lest you think his account was mistaken, he records them singing the Song of the Seraphim, 'holy, holy, holy.' He is not confused in his vision, but rather is describing a mysterious transfiguration, a Paschal Glorification. In the description of the Four Living Creatures, we learn of their unique conformity to the Christ, bearing His Gospel, becoming the Four Gospels of His Word, and it is this absolute conformity to Christ that in lies the secret. For, as Christ rose from the dead—body, blood, soul, and divinity—transfigured in Glory, so, too, the Gospels were transfigured in Glory, and so the Four Living Creatures who bear the Gospels were transfigured in Glory. Thus, much like the Three Archangels who are both Seraphim and Archangels, the Four Living Creatures are glorified with Christ in the Seraphic flame, who now bear six wings and find upon their lips the Song of the Seraphim. Most importantly, this glorification reveals a hallowed secret held at the very core of the person of Christ—Truth is glorified when it gives itself over to Love.

570   Ezekiel 10:6 "Then [God] commanded the man clothed in linen, 'Take fire from within the wheelwork, from among the Cherubim.'" The sacred fire of God is actually housed within the great wheelwork of the Cherubim, which later will transfigure the Four Living Creatures when Christ Himself is transfigured in Glory at the Resurrection.

Daniel
...3:46...

Yet, the Lord God kept stoking the fire and soon the flames poured out forty-nine cubits high and spread out, enrapturing the Four Living Creatures, enkindling the Seraphim, and illuminating the Cherubim who were near the Altar. The Lord then came down upon the Altar to be with Michael and his companions, who could be seen walking amidst the flames with them.

Daniel
3:91

The Four Living Creatures then said, "Was it not three angels we threw into the fire? Yet we see four beings dancing admits the flames, and they are overjoyed. The fourth is not like the others He is in the form of God!"

The Spirit of the Lord then gathered together the seven-times greater flame that swirled about the Altar and divided it into seven scions burning as Tongues of Fire.[571] He then took the sevenfold flame and gave each angel a portion of His Spirit, which came to rest upon the seven torches before the Altar.[572] The Spirit of the Lord remained there upon the Altar, bestowing the seven angels who held the seven torches with the spirit of *wisdom* and the spirit of *understanding*, with the spirit of *counsel* and the spirit of *fortitude*, with the spirit of *knowledge* and the spirit of *piety*, and with the spirit of *fear of the Lord*.[573]

Acts of
the Apostles
2:2

Revelation
4:5

Isaiah
11:2

571 Acts 2:2 The tongues of fire are a great truth revealed about the Holy Spirit, for we see that the Holy Spirit is Fire, an ardent flame burning with the all-consuming love of God. This is an eternal fire flowing straight from the intimate union of the Most Holy Trinity. This eternal and Divine fire is the reason why the Holy Altar in Heaven is ablaze as seen in the Book of Isaiah, where one of the seraphim takes an ember from the burning Altar and purges the sin from Isaiah's lips, and is in fact the reason why the Seraphim themselves are aflame. This holy and ardent love of the Holy Spirit is the sacred flame of Seraph and Madonna.

572 This is the eternal fire of the Holy Spirit coming down to set the heavenly Altar ablaze. The seven flaming torches mentioned in Revelation 4:5 are the Seven Gifts of the Holy Spirit given to The Seven Angels "who stand before the Glory of the Lord;" thus, such torches symbolize both the fire of the Holy Spirit and the bearers of such fire: The Seven Holy Angels, "seven unlit torches awaiting the Lord to kindle them with the flames of His Spirit."

573 Isaiah 11:2 reveals the Seven Gifts of the Holy Spirit.

NOTES

Tobit
12:15

So the Spirit of the Lord filled Michael, Gabriel, Raphael, and the Four Living Creatures, enrapturing them as the Seven Holy Angels who stand before the Glory of the Lord.[574]

Those Seven who stand before the Lord

574 Ever since the words of St. Raphael "I am one of the Seven..." were recorded in the Book of Tobit, many have pondered the great mystery of the Seven Holy Angels who stand before the Glory of God. There have been many attempts to understand their natures, and some have even speculated their names like in the Book of Enoch, but these spurious attempts are clearly derived from the minds of men and are not part of the sacred canon of Scripture. How strange a thing to be told there are Seven Angels at the very pinnacle of the Celestial Hierarchy that direct the flow of grace for the entire Universe but whose names are not revealed in Scripture. At best, most Theologians had to resign themselves to the answer: 'Well, their names must not be beneficial for our Salvation if they are not revealed in Scripture.' This, however, seems even more peculiar. To be told that such instrumental angels as Michael, Gabriel, and Raphael would be accompanied by four irrelevant angels who are extraneous to the Salvific Plan of Christ, seems to be a grave misunderstanding of Scripture, especially when the Celestial Hierarchy itself is built on Christ, the angels of God ascending and descending upon Christ Himself. What then can be said for those faithful to Scripture and hopeful that all things are revealed in Christ?

Let us contemplate the Three Archangels who are named in Scripture, how they are the three most influential angels and reflect the most intimate virtues of Christ. Scripture reveals Michael to be Prince of the Heavenly Host and of the family of Israel. In Revelation, Michael is revealed defending *the Woman* with Child, our Lord Jesus Christ. Scripture reveals Gabriel to be the Archangel entrusted with the Incarnation itself, both in the Old Testament and in the New. Gabriel heralds the most important message ever given to man and angel, the Logos of God Himself, incarnate of the Virgin Mary. Raphael is the Archangel that reveals that there are Seven who stand before the Glory of God, without which we would have no knowledge of such holy angels. Raphael is entrusted with the 'King's secret,' namely that Christ is coming as Bridegroom to heal and marry the human race. All three of these angels are Archangels devoted to the Family of God, burning with the spousal fire of the Holy Spirit, and so take their place not only as head of the Celestial Choir of Archangels but of the entire Celestial Hierarchy as inflamed Seraphim.

It is not by accident that, according to Scripture, a similar transfiguration is revealed about the Four Living Creatures. For the acute Christian reader, there arises a unique peculiarity between Ezekiel's description of the Four Living Creatures and St. John's account of the Four Living Creatures in the Book of Revelation. Ezekiel describes them having four faces and four wings, yet after the Paschal Victory of Christ the description of the Four Living Creatures changes to reflect the unique characteristics of Seraphim possessing six wings and singing the *Song of the Seraphim*: "Holy, Holy, Holy." This transfiguration is undoubtedly due to Christ's own transfiguration in the Resurrection, for as Christ the Word was transfigured in Glory so, too, was the Gospel and those holy angels that bear the Gospel: for Christ is the Gospel, the Living Word of God, the very source of *Life* of the *Four Living Creatures*. Thus, just as His life was glorified in the Resurrection, so, too, would their life be glorified. Thus, just as it is the three Archangels' unique conformity to Christ as family which causes their glorification, so, too, it is the Four Living Creatures' unique conformity to Christ as Gospel that causes their seraphic glorification. Therefore, with a proper understanding of seraphic glorification, it becomes clear: Scripture has revealed the Three Archangels and the Four Living Cherubim to be the Seven Holy Angels that stand before the Glory of God.

Daniel
...3:52...

The Seven Holy Angels then began to praise, to bless, and to glorify the Lord God upon the Altar:[575]

"Blessed are You, O Lord, God of our creation, worthy to be praised and glorified, and highly exalted forever; and blessed is Your Glorious and Holy Name; alone are You worthy to be highly praised and exalted above all and through all ages!

Blessed are You in the Holy Temple of Your Glory,[576] to be extolled and exceedingly glorified forever!

Blessed are You who behold the Depths from Your throne upon the *Cherubim*,[577] to be praised and exalted above all forever!

Blessed are You on the *Throne*[578] of Your Kingdom, to be extolled and exalted above all forever!

Daniel
...3:56...

Blessed are You in the Firmament of Heaven,[579] to be serenaded and glorified forever!

Let all you *Workers* of God,[580] bless the Lord: sing praise to Him and exalt Him above all forever!

O you heavens, bless the Lord: sing praise to Him and exalt Him above all forever!

O you *Angels* of the Lord,[581] bless the Lord: sing praise to Him and exalt Him above all forever!

O all you waters over the heavens, bless the Lord: sing praise to Him and exalt Him above all forever!

O all you *Powers* of the Lord,[582] bless the Lord: sing praise to Him and exalt Him above all forever!

O you Sun and Moon, bless the Lord: sing praise to Him and exalt Him above all forever!

O you stars of heaven, bless the Lord: sing praise to Him and exalt Him above all forever!

O you rain and dew, bless the Lord: sing praise to Him and exalt Him above all forever!

O all you winds, bless the Lord: sing praise to Him and exalt Him above all forever!

575   Let us turn to contemplate the prayer of The Seven holy angels who stand before the Glory of the Lord. This holy prayer is a full account of the ordering of creation, beginning with God and ending with man upon the Earth. The prayer so begins with the great invocation of God as Creator, extolling His holy name, which as we know is "I Am Who Am": the name of Being itself. From there it systematically goes through the First, Second, and Third Heavens, calling each choir by name to pray. However, this prayer does something that our modern minds find very difficult—it seamlessly intertwines the natural and the supernatural, invoking both the various angels and the various forces of nature to praise and bless the Lord. This is one of the greatest truths lost in the modern world: how perfectly interwoven the natural is with the supernatural. Finally, it ends with invoking mankind upon the Earth to bless the Lord, showing that all of the First, Second, and Third Heavens—and all of nature itself—is ordered for the flow of grace upon the Earth, specifically for the benefit of mankind.

576   The Seven are calling upon the most holy Seraphim to Bless the Lord forever. Note in the Third Heaven each invocation is directed to the Lord but speaks also to the angels which adhere themselves to Him. Consider, then, the profound unity of the Seraphim with God, how they are not even distinguished as separate but simply dwell with God in His holy Temple.

577   The Seven are calling upon the holy Cherubim to Bless the Lord forever. Even though the invocation is to the Lord, the Cherubim are distinguished as the foundation of His Throne.

578   The Seven are calling upon the holy Thrones to Bless the Lord forever. The invocation is still directed to the Lord, yet is also addressing the holy Thrones, and shifts from the Heavenly Temple to the extended notion of God's Kingdom.

579   The prayer now transitions from adoring God in the Third Heaven to blessing Him in the Second Heaven. The Second Heaven exists alongside the Firmament, which shows the convergence and union of the very heights of our physical realm and the metaphysical realm, both of which share the very name 'heavens.' As Flannery O'Connor said, "Everything that rises must converge."

580   The Seven are calling upon the heavenly Dominations to Bless the Lord forever. Note how the Scriptural name given to the holy Dominations is 'Workers of God,' denoting their unique manifestation of God's dominion throughout the Universe.

581   The Seven are calling upon the heavenly Virtues to Bless the Lord forever. The holy title of 'Angels' is given to the Choir of Virtues, firstly because they uniquely fulfill the role of angel, most adeptly transmitting God's grace throughout the cosmos, and secondly because they are the middlemost choir of the entire Celestial Hierarchy, and, thus, Virtues stand as an archetype for all angels.

582   The Seven are calling upon the heavenly Powers to Bless the Lord forever. The heavenly Powers stand at the gate of the Second Heaven, guarding its purity and integrity. This is why they are invoked even before the Sun and Moon, which stand as the height of the physical cosmos.

O you fire and heat, bless the Lord: sing praise to Him and exalt Him above all forever!

O you winter cold and summer heat, bless the Lord: sing praise to Him and exalt Him above all forever!

O you dews and hoarfrost, bless the Lord: sing praise to Him and exalt Him above all forever!

O you ice and cold, bless the Lord: sing praise to Him and exalt Him above all forever!

O you frost and snow, bless the Lord: sing praise to Him and exalt Him above all forever!

O you Night and Day, bless the Lord: sing praise to Him and exalt Him above all forever!

O you Light and Darkness, bless the Lord: sing praise to Him and exalt Him above all forever!

O you lightning and cloud, bless the Lord: sing praise to Him and exalt Him above all forever!

Daniel
...3:74...

Let then the Earth[583] bless the Lord: sing praise to Him and exalt Him above all forever!

O you mountains and hills, bless the Lord: sing praise to Him and exalt Him above all forever!

O you verdure of the Earth, bless the Lord: sing praise to Him and exalt Him above all forever!

O you fountains and springs, bless the Lord: sing praise to Him and exalt Him above all forever!

O you rivers and seas, bless the Lord: sing praise to Him and exalt Him above all forever!

O you sea monsters and all that swim the depths, bless the Lord: sing praise to Him and exalt Him above all forever!

O you birds of the air, bless the Lord: sing praise to Him and exalt Him above all forever!

O you wild beasts and cattle, bless the Lord: sing praise to Him and exalt Him above all forever!

583 The prayer now transitions from the Second Heaven to the First Heaven, invoking the Earth to bless the Lord.

───────── ❧ *NOTES* ❧ ─────────

O you *Princes and Peoples* on the Earth,[584] bless the Lord: sing praise to Him and exalt Him above all forever!

O let Zion bless the Lord: sing praise to Him and exalt Him above all forever!

O you Priests of God, bless the Lord: sing praise to Him and exalt Him above all forever!

O you *Servants of God*,[585] bless the Lord: sing praise to Him and exalt Him above all forever!

O you *Spirits and Souls* of the Just,[586] bless the Lord: sing praise to Him and exalt Him above all forever!

O you holy and humble of heart, bless the Lord: sing praise to Him and exalt Him above all forever!

O you Michael, Gabriel and Raphael, bless the Lord: sing praise to Him and exalt Him above all forever! For He has saved us from Hell, from the power of Death, and delivered us from the burning fires of Hell; from the midst of Hell He has delivered us. Give thanks to the Lord for He is good—His mercy endures forever!

All who worship the Lord, bless the God of gods, sing praise to Him and give thanks to Him, for His mercy endures forever!"

Daniel
...3:90

So it was through the prayer of the Seven Holy Angels who stand before the Glory of the Lord that all of Heaven learned to pray and sing a new song of mercy before the Lord.

584 The Seven are calling upon the holy Principalities to Bless the Lord God forever. The Principalities are invoked right alongside the peoples whom they serve and watch over.

585 The Seven are calling upon the holy Archangels to Bless the Lord God forever. This unique and holy choir is referred to as Servants of God, denoting their unique humility before and service to the Lord.

586 The Seven are calling upon the Guardian Angels to Bless the Lord God forever. Much like the Principalities, the Guardian Angels are invoked right alongside their individual person whom they serve and protect. Note, however, only those angels and souls who choose to serve God's justice are specifically invoked.

NOTES

The Beatific Vision[587]

2 Samuel
5:1...

Thus, all the choirs of Heaven gathered themselves to Michael and said: "We have been preserved through your own grace and glory.[588] In the past, while Lucifer was king over us, you rose up, the one who was to lead the armies of Heaven. And the Lord said unto you, 'You will shepherd my angels in Heaven, and you will become their Prince.'"

Then all the Ancients of Heaven and all the choirmasters came to Michael their prince, and they made a covenant with him before the Lord, and so they anointed Michael as Prince over all of Heaven.[589]

2 Samuel
...5:3

1 Chronicles
29:10...

Michael then turned and blessed the Lord in the presence of the whole assembly, saying: "Blessed are You, Lord God, *the Father*[590] who dwells in Heaven forever and ever! Yours, Lord, is the greatness, and the power, and the glory, and the victory, and the majesty, for everything in Heaven and on Earth is Yours. Yours, Lord, is the kingdom; You are exalted as head over all. Prosperity and power come from You; You rule over all things. In Your hand rests power and might, and it is in Your hand to glorify and give strength to all. And now, our God, we give You thanks and praise Your glorious Name forever!

1 Chronicles
...29:13

1 Chronicles
29:20

Then Michael turned and spoke to the whole assembly, instructing them saying: "Bless the Lord your God!" So they all blessed the Lord, the God of creation, and bowed down, prostrating themselves before their Lord and King.[591]

IGNATIAN CONTEMPLATION

587 The Beatific Vision is the source and summit of Heaven; it is the pinnacle of the entire created order, the climax of creation. It is that to which the whole Celestial Hierarchy is built toward, yet, the Beatific Vision is also that which Heaven is built upon, the sure and unshakable foundation of Heaven's holiness. The Beatific Vision is the telos or the end of all Creation, that to which all creation is ordered; it is the culmination of existence by which creature looks upon Creator face to face. For it is written in 1 Corinthians 13:12: "Now we see through a dark mirror dimly, but then we shall see face to face," and in 1 John 3:2: "When He shall appear, we shall be like to Him, because we shall see Him as He is." This is the common desire of the saints: to see God in His essence, according to Exodus 33:13, "Show me Thy glory"; Psalm 79:20, "Show Thy face and we shall be saved"; and John 14:8, "Show us the Father and it is enough for us."

Therefore, according to Scripture, the Beatific Vision is seeing God in His essence, face to face. This supreme and edifying vision is God dwelling within our intellect, being both *that which is understood*, and *that whereby He is understood*, meaning God is both the object of sight and the object received in our intellect. The proportion of the Divine Essence to our intellect is as the proportion of *form* to *matter*, meaning the Intellect receives the Divine Essence as the body receives the soul, vivifying it and perfecting it. Things are only intelligible according to their *actuality*, which is bestowed by the *form*, and since the Divine Essence is *pure actuality*, it is the *form* whereby the intellect receives *pure understanding*, and this Divine indwelling is the Beatific Vision. Therefore, the Beatific Vision is the unique indwelling of God Himself within the intellect of the beholder, uniting Himself and so perfecting the creature according to its capacity. This is why the theologian has always said the angels were not created with the Beatific Vision or a third of them would not have fallen, for one cannot gaze upon the Face of God, the perfection of Beauty, and look away.

588 Recall now the old order of which Lucifer found himself chief, how it was according to knowledge of God, a hierarchy of light, the new order is according to love of God, a hierarchy of grace, of which Michael is now prince. Thus, just as all knowledge of the Divine was held and so received from the Light Bearer himself, so, too, Michael is the first angel to receive such grace. He in turn gathers together all the various choirs of angels to receive such grace. [From whence the Prince receives such grace is yet to be revealed.]

589 2 Samuel 5:1 The kingship of Michael as Prince of the Heavenly Host is both Divine Right and public confirmation; he was chosen by God and thus was blessed with a superabundance of grace, but all the angels in Heaven choose to follow Michael because he saved them from the fires of Hell defeating the great dragon. The covenant they make is an exchange of persons—they give themselves over to Michael, submitting themselves to receive knowledge and grace of God through him, and he gives himself to them to be their prince and lead them closer to God in all things.

590 St. Michael uses the holy and revered title of Father, a concept no angel could reason to, but had to be revealed to him through his holy service of God as an Archangel, guardian of the holy family. Only through seeing Christ can one comprehend truly the Divine Fatherhood of God—it is the boast of the Christian alone to call God Father.

591 1 Chronicles 29:10 St. Michael's first act as Prince of the Heavenly Host is to teach all the angels how to pray and how to relate to God. He exhorts them to prostrate themselves before the Lord and bless Him, giving all that they have to God as the source of their very existence.

Leviticus
9:23...
Michael and Gabriel then entered the *Holy of Holies* and prayed before the Lord to reveal His Face[592] to the assembly and confirm them in the *good news* first preached in Eden, the Garden of God.[593] After

Numbers
6:24
they came out, they blessed the many angels saying: "May the Lord bless you and keep you! May the Lord make His Face to shine upon you and be gracious to you! And may the Lord turn His Face toward you and grant you peace!"[594]

The glory of the Lord then appeared to all the angels. Fire came out from the Lord and consumed the Sacrifice upon the Altar, and,

Leviticus
...9:24
when all the angels saw it, they shouted and fell on their faces.[595]

Isaiah
7:10...
Then the Lord spoke to Michael, saying: "Ask a sign of the Lord your God; let it be as deep as Hell and as high as Heaven!"[596] And so, Michael obediently asked of the Lord a great sign.

So the Lord called forth the Ark of the Covenant and declared: "Look, therefore, the Lord Himself shall give you a sign: *the Virgin* will conceive and shall bear forth a Son, and His name shall be

Isaiah
...7:14
Immanuel!"

Revelation
11:19...
At that decree, the Temple in Heaven was opened, and the Ark of the Covenant was seen within the Temple; and there were great flashes of lightning, rumblings, peals of thunder, a mighty earthquake, and a heavy hailstorm.[597] And so, from the heights of Heaven to the depths of Hell, all creation shook at the sight of the Ark of the Lord.

592 To see God's Face is nothing other than the Beatific Vision: the source and summit of all beatitude and joy in Heaven. Once an angel looks upon the Blessed Face of God, it is impossible for the angel to do anything but love and serve the Lord. Receiving the Beatific Vision is the hallowed reward given to those holy angels that chose to serve the Lord under Michael their Prince.

593 Recall the Protoevangelium, the promise of an immaculate woman, not stained by Satan's sin, who will conceive and bear forth a seed, of her own flesh, who will destroy the very head of the Serpent. This first Gospel, as the Church Fathers explained, is a holy and solemn promise for Mary and the Union of God and Man: Jesus Christ.

594 Numbers 6:24 Michael and Gabriel are the two highest angels in the new Order of Grace; they enter into the Heavenly Temple's Holy of Holies, a chamber at the very center of the God's House. The Holy of Holies is the Heart of the Temple, a place where the fire of God's love burns for the Heavenly Ark of the Covenant, His holy Theotokos. They enter this most holy and sacred space pleading that the Lord would reveal this same intimate love to all the holy angels in Heaven.

595 Leviticus 9:24 Recall the contemplation on the most holy Seraphim, how such fire is the source of all Love in Heaven, burning with the selfsame ardor as the Sacred Heart of Jesus. The Holy Spirit descends upon the Altar of Sacrifice in Heaven and from this holy fire the Seraphim are set ablaze, but now all of Heaven bears witness to such fire, such love of God.

596 Isaiah 7:10 The Lord makes plain His great gift of holy Fire from the Holy Spirit, granting Michael the opportunity to ask of the Lord an even greater sign. Michael, unlike Ahaz, obeys and asks for the great sign. God then gives a vision that sums up the entirety of Scripture: Mary's espousal to the Holy Spirit, conceiving and bearing the Son of God. In this one vision, the entire Salvific Plan of God is revealed to the angels, and, for the first time, they see it as it was intended through the eyes of Michael their Prince.

597 Revelation 11:19 The Heavenly Temple is the abode of God. It stands as His castle, His capital, and His sanctuary; it alone is worthy to house His Throne and the train of His garment. The Heavenly Temple is the most holy place in all of creation, the very reason why Heaven itself is holy. Thus, when it is opened, it unveils to the whole multitude of Heaven the innermost sanctuary of God's House, that which is the center, source, and summit of God's Presence: the Ark of the Covenant. The Temple was built for a single purpose: to house the heavenly Ark of the Covenant, which is the source of the Temple's own holiness. Now the Heavenly Ark, much like the Earthly Ark, is the Holiest of Holies; it is the nexus of God's very Presence within the Heavenly Temple dwelling with His angels, or the Earthly Temple dwelling with His chosen people. In a very profound and mystical sense, the Ark of the Covenant is that which bears God, and is the means by which God chooses to dwell with His people, in Heaven and on Earth. This is why it is so shocking that above the Ark of the Covenant God reveals the Immaculate Woman, the holy vessel chosen to bear His own Son. This is the single greatest insight into the heart of God: the Ark of the Covenant is Mary, Theotokos and Mother of God. She is the Heavenly Ark, not of this creation—the Immaculate Conception. She is the means by which God has chosen to dwell with His creation, the cause of the Heavenly Temple's sanctity, and is in fact the cause of all Heaven's sanctity, for she has been chosen to hold the Lord God within her.

Revelation
...12:1...

Then a great revelation appeared in a pillar of cloud above the Ark: *the Woman* clothed in the sun with the moon beneath her feet, and on her head rested a crown of twelve stars. She was with child,[598] and wailed aloud in birth pangs, her voice crying out in agony to give birth.

Immediately, Gabriel fell to his knee and proclaimed before all the angels of Heaven: "All Hail, *Grace the Overflowing*,[599] the Lord is

Luke
1:28

with her!"[600]

Hail Kecharitōmenē

598 These descriptions of being clothed in the sun and standing upon the moon with a crown of stars are eternal descriptions; she is revealed to all of heaven already possessing these honorable and exalted virtues. Mystically, from the moment of her Immaculate Conception, God has already given her the grace of the sun, made her the fulfillment of the moon and queen of the stars, but most importantly she already is mother and is with child. It is part of her very nature—who she is—that she is the Mother of God. In God's mind, there was never a 'time' where Mary wasn't the mother of His Son.

599 The specific word used by St. Gabriel at the Annunciation is "kecharitōmenē," which is translated "Full of Grace" in the Holy Scriptures. Kecharitōmĕnē, the perfect passive participle of charitŏō, denotes one who has been and still is the object of Divine grace, one who has been favored and continues to be favored by God, one who has been granted supernatural life and remains in this state. Verbs ending in ŏō—such as haimatŏō (turn into blood), thaumatŏō (fill with wonder), and spodŏōmai (burn to ashes)—express the full intensity of the action. Thus, the perfect passive state of Kecharitomene denotes the fullest intensity of grace and the continuance of such grace for all perpetuity. This most hallowed title given to Mary by the Archangel Gabriel denotes the Mother of God's role as the Fount of Grace. Mary is she whose name, whose title, whose office, whose very person, is one who has been endowed with grace in anticipation of her role as Mother of God and Mother of the Church. The English translation of "Full of Grace" does not go far enough, appearing adjectival and lacking in its perpetuity and super-inundation. Only in the original Greek does the Archangel Gabriel's words unveil such a sublime and edifying truth as the plenary redoundingness of grace contained within Mary. Let us turn then in contemplation of the earth-shattering salutation of the second highest angel of the Most High God, who kneels before Mary and hails her as Kecharitomene, a proper noun, revealing to the Church and all Christians their Mother's heavenly name.

600 Luke 1:28 Gabriel actually gives the cause of such sanctifying grace, namely the Presence of the Lord within her. Recall that the cause of the Seven Holy Angels' extreme holiness is that they stand before the Presence of the Lord. How much more exalted must Mary be if she contains within her the very Presence of God? It is for this reason Mary is so 'full of grace' that she is grace overflowing, the fount by which Michael first received the grace necessary to contend with the great dragon, depose Lucifer, and establish a new order with Mary as their Kecharitomene, their new Fount of Grace. Thus, Mary is not only the source of grace for all of mankind, but for all the angels as well. Therefore, when Gabriel kneels before Mary and declares her heavenly name: Kecharitomene, he is kneeling before the source of his own grace that preserved him from following Lucifer and becoming a demon in Hell.

Luke
1:42

"Blessed is she among women[601] and blessed is the fruit of her womb!"[602] Michael exclaimed in a loud voice. "Why has this happened to me, that the *Mother of God* has come unto me? For the moment I heard the sound of her voice, my heart leapt for joy at the child in her womb! Blessed is she who believed that there would be a fulfillment of what was spoken in the garden by the Lord."[603]

Michael then recounted his battle with Leviathan, saying: "It was through her grace I was preserved! By her favor I was set apart.

Sirach
24:24...

It was for her sanctity that I contended with the Dragon, and by the blood of her womb that I overcame him, for she is the mother of all fair love, and of fear, and of knowledge, and of holy hope! In her is all grace of *the way* and of the truth; in her is all hope of life and of virtue. Go to her, all those who desire; be filled with the fruit of her womb, for her spirit is sweet beyond honey, and her inheritance beyond honey and honeycomb! Her memory shall be

Sirach
...24:28

unto everlasting generations!"[604]

Revelation
12:5

The Woman then gave birth to a son, a male child, who was destined to rule all the nations with an iron rod; her son was caught

Luke
2:13

up to God and His Throne. So the many angels began praising God and singing: "Glory to God in the highest and on Earth peace to men of God's good will!"[605]

Matthew
3:17

The Lord God then declared: "This is My beloved Son with whom I am well pleased!"

So the great multitude beheld *the Woman* for the first time through the eyes of Michael their prince, and falling to their knees, acclaimed,

Luke
1:35

"*Theotokos*! She is the Mother of God!"

And so, the Lord declared: "Of old has the Spirit of God courted her, enveloping her, and the power of the Most High has overshadowed

Proverbs
3:18...

her. She is the Tree of Life to those who grasp her, and felicity to those who cling to her.

601 Luke 1:42 Michael here extols her as blessed among all women, which, if we recall the centricity of Creation, woman is created from the center of man, who dwells in the Garden, which is the center of the Earth, which is the center of the Cosmos itself. Thus, Michael is proclaiming that this Woman is the 'New Eve' created to be the new center of Creation. This, coupled with the words of St. Gabriel that the 'Lord is with her,' shows God's true plan of Salvation: for by God dwelling within this Woman, the New Eve, God is dwelling within the very center of Creation, and, from this Immaculate Woman, He is able to inundate all of Creation with His grace.

602 Let us contemplate the hallowed salutation of the Archangel Gabriel and the words of St. Elizabeth, for their words form a most significant prayer for all true Christians. It is the most recited prayer on the planet and has been since the earliest days of Christianity; it is the Hail Mary. We so often forget the overwhelming and crippling nature of an angelic visitation; throughout the whole Old Testament, when an angel appears to an individual, they fall on their faces and worship the Lord by worshiping the angel (cf. Joshua 5:14 & Genesis 18:2). Only at the Annunciation do we see an angel kneeling before a human being, but not just kneeling, actually heralding her as Kecharitomene, the source of the angel's own grace. The Archangel Gabriel proclaims: "Hail, Full of Grace, the Lord is with Thee!" These are words from heaven, hand-delivered by the second greatest angel in the entire Celestial Hierarchy. That we can even repeat such holy words is a gift from God.

   The second phrase is from the mouth of St. Elizabeth, who after hearing Mary's voice, feels her child leaps in her womb and is filled with the Holy Spirit. Thus, Scripture is very clear that the Holy Spirit speaks through Elizabeth, as an enamored husband before his wife, saying: "Blessed are you among women and blessed is the fruit of your womb!" These holy and venerable words are not from any mortal mind but are inspired by the Holy Spirit, for Elizabeth could never have fathomed Mary to be the Theotokos, the Mother of God, carrying God in her womb. Thus, we see the *Hail Mary* is not just Scriptural, but is comprised of the heavenly words of the Archangel Gabriel and the Divine words of the Holy Spirit Himself.

   Let us turn then and pray with St. Michael and St. Gabriel this holy and venerable prayer: "Hail Mary, *Full of Grace*, the Lord is with Thee. Blessed art Thou amongst women and blessed is the fruit of Thy womb, Jesus. Holy Mary, *Mother of God*, pray for us sinners, now and at the hour of our Death. Amen."

603 Luke 1:42 St. Michael finishes this most perfect prayer by echoing the words of King David in finding the Ark and St. Elizabeth in receiving Mary into her home. This shows Mary's unique role as the true Ark of the Covenant, which Michael now heralds to the multitude of angels.

604 Sirach 24:24 Mary herself draws our attention to this passage of Sirach in her 'Magnificat' prayer in the Gospel of Luke 1:48, stating, "Because He has regarded the humility of His handmaid; henceforth all generations shall call me blessed." She recognizes the marvelous work of the Holy Spirit within her, courting her, espousing her, and conceiving within her the Son of God. Truly she is Lady Wisdom in whose tabernacle the Lord has chosen to rest.

605 Luke 2:13 This is the song of the angels sung to herald the birth of Christ.

I founded the Earth with her in mind, established the Heavens with an understanding of her; for her were the depths split open, and the clouds drop down their dew. Go to her, all those who desire, and be filled with the fruit of her womb!"

Proverbs
...3:20
Sirach
24:26

And, looking upon the face of her Son,[606] the great multitude of angels sang out in acclaim: "Truly, we have seen the Face of God!"[607]

John
14:9

Thus, the great Celestial Hierarchy was complete, so the Lord looked upon the *Theotokos*[608] and all her angels and found them to be very good.[609]

Queen of Angels

606 Let us turn in contemplation to the most holy Face of Jesus, which is the very Face of God. Held within the Face of Christ is all the perfection and beauty of the Father, for anyone who has seen Christ has seen the Father. Anyone who has looked upon the Face of Christ has entered into that most loving gaze between creature and Creator that is the complete and utter fulfillment of the soul. It is this most holy face—the face of the child of Mary, the face that would be bloodied for our sins—that gives eternal beatitude and glory to all the angels and saints in Heaven.

607 To behold the Face of God is the Beatific Vision, the source and summit of the Celestial Hierarchy, of Heaven itself, that to which all the Cherubim, all the Seraphim, and all the host of Heaven aspire. It is the perfection and culmination of existence itself, for within the ineffable Face of God is contained the entirety of Goodness, the entirety of Truth, and the entirety of Beauty, unseparated and absolute, God's own transcendent perfection so potent, so pervasive, that to merely look upon His Face transfigures the soul, placing the Logos of God within the intellect and the charitas of the Holy Spirit within the will of the beholder. Thus, through beholding the most sublime Face of God, the creature receives within its mind God the Word and within its heart God the Spirit. This is the Beatitude of Beauty in the Beatific Vision, a true and mystical Theosis of creature with Creator.

608 Let us turn to our final contemplation of Mary, the Mother of God, for whom this book has been written and by whom this book has been inspired. What then can be said, standing atop the Celestial Hierarchy, gazing at our Blessed Mother? To say she is the Pinnacle of Creation simply isn't enough. To recall all that was said about the Good, the True, and the Beautiful, the Transcendent Being of God desired by the Thrones, contemplated by the Cherubim, and adored by the Seraphim and to say she is the Dispenser of all such grace still isn't enough, for, when all of Heaven is contemplating the sublime Face of her Son, adoring Him in existential bliss, He, God Himself, is gazing upon her face with a love so profound it spills over into all women, specifically the love of mother and child. (This is not poetry; the unique love of God and His Mother is the metaphysical source of love that so inspires the unique love of mother and child recognized by all throughout the world.) Thus, we see from atop the Celestial Hierarchy that God Himself looks upon Mary in a unique way, beyond that of any angel or saint. Yet, God is a Trinity of Divine Persons, so there must be three unique ways God relates to Mary. All three have been explicitly expounded upon in this book, for they are the three Names derived from the Holy Spirit in Sacred Scripture, Tradition, and the Magisterium—the Three Pillars of Christendom.

The First Triune Name for Mary is Kecharitomene, bequeathed to us by the Holy Spirit in Sacred Scripture, revealing the full redoundingness of grace poured into Mary from all eternity, to such an extent that Gabriel, one of the Seven, kneels before her. This most hallowed Salutation delivered by an angel is actually the word of the Holy Spirit, for Kecharitomene is the nuptial name the Holy Spirit whispers to Mary as husband to spouse. (Our God is not a character of mythology coming down like Zeus and conceiving children upon the Earth. YHWH, God, the Architect of Family and Institutor of Marriage, would never allow His Son to be conceived out of wedlock, and to think otherwise is to misunderstand God, the Faith, and the Bible.) . . .

. . .The Second *Triune Name* for Mary is *Theotokos*, handed over to us
by the Holy Spirit in 431 A.D. at the Council of Ephesus. The Council
was called due to the Heresy of Nestorianism, which spread like a cancer
throughout the Church, claiming that Jesus was in fact two persons, a
Divine person and a human person. This fundamental misunderstanding
of Jesus resulted in the claim that only the human Jesus was born of
Mary, suffered, and died on the Cross. Thus, the Council was called to
determine who Jesus really was, and, as the Holy Spirit moved throughout
the Council inspiring the Bishops on the *Hypostatic Union* of Jesus—
which is the complete union of the human nature and Divine nature
held within the single Person of Jesus—the answer actually came in a
single word: *Theotokos*! This Divinely revealed name of Mary contains
the entirety of truth on the Person of Jesus, namely that, because Mary
gives birth to the Person of Jesus—and contained within that person is
the hypostatic union of God and man,—Mary *the God Bearer*, really and
truly gives birth to God Himself. At this Inspiration of the Holy Spirit
the church bells rang out, and the entire city celebrated, cheering the
hallowed name *Theotokos* through the streets.

The Third *Triune Name* of Mary is *Immaculate Conception*,
bequeathed to the Church through a series of visions, councils, and
theological inspirations starting with the Church Fathers and ending with
Mary revealing herself as the *Immaculate Conception* to St. Bernadette at
Lourdes. First spoken of by God the Father in Genesis 3:15, God punishes
Satan by promising a woman who will be conceived completely separate
from the Devil and Sin, and it will be through her seed that his head shall
be crushed, defeating sin and death. *The Woman* spoken of by God the
Father is *the Immaculate Conception*, preserved from all imperfection
and sin for her role as the Heavenly Ark of the Covenant, without
which she would have been immediately obliterated to house the Lord
God incarnate. This the Church Fathers recognized and proclaimed: St.
Irenaeus in the exegesis of Mary as the New Eve, St. Ambrose defending
her purity and even immaculate state, and St. Augustine and St. Anselm
stating explicitly that she was free from Original Sin. In the 12th century,
various European countries began celebrating the Feast of the Conception
of Mary, until the necessity of Christ's universal redemption was called
into question. This was eventually resolved by Blessed Dun Scotus, who
explained that Mary was preemptively preserved from sin by Christ's
Victory on the Cross, a 'redemption by exception.' Mary herself appeared
to St. Catherine Laboure in 1830, entrusting her with the Medal of the
Immaculate Conception, exhorting her to promulgate such a devotion
for the outpouring of grace. Eventually, in 1858, all such theology and
visions culminated in the Magisterium of the Church proclaiming the
Dogma of the Immaculate Conception *ex cathedra* by Pope Pius IX, . . .

608 concluded. . . . and, as if in Divine confirmation, Mary appeared to St. Bernadette at Lourdes, and, when asked her name by the child, replied: "I am the *Immaculate Conception.*"

Therefore, we see these are the three cardinal names of Mary from which all reverence and devotions are derived, yet contained in these three names is a pearl beyond price, for in prayer and humility we begin to realize these names are familial—*Divinely familial*—each title a mystically intimate name given to Mary by each Person of the Most Holy Trinity. God the Father calls His *Daughter* from all eternity to sit upon His lap without blemish in a loving embrace of paternal joy, cradling her and calling her His '*Immaculata.*' And so, we see she alone was preserved in such pristine perfection from the first moment of her conception, both in that first moment she was conceived of in the Mind of the Father and the first moment she was conceived by the love of her parents, Sts. Joachim and Anne. God the Son, too, calls out to His one and only *Mother* in such filial affection, desiring only to rest His head upon her breast and whisper to her heart, '*Theotokos.*' So, we begin to see the profound intimacy of *Mother and Son*, a relationship that no creature can claim with the Lord God or even begin to approach. God the Spirit, too, beacons to His *Spouse*, courting her in nuptial bliss, desiring nothing more than to possess her entirely, stirring up in her the flames of love to overshadow her and whisper in her ear, '*Kecharitomene.*' Before such love, we glimpse for the briefest moment the ineffable glory of being Married to God, before we recoil, blinded by such incomprehensible intimacy. Thus, we see these holy names are not only the three most holy names of any creature, but are the three most holy names that could ever be given to any creature, for each name is the dyadic object of each Person of the Trinity. Mary is the *Immaculate Conception* of God the Father, receiving all the paternal love of God and actually becoming the *Daughter of God*. Mary is the *Theotokos* of God the Son, receiving all the filial love of God and actually becoming the *Mother of God*. Mary is the *Kecharitomene* of God the Spirit, receiving all the nuptial love of God and actually becoming the *Spouse of God*. Finally, it is standing atop the Celestial Hierarchy, born up by the wings of Michael, *Archangel of the Family*, that we see the Most Holy Trinity as *Holy Matrimony* bound in love to Mary, pouring themselves into her as *Daughter of the Father, Mother of the Son*, and *Spouse of the Holy Spirit*.

Mother of God

609 This, then, is the summary of the entire Celestial Order, mystically revealed to mankind in Scripture, from the structure of Heaven in its multifaceted tiers to the intricate channels of grace by which the human person receives the transcendent Being of God infused into their souls as the Theological Virtues of Faith, Hope, and Charity. The entire Spiritual realm is structured according to the Order of Grace, which is the participation in God's own Life, first poured out from the side of the Sacred Heart of Jesus, filling and overflowing upon all those blessed angels and saints in Heaven. Christ is the source of all grace in Heaven and on Earth; He is the Way, the Truth, and the Life; there is no way to the Father except through the Son. Yet, in an act of pure love, Christ hands over all grace to His mother, Kecharitomene, the 'plenary redoundingness of grace' herself, for by choosing to be born of her, God the Son places His own Life in her hands, allowing Himself to be formed in her womb—His Life, His grace, completely entrusted to her. This is the meaning of the Vision of the Woman above the Heavenly Ark of the Covenant; Christ, God the Son, has chosen from all time to make His abode within the immaculate tabernacle of her womb, and, by such an overwhelming act, she is so wholly filled with Divine Life that she overflows with the totality of grace. This is why all saints will pray for her intercession in due time and why it is said that the way to Christ's heart is through Mary, for no one can have Christ as a brother without having Mary Immaculate as their Mother. Thus, we see Christ is the Wellspring of Grace and Mary the Dispenser or Fount of Grace, for, just as Lucifer—the Light Bearer—was the nexus by which all knowledge of God entered the Universe, and it was according to his discretion to dispense such light, so, too, it is Mary—the God Bearer—the true Ark of the Covenant, who is the fount by which all grace enters the Universe, and it is at her discretion how to direct the flow of grace. Hence, every holy angel—from St. Michael, to St. Gabriel, to St. Raphael, to the Four Living Creatures, to all the Seraphim and Cherubim, every Throne and Dominion, each Virtue and Power, all Principalities and Archangels, and even the lowest Choir of Guardian Angels—hails Mary as queen, for it was through her grace that each and every angel in Heaven was preserved from the fires of Hell.

EXILE
God's Mercy

Therefore, seeing the man and his wife clothed and the Heavens declaring the Glory of God, the firmament of Heaven made perfect by the work of His hands,[610] the Lord God then turned inward and spoke amongst Himself, saying: "Behold, man has become like One of Us, knowing good and evil.[611] Now, therefore, lest perhaps he stretch forth his hand and take also from the Tree of Life, eat of it, and live forever?"[612]

Genesis
3:22...

Note 612 If such Knowledge of Good and Evil was so dangerous and could throw humanity into such a wretched state, why was the Tree of Knowledge even in the garden, moreover at the center of the garden? First, we must recall that everything in the Garden was made by God specifically for the good of mankind, especially the two sacramental Trees at the center of the Garden. This is why we can say with certainty that we were intended to receive the Fruit of the Tree of Knowledge of Good and Evil, but there are things which are too precious to be taken and can only be given, and it was in taking that we transgressed. Yet, how good the fruit must be, that even in our sin it still transformed our souls to be like God! Confirmed by God's own words: "Behold, man has become like One of Us..." How much more would have been bestowed on us if we had received the fruit as a proper sacrament? Based on the effects of the fruit, we can say with certainty its purpose was to reveal and perfect the Image and Likeness of God in man as that of the Son to the Father: a most hallowed truth which can only be truly understood in the Incarnation of the Godman, Jesus Christ. Therefore, it must be said that, if the fruit from the Tree of Knowledge of Good and Evil was received properly, it would have revealed the knowledge of the Incarnation of God the Son. However, it was received improperly, and we beheld our flesh with shame instead of Incarnational wonder. So, in an act of pure mercy, God exiled us from Eden, for in such a fatal state of mortal sin we could not be permitted to take from the Tree of Life, for it would have cemented us in an even worse state of permanent death. What, then, is the Tree of Life and the fruit upon its branches? The Book of Proverbs chapters 3, 11, & 13 tell us that Wisdom "is the Tree of Life for those who grasp her," that "the fruit of the righteous is the Tree of Life," and that "hope deferred sickens the soul, but hope's desire fulfilled is the Tree of Life." This, coupled with St. John's discourse on the Eucharist, which culminates in Jesus' sacrifice on the cross as the 'Fourth Cup of Passover'—the fruit of the vine poured out for the salvation of the many—reveals that the wood of the Cross is indeed the Tree of Life, and the fruit upon its branches is Jesus Himself. Thus, we see that the Tree of Knowledge held in its branches the Mystery of the Incarnation, and the Tree of Life the Paschal Mystery, which when received together impart the whole Christ, Head and Body. This is confirmed in the Gospel of John, where, upon receiving first the fruit of the Cross, . . .

610 Let us reflect, now that we have worked our way from the depths of the Universal Fall up through the Celestial Hierarchy past the Seven Holy Angels to the very heights of Heaven, where we glimpsed the Immaculate Woman, Seat of Wisdom, shining like the Moon resplendent in the sky, replete with all the stars of Heaven. It is here at the pinnacle of Creation, in the lap of the Mother of God, that we can hear the Lord God speak mercy amongst Himself as Trinity. This mercy found at the very center of the Trinity is not only care and concern for humanity but is action, the first steps necessary to restore mankind into right relation with God.

Examining the nine choirs as a whole reveals a striking revelation about how all existence is instrumentally maintained through these faithful servants. Whether it be through the *guarding of men* as individuals, families, or communities; or the *preservation of the Universe* through predominant order, the maintenance of the entire physical universe, or even the delegation of the angels themselves; or the *worship of God Himself* through the adoration of His goodness, His truth, or His beauty. This is all that exists, all that could exist, both visible and invisible. Thus, we see that there are nine ways to come to love and serve the Lord.

611 This Scripture passage helps to reveal what actually transpired in the eating of the forbidden fruit, and a clue to what the fruit actually is. God says man is now like a person of the Trinity; this alone is profound, and astonishingly good! The divinizing fruit has made man similar to God insofar as he now knows the truth between good and evil, and there is no knowledge more precious to mortal men than this. First, such knowledge is how we relate to God and to the world, for evil is a very destructive force both to us and to the world. Second, it is for our own benefit because a proper understanding of what is good and what is evil bestows happiness upon a person in the most profound way. Thus, if someone were to obtain perfect knowledge of good and evil, that is to say perfect virtue, they would first have a perfect relationship with God and understand exactly how they fit into the world as a body-soul composite, and, second, have perfect happiness because of such a habit in their soul. However, Adam and Eve did not come to this precious knowledge virtuously, but viciously, and the manner one receives knowledge affects the character of the knowledge received. For example, molestation takes what ought to be the most beautiful and holy part of human relationship and corrupts that knowledge, transforming sex from self-giving love into selfish usury. Thus, when Adam and Eve came to know evil improperly, finding it within themselves through their own actions, it tainted their ability for virtue: to choose good and avoid evil. This skewed their relationship with God, who is the Good, their relationship with the world, their relationship with each other, and their relationship with themselves. No longer could they see themselves as God saw them, as His crowning jewel of creation bridging the spiritual and material. No, in this fallen state they saw their bodies as deplorable, eagerly covering themselves with fig leaves. This not only distorted the relationship between God and man, but also body and soul, reducing man to little more than an animal. Yet, evil is corrosive, and the sin of disobedience was quickly multiplied by the sin of obstinance, refusing to apologize or ask for forgiveness. This is why there is a tone of regret in the Trinity's voice, because in this distorted and ever-worsening state man could not be permitted to live forever.

---

612 cont. ... which is the Tree of Life, Mary so receives from God a son, the beloved disciple, and becomes the Mother of the Church. Thus, we see Mary gives birth to the Whole Christ, in splendor to Christ the Head in the manger, and in agony to the Church, the Body of Christ, on Calvary. Hence, we see the prolific life contained within the Tree of Life, not only the Source of Eternal Life, but of such abundance that it imparts a new life—Christ's life—to those who receive it. This is why Leviathan attacks Eve, and why Mary is referred to as the New Eve and Christ the New Adam. Leviathan purposefully set out to stop the Incarnation, to corrupt Eve before she could become like Mary—the Theotokos—bearing God into the world.

The man and his wife now subject to death looked from under the fig tree and beheld the Tree of Life. Yet, up above the fruit of the Tree of Life they beheld the heavens, and the angels of God ascending and descending on what appeared to be the Son of Man.[613]

The Lord then declared: "I have seen you while you were under the fig tree."

He then stood beside the man and said: "I am the Lord, the God of all the Earth; the land on which you stand I must take from you and from your offspring; your offspring shall be like the dust of the Earth, and you shall spread abroad to the East and to the West, to the North and to the South; and all the families of the Earth shall be born from you, your offspring. Know that I am with you and will keep you wherever you shall go, and will again bring you back to this land; for I will not leave you until I have done what I have promised you!"

Thereupon the Lord God exiled Adam from the Garden of Paradise, to till the ground from which he came. He exiled the man east of Eden,[614] . . .

John
1:50

John
1:48

Genesis
28:13...

Genesis
...28:15

Genesis
3:23...

Note 614   This First Contemplation has been devoted to our Christian Cosmology, meditating upon the First Things under the discipline of St. Ignatius, and under such saintly guidance we contemplated the Preternatural State of Man and Angel. Yet, here at the end of such a contemplation, we see a Second Contemplation is needed on the Fallen State of Man and Angel. This, however, will be a great endeavor, so let us for now briefly consider the world to which Adam and Eve are now exiled. The Universal Fall of man and angel results in an upheaval of all right relations within Creation. No longer is Man in harmony with God, with Nature, with his wife, or with himself, which mars and distorts the world to which man is now exiled, but this is not the only effect of the Universal Fall. The Fallen Angels, too, are now no longer in harmony with God, with Creation, with Mankind, or with themselves, and this affects the world just as much if not more than fallen man, for, in man's transgression, he loses his kingship of the Earth, and, due to his particular sin, he loses his kingship to Satan, who in turn opens up the Earth to the entire cohort of Demons. Let us then consider the new state of the Earth, whose King is no longer Adam but Satan. Recall what we have learned about the Celestial Hierarchy, for, as the holy angels are gathered together according to their specific loves for God and creation, so, too, are the fallen angels gathered according to those same loves, which are now corrupt, twisted into hatred for God and creation. It becomes clear, then, that there is a staggering multitude . . .

613   John 1:50. Only in light of the fruit of the Tree of Life, which is Christ Jesus, can one see that the angels and the very Heavens themselves are constructed around Jesus, the only way to the Father.

---

614   ... of demons who would be specifically devoted to the corruption of humanity, for
cont.   the entire First Heaven, a third of the Celestial Hierarchy, is devoted to the service and protection of humanity as individual, family, and nation. The lowest demons incite individual men to the deadliest sins of pride, envy, wrath, sloth, greed, lust, and gluttony. While archdemons deform the family, corrupting monogamy into polygamy and inciting licentiousness inside and outside of marriage, Demonic Principalities play war with peoples and tribes, amassing power in a cruel game of thrones, demanding all peoples of the Earth pay them homage. Yet, there are some greater demons who would desire the destruction of God's power and influence in the world, devoting themselves to the undoing of Divine justice and order, to which the heavenly Powers devote themselves in service. And there are greater demons still who would desire the corruption of the natural order, diverting and depleting its grace, twisting it against itself and mankind, to which the heavenly Virtues tirelessly work to maintain its laws. The greatest demons, however, would desire the accumulation of other demons, gathering unto themselves as much dominion as possible, commanding legions of fallen angels, an authority which the holy Dominations alone ought to direct. The demon king, of course, is Satan, the great Red Dragon. He is concerned in particular with the Protoevangelium, frustrating the Salvific Plan of God to deter the coming of the Immaculate Woman who could birth the Son of God. Yet, we mustn't forget there is no unity or order amongst evil; these fallen angels owe no allegiance to God, to creation, to man, or to themselves, and so they were recklessly free to act upon every impetus, carving up the Earth into a grab bag of demonic occupation. This horrific reality has been chronicled throughout all the world's histories: every people, tribe, and tongue has recorded this pandemonium, though unwittingly ascribing it as the reign of gods over nature and nations. There is no greater truth modernity has forgotten than this, masterfully erased from the memory of man: All the pagan gods were Demons. Every ancient religion, every mystical and philosophic order, has been instituted for the enslavement of humanity, either degrading humanity into animalism or seducing humanity to spiritualism, both of which subjugate mankind to demonic superiority. Israel alone was chosen, set apart, by God to be His chosen people, free from demonic rule. This is the context for the whole Old Testament, God calling His people into Covenant with Himself despite their constant failure of adultery with foreign demons. And this is the Good News: God deemed in an act of pure love to send His only begotten Son to free us from sin and slavery. How potent a message when properly understood! Praise be to our Lord Jesus Christ! This is also the great divide between antiquity and modernity—Christianity—the Triumphant Victory of Jesus Christ upon the Cross, subjugating all Principalities, Powers, Dominations, and demonic forces of this present darkness to the Authority of St. Peter in the Holy Roman Catholic Church—for, wherever the Church spreads, paganism is almost immediately abolished—first in the Middle East, then in Europe with the conversion of the Roman Empire, and finally in the Americas with the coming of our Lady of Guadalupe; all that is left is Africa and Asia. (The conversion of Africa we can actively see taking place before our very eyes.) Further, without the impediment of demons meddling with the Laws of Nature, the birth of science could take place, and, through the education of the Church, the scientific method could be established. Astonishingly, all history falls into place with this one missing piece of lost truth, but most importantly we see the absolute necessity for the coming of Christ.

. . . and placed at the entrance of the Garden a Cherubim with a flaming sword,[615] which turned every way, to guard the way to the Tree of Life.[616]

Angel of Truth and Love

615 This is the first time Scripture mentions a specific choir of angels, which means we definitively know that by this point the Celestial Hierarchy is fully formed. Further, the specific angel placed to guard the Tree of Life is a Cherubim, an angel of truth, just as Lucifer guarded the Tree of Knowledge of Good and Evil on account of his intellect. The question then arises: Is this Cherubim simply to keep Adam and Eve out of the Garden, or is it to keep Leviathan out as well? It seems at first glance that, if God was concerned with barring Leviathan from the Garden, He would have stationed a more powerful angel, such as a Seraphim or an Archangel like Michael, to guard the Tree of Life; there seems to be an implicit role reserved for angels of truth to guard and protect. However, it is not simply a Cherubim, but a Cherubim that wields a fiery sword. This sword shows that this particular Cherubim is enraptured with an ardent love just like the Seraphim, and it is this unquenchable flame that Leviathan cannot defeat. This is fitting, for it is not the role of a Seraphim to brandish a sword; love never defends itself, for it is pure and undefiled (1 Corinthians 13:4). Such a role is reserved for truth, which is itself referred to as a sword, meaning this Cherubim specifically represents truth that has given itself over to the fires of love. Ironically, therefore, this mighty Cherubim wielding a flaming sword is the perfect defense against Satan, the watery dragon, for it is in fact the righteous paragon of which Lucifer himself would have become, had he not chosen rebellion.

616 This is the set up for the entire Old Testament and is the reason that Christ's sacrifice is so pivotal. Every word in Scripture after this point is driven with an undercurrent of returning to the Garden, and to the Tree of Life. It is for this very reason that when Israel was finally allowed to build the Temple (God's dwelling on the Earth), Solomon built it on a mountain and spared no expense to turn it into a garden, covered in golden palm trees and carvings of Cherubim. The most striking description comes in 2 Chronicles 3:14, where we learn that on the Temple veil separating the Holy of Holies from the people was embroidered the image of a Cherubim, the very same Cherubim stationed at the entrance of Eden in Genesis 3:24. This is the true significance of the rending of the Temple curtain upon Christ's death; it is the restoration of God's people to the Garden of Eden. Christ tears away that great barrier which separated the people from the Tree of Life, opening the way to Eternal Life.

I write in the great hope that these 'milk and morsels' I offer you might make you strong, so that you might continue to seek out such solid food of the Faith. "For everyone who lives on milk alone is still an infant unskilled in the Word of Righteousness. But meat is for the mature, for those whose faculties have been trained by practice to distinguish good from evil." Hebrews 5:13—Seek out the rich meats of our Faith!

In the great tradition of St. Ignatius, I have attempted to guide the student of Christ through a proper contemplation of Genesis, yet there are many things on which I did not write, for, in the use of Holy Scripture to recount the Preternatural State of man and angel, there so opened up a wellspring of understanding ever deepening and ever widening as it flowed—For who could ever exhaust the infinite treasury of God's Wisdom housed in Holy Writ? Yet, these meditations are written so that you may come to believe that Jesus is the Christ, the Son of the Living God, and that through such belief, you may have Life in His Name.

May the Lord Jesus Christ be with you always and bestow upon you every Spiritual Blessing in the Heavens.

God be ever with you,
Luke

APPENDIX

Angelic Apologetics

Cosmology
¿ Part I ǰ

In the West and throughout all of Christendom there has sprung a great chasm dividing faith and reason, a schism which has left faith ostracized and roundly mocked. Truth, now esteemed to be held within the halls of science rather than the Church, has become the focus of Western Civilization. Thus, having been set apart and unable to fulfill its purpose of guiding mankind, faith was forced to pursue its own endeavors bereft from the social and scientific progression of the West. This left reason to wander aimlessly throughout the age pursuing whatever slight trifle caught its fancy. A proper cosmology will set straight these paths, as two tracks of a train, both necessary for the progression of mankind. A comprehensive cosmology will afford humanity with the opportunity to bridge the chasm, and to unite faith and reason once more.

A true and authoritative cosmology will set forth, free from error, a model of the Universe, both physical and metaphysical. It will elucidate the origin of the Universe, while simultaneously expounding upon the process by which the Universe exists. However, a fully Christian cosmology is not at liberty to ignore man's significance, as all other scientific models do; an absolute cosmology will not shrink from the task of explaining mankind's purpose in the Universe. This includes both what man is, as a body-soul composite, and what man was intended for, as the culmination of embodied life.

The purpose of such a cosmology is to provide conclusively a precise and reliable answer to our place and purpose in the Universe. This therefore requires a rigorous ordering of what is above man and what is below man. To establish a trustworthy understanding of what lies below man, we must have strict confidence in the scientific model of the Universe, which the physical sciences have worked tirelessly to procure. From such secure principles, it is within man's power to work up to a systematic understanding of the Universe's metaphysics;

however, this is very difficult, and has yet to be accomplished. To ascertain what lies above man, we are faced with a far greater dilemma, for man's sight begins to wane in the pursuit of such sublime truths.

Fortunately, in the pursuit of such a lofty discipline as Metaphysics, man is not abandoned to the deliberative sciences alone, but through Faith has been given the very source and summit of all metaphysical knowledge. The Divinely revealed principles of Theology provide humanity with just such a trustworthy basis to understand the Universe. These principles, having their origin in the Omniscient, can be taken up securely, if not with greater certainty than the principles derived from man's specious senses. Thus, in great confidence we proceed, secure in our ability to delineate the framework of a metaphysical cosmology.

Such a metaphysical cosmology will, by necessity, resemble our physical cosmology, which is composed of three main sciences: Biology, Chemistry, and Physics. These, simply put, are organic matter as being, inorganic matter as being, and the function of such matter within the Universe. A true metaphysical cosmology will concern itself with being as being, and therefore encompasses not only the physical sciences, but their metaphysical counterparts as well, which shall be named: Subsistence and Metaphysics. Subsistence will, by necessity, encompass the principles of Biology and Chemistry, namely life and form. While Metaphysics will, by necessity, encompass the principle of Physics, namely the function of the Universe. However, these metaphysical sciences have come to be known by different names according to the Divinely revealed principles of Theology, namely: Angelology and Celestial Hierarchy. Angelology is the study of metaphysical existence as it subsists without matter, and Celestial Hierarchy is the study of metaphysical operation as it sustains the Universe in its function.

Therefore, it will be necessary to expound upon the sciences of Angelology and Celestial Hierarchy in order to ascertain a true and authoritative Metaphysical Cosmology.

Angelology
℘ Part II ℘

Now raising our eyes to peer past all material obscurity in feeble hope of comprehending such transcendent truths, we look through a fogged glass dimly. Therefore, only by the light of Faith and the rigors of reason do we attempt an understanding of the Metaphysical Cosmology surrounding man.

First and foremost, among the limitless expanse of the Universe, both visible and invisible, there can be no absence of existence. Easily observed within the physical world, a natural hierarchy is formed within the mind, for stars and planets are nobler than the emptiness of space, and life itself is still more precious than the inorganic. Among the living, soul possesses three powers: the nutritive, the appetitive, and the deliberative. These are the natural divisions observed in Nature: plants possess the nutritive but lack the appetitive, while animals possess both the nutritive and appetitive but lack the deliberative. Only man possesses all three powers and thus is crowned above all ensouled life.

Before proceeding, man's peculiarity ought to be noted. Man alone possesses the deliberative faculty among all such ensouled creatures and thus is precariously perched betwixt the animal and spiritual realms. It was for this reason the Philosopher named man the rational-animal; man alone participates in both the physical realm—subject to hunger and thirst—and the metaphysical realm: comprehending Truth, imitating the Good, and loving the Beautiful.

Returning then, this natural hierarchy does not terminate with the visible realm but continues, in due order, into the invisible realm. Further, every higher echelon in the pyramid of nobility possesses the faculties of all lower echelons, and thus when proceeding into the metaphysical realm all such existence will, by necessity, possess the three aspects of life. A strange thought indeed, but every existent 'thing' within the metaphysical realm is alive, principally possessing the faculty of mind. And thus, these luminous creatures of supreme brilliance are duly designated Celestial Intelligences.

However, since the principle division between the physical and metaphysical is body, animal possessing body and spirit the lack of, when attempting to comprehend such metaphysical existence it is advantageous to begin to think about life apart from body particularly with regard to the three aspects of life: the nutritive, the appetitive, and the deliberative faculties.

We, being creatures of body, learn through induction, a synthesis of sensory experiences stretched throughout time. Simply put, we work from the particular to the universal. Creatures of pure intellect, not dependent on such bodily senses, learn deductively, comprehending the universal alongside the particular instance. For example, when a Celestial Intelligence first considers triangle, it would instantaneously and precisely comprehend all mathematical truths concerning triangle, all principles of it, and indeed the whole science of rectilinear shape, of which triangle is the cause.

Further, being creatures of body, our position and locomotion is determined by spatial proximity to other objects, but, with regard to incorporeal beings such a locus-identity is not applicable. Rather, these Celestial Intelligences lacking any physical form are differentiated and ranked according to their capacity for knowledge. A metaphysical position, unlike a physical position, describes the very essence of a metaphysical being according to the internalization and manifestation of knowledge each Celestial Mind possesses. What a metaphysical being knows and internalizes so too it externalizes actually becoming what it knows—it is for this reason that they have been duly named Celestial Intelligences.

Lastly, with regard to locomotion, one must distinguish between metaphysical locomotion and physical locomotion. The prior would be determined by a coming to of knowledge, but since such creatures learn deductively, comprehending the universal alongside the particular, their knowledge is only limited to their vision. This, however, would mean that, in order to learn continuously, they would have to continue to see beyond their ability, thus exceeding their natural capacity for knowledge, which is absurd. Indicating the necessity of a strict hierarchy of metaphysical beings according to the knowledge they possess. With regard to the latter, physical locomotion would not occur naturally, though if so willed such a superior being, existing beyond the physical plane, not being subject to any physical constraints could so choose to manifest themselves and locomote according to their will, uninhibited by any such laws of physics.

With respect to the nutritive faculty, such creatures would have no need for material sustenance or restorative dormancy. They do not experience growth, decay, or even aging, for all are consequences of body. Even death is a consequence of bodily nature, for death is the separation of soul from body. The nutrition of such a being does not come from without, as with material organisms, but rather is sustained from within. Thus, upon its genesis such a creature is a perpetually subsistent being, incapable of death, unconstrained by time or space, and is principally an uninhibited mind.

Having then established the *intrinsic* modes by which such metaphysical principles exist, it is necessary to examine the *extrinsic* modes such metaphysical principles possess, namely quantity and relation. First, with respect to quantity, if such perpetually subsistent beings exist and lack any distinction according to physical location, how then can one have certainty of whether they are many or one? And if many, what number do such Celestial Intelligences possess?

Again, it is necessary to begin from what is known. Science is of its subject, and thus for every higher echelon in the natural hierarchy of existence, there too follows a corresponding science. Likewise, every higher science subsumes the lower and demonstrates the lower science's principles. For example, Biology subsumes Chemistry, utilizing all such truths to explain the function of organic life according to the various chemical reactions necessitated from such inorganic particles. Correspondingly, Physics subsumes both Biology and Chemistry, utilizing all such truths to explain the total function of all matter within the universe.

Turning then and looking down, the higher science of Physics provides the principles for each of its lower sciences, for it is not within the jurisdiction of Chemistry to prove the existence of the Elements, only to demonstrate the assorted properties and various interactions of such atomic structures. Thus, it falls to the higher science to describe the cause of such elemental particles. Physics, being of a greater subject—namely the material universe—demonstrates the origin of such Elements to arise from the hearts of stars, according to a process called nucleosynthesis.

Hence, it is the function of higher sciences to explain the principles taken up by the lower sciences, and so following the natural progression established in the physical sciences and continuing it beyond the material, the principles of Physics must be upheld by the Science of Metaphysics. Therefore, it is necessary to state that all physical processes and interactions in the material universe are perpetually upheld by the care and maintenance of the Celestial Intelligences— both the organic and inorganic—and dynamic forces. For every cellular mitosis, molecular compound, and magnetic polarity, for every strand of DNA, atomic structure, and gravitational field, there must—by necessity—be a metaphysical cause upholding the physical process taking place. Thus, the multitude of such metaphysical creatures can be ascribed to be, at the very least, the number necessary to cause all physical effects within the Universe.

Having then established the abundance of such incorporeal beings, it is necessary to ascertain their relation to one another, for when contemplating such metaphysical necessities as these, there can be the temptation to assume such life will duplicate our own ensouled life. For example, when regarding ensouled life which share in the same species yet differ in number, such beings always agree in form, thus their individuality is found not within their form, but in their matter. This, however, is impossible when regarding metaphysical beings, for, since they principally do not possess body, their individuating principle must arise from within their form itself, necessitating that no two metaphysical beings can share in the same species, each being completely unique unto itself. Therefore, among the superabundance of Celestial Intelligences, each is, by necessity, its own species, administering unto all physical existence the metaphysical continuity necessary for the Universe to be sustained in its function.

This so much the Theologian always understood, for Theology has always attributed the care and maintenance of the Universe to such metaphysical beings, though referring to them by a different name. These creatures have traditionally been called by their Divinely ordained title of 'Angels', denoting their mediating principle of serving the Universe and the Divine Godhead. As for the science of how these creatures maintain the function and administer the Divine Will unto creation, one cannot simply rely on the science of Angelology, but rather must peer even farther into the metaphysical realm, turning to the study and science of Celestial Hierarchy.

Celestial Hierarchy
⸎ Part III ⸎

Turning lastly to the highest study of Metaphysics, and so ascending to the farthest reaches of understanding, we attempt to comprehend the infinitely perfect process by which the Omnipotent Godhead has deemed for the Universe to function.

Recalling then all that was previously mentioned, it is necessary to first establish the proper categories of existence in order to understand in what manner the Celestial Intelligences tirelessly work to maintain the Universe. The aforementioned distinction of body will prove optimal for the initiation of our investigation.

The first and most broad division of the Universe is that according to body, namely that which possesses body and that which does not. According to that which possesses body, the most immediately apparent operation of such metaphysical beings is to uphold and maintain the proper function of all such physical processes in our visible universe. The entire physical universe, all that is known and knowable by what we call 'Science' functions in *virtue* of these very real and specific metaphysical beings. For this reason, the Theologian has always referred to these Celestial Principles tasked with the preservation of the physical universe as *The Celestial Choir of Virtues*.

Before proceeding, the simple division of material and immaterial will not suffice in a proper accounting of our Universe, for there exists an anomaly called man. This creature properly belongs to neither the physical nor the metaphysical realms alone; he is neither simply an animal nor a spirit but is a strange synthesis—an amalgam all his own. Therefore, within our Universe according to the distinction of body, there arise three categories: physical existence below man, man, and metaphysical existence above man.

Thus, it is necessary to delve deeper into the singular category of man. However, since man is a unique synthesis of body and soul—both parts of which are so hermetically joined neither can function on its own—there inevitably arises unique peculiarities not found in any other category. The rational soul possesses the powers of Intellect and Will, this in a Celestial Intelligence is fulfilled when apprehending the Truth and choosing the Good. Hence, when rationality is joined to body the desire for Truth remains the same, being that of an individual nature, but when volition is joined to body, and so belongs to a larger species, there naturally arises a desire for Love and communion with others. This desire for Love is specifically fulfilled within the bonds of Matrimony, fulfilling the person as individual and lover. However, man is not meant to simply love one individual, but finds in his heart the desire to love friends and family, even strangers—his love eventually extending to his entire community. Thus, since man draws his fulfillment from knowing and loving, he must therefore be sustained by such metaphysical interactions as well. Namely as *Individual* knowing truth and choosing the good, as *Family member* knowing self and loving another, and as *Statesman* loving his neighbor. Thus, these are the three natural divisions of man's existence that, by necessity, must be maintained by three separate categories of Celestial Intelligences known as *The Celestial Choirs of Guardian Angels, Archangels, and Principalities.*

Further, with the introduction of man comes a unique opportunity to acknowledge the existence of evil, a topic most cosmologies are not at liberty to discuss since they do not take into account man, other than as glorified ape. Evil, as observable in the world of men, is a consequence of the intelligent soul willingly dissenting from choosing the Good. Evil, thus, does not exist in the physical realm below man, because all such existence lacks the highest power of life, the volition of the rational soul. This, however, has immense consequences for the metaphysical realm above man, recalling the hierarchy of life which proceeds, in due order, into the invisible realm. If man possesses the power of evil because of the deliberative nature of his soul, so too must the Celestial Intelligences possess the same power and be capable of birthing evil into the Universe. Thus, there is a real threat of existential evil, for such beings would not simply cause evil in the physical plane but the metaphysical one as well. Thus, in order, to preserve the well-functioning of the Universe, such a threat of evil must be counterpoised by a category of Celestial Intelligences tasked with the protection of the existential good of the Universe, and these honorable creatures are known as *The Celestial Choir of Powers.*

Having mentioned the categories of man and what lies below him, next it is necessary to discuss what lies above him. This is a far more difficult endeavor requiring an acute knowledge of Divine principles, namely the ceaseless flow of Divine ordinances, which emanating from the Omniscient confer directly unto the first of the Celestial Hierarchy and, so filling, overflow down unto the rest of creation.

Beginning then, if all that exists is maintained by the metaphysical principles of Celestial Hierarchy, then the Celestial Intelligences themselves are no exception, and they too must be maintained by similar metaphysical principles. Such a metaphysical necessity is easily overlooked under the assumption that the metaphysical realm is maintained directly by the Supreme Godhead, but this is not how the Omnipotent Godhead has deemed for the Universe to function. Lacking all contradiction, the Metaphysical Laws which He has established are as irrefutable as the laws we observe in the physical universe. Thus, there must be, by necessity, a special category of Celestial Intelligences tasked with the governance and preservation of all subsequent Celestial Intelligences, known as *The Celestial Choir of Dominations.*

Having therefore the addition of *The Celestial Choir of Dominations*, the totality of the Universe is now accounted for; everything visible and invisible is preserved by the ceaseless maintenance of the Celestial Hierarchy. The Universe in its entirety is hence upheld by six principle categories of Celestial Intelligences maintaining both physical and metaphysical existence, extending without interruption unto the very source of existence: the Supreme Godhead.

Thus, with the entire Universe accounted for we must speak of the origin of the metaphysical, the foundation of all existence, the Prime Mover and First Cause, the Triune Godhead Himself. Having so traversed the metaphysical bounds and reached the apex of the created order, it is necessary to describe the three Transcendentals, which flow preeminently from the Supreme Source: *the*

Good, the True, and *the Beautiful.* These three attributes transcending all created existence permeate all things, binding them together and drawing them up toward unity with the Grand Architect. They are the source and summit of all metaphysical existence and that from which the Celestial Hierarchy draws life itself. Hence there must be, by necessity, three categories of Celestial Intelligences that adhere themselves most perfectly to these three Transcendentals, receiving— and so passing down—such divinely subsistent principles unto the rest of creation. The first would adhere themselves most properly to the *Divine Good* and serve as creation conforming itself to the *Good* of the Creator. This category of Celestial Intelligences has come to be known as the *Celestial Choir of Thrones.* The second would so adhere themselves to the *Omniscient Truth* of the Supreme Godhead and serve as luminaries of intelligibility reflecting the very mind of God in creation; such Celestial Intelligences have come to be known as the *Celestial Choir of Cherubim.* The third and highest would so perfectly adhere themselves to the *Divine Beauty* that they themselves would become enamored with the all-consuming ardor of *Omnipotent Love,* which so enkindled in the highest Celestial Intelligences would disseminate igniting and enrapturing the whole of creation up toward the *Divine Love.* Such privileged and paramount Celestial Intelligences have duly come to be known as the *Celestial Choir of Seraphim.*

This, then, is the summary of the whole created order, a ceaseless Hierarchy emanating and disseminating from the Supreme Godhead, through the physical and metaphysical, bestowing upon every aspect of creation *being itself.* Among such transcendent couriers ascending and descending on such a sublime and perfect hierarchy, man is found to be the primary beneficiary of all transmitted grace of the Celestial Hierarchy. Whether it be individual, family, or nation, existential safeguard, material subsidiary, metaphysical propriety, or imbued Transcendental aspiration, all are directed at man as prime recipient. And so, recalling man as the culmination of embodied life and that to which all material existence builds toward, it follows, thus, that man is found to be at the very center of the consummate Universe, uniting within his very self both the physical and metaphysical.

This then is the limit of our knowledge, and, having reached the height of human understanding, it is thus necessary to take the last step by Faith, uniting within ourselves both Faith and Reason, born up on both pinions to ascertain, by Divine Revelation, the secret counsels of God's own Mind. Therefore, holding fast to the centripetal value of man attained through Reason, and the abounding nature of Love held within the Triune God revealed in Sacred Scripture, we have the courage to say: The Almighty, Ever-living God, cause of all existence, so wishing to draw all things back unto Himself in perfect Love, so chose to become man, that so uniting Divinity with humanity all existence, physical and metaphysical, could in turn be reconciled to the Supreme Godhead, source of all existence, through the Godman, Jesus Christ our Lord.

ANGELIC PRAYERS

† *The Angelus* †

V. The Angel of the Lord declared unto Mary.

R. And she conceived of the Holy Spirit.

Hail Mary, Full of Grace, the Lord is with Thee;

Blessed art thou among women,

And blessed is the fruit of thy womb, Jesus.

Holy Mary, Mother of God,

Pray for us sinners,

Now and at the hour of our death. Amen

V. Behold the handmaid of the Lord.

R. Be it done unto me according to thy word.

Hail Mary, etc.

V. And the Word was made Flesh.

R. And dwelt among us.

Hail Mary, etc.

V. Pray for us, O holy Mother of God.

R. That we may be made worthy of the promises of Christ.

Let us pray:

Pour forth, we beseech Thee, O Lord, Thy grace into our hearts, that we to whom the Incarnation of Christ Thy Son was made known by the message of an angel, may by His Passion and Cross be brought to the glory of His Resurrection. Through the same Christ Our Lord.

Amen.

† *Sanctus* †

Sanctus, Sanctus, Sanctus,	Holy, Holy, Holy,
Dominus Deus Sabaoth	Lord God of Hosts
Pleni Sunt Caeli et Terra, Gloria Tua	Heaven and Earth are Full of Your Glory
Hosanna in excelsis	Hosanna in the Highest
Benedictus qui venit in	Blessed is He who comes in the
Nomine Domini	Name of the Lord
Hosanna in excelsis.	Hosanna in the Highest

† *Prayer to Saint Raphael the Archangel* †

Glorious Archangel, St. Raphael, great prince of the heavenly court, illustrious by thy gifts of Wisdom and grace, guide of travelers by land and sea, consoler of the unfortunate and refuge of sinners, I entreat thee to help me in all my needs and in all the trials of this life, as thou didst once assist the young Tobias in his journeying. And since thou art the "physician of God," I humbly pray thee to heal my soul of its many infirmities and my body of the ills that afflict it, if this favor is for my greater good. I ask, especially, for angelic purity, that I may be made fit to be the living temple of the Holy Ghost. Amen.

† *Prayer to the Archangel Gabriel* †

O blessed Archangel Gabriel, we beseech thee, do thou intercede for us at the throne of Divine mercy in our present necessities that, as thou didst announce to Mary the mystery of the incarnation, so through thy prayers and patronage in Heaven we may obtain the benefits of the same, and sing the praise of God forever in the land of the living. Amen.

† *St. Michael the Archangel* †

St. Michael the Archangel, defend us in battle;

be our protection against the wickedness and snares of the Devil.

May God rebuke him, we humbly pray;

and do thou, O Prince of the Heavenly Host,

by the Power of God,

thrust into Hell Satan and all the other evil spirits

who prowl about the World seeking the ruin of souls.

Amen.

St. Michael the Archangel

† *St. Michael Prayer* †

O glorious Prince of the heavenly host, Saint Michael the Archangel, defend us in battle and in the fearful warfare that we are waging against the Principalities and Powers, against the rulers of this world of darkness, against the evil spirits.

Come thou to the assistance of men, whom Almighty God created immortal, making them in His own image and likeness and redeeming them at a great price from the tyranny of Satan. Fight this day the battle of the Lord with the legions of holy Angels, even as of old thou didst fight against Lucifer, the leader of the proud spirits and all his rebel angels, who were powerless to stand against thee, neither was their place found any more in heaven.

And that apostate angel, transformed into an angel of darkness who still creeps about the earth to encompass our ruin, was cast headlong into the abyss together with his followers. But behold, that first enemy of mankind, and a murderer from the beginning, has regained his confidence.

Changing himself into an angel of light, he goes about with the whole multitude of the wicked spirits to invade the earth and blot out the Name of God and of His Christ, to plunder, to slay and to consign to eternal damnation the souls that have been destined for a crown of everlasting life. This wicked serpent, like an unclean torrent, pours into men of depraved minds and corrupt hearts the poison of his malice, the spirit of lying, impiety and blasphemy, and the deadly breath of impurity and every form of vice and iniquity.

These crafty enemies of mankind have filled to overflowing with gall and wormwood the Church, which is the Bride of the Lamb without spot; they have laid profane hands upon her most sacred treasures.

Make haste, therefore, O invincible Prince, to help the people of God against the inroads of the lost spirits and grant us the victory. Amen.

† *Consecration to St. Michael the Archangel* †

O most noble Prince of the Angelic Hierarchies, valorous warrior of Almighty God and zealous lover of His glory, terror of the rebellious angels, love and delight of all the just angels, my beloved Archangel Michael, desiring to be numbered among your devoted servants, I, today offer and consecrate myself to you, and place myself, my family, and all I possess under your most powerful protection.

I entreat you not to look at how little, I, as your servant have to offer, being only a wretched sinner, but to gaze, rather, with favorable eye at the heartfelt affection with which this offering is made, and remember that if from this day onward I am under your patronage, you must during all my life assist me, and procure for me the pardon of my many grievous offenses, and sins, the grace to love with all my heart my God, my dear Savior Jesus, and my Sweet Mother Mary, and to obtain for me all the help necessary to arrive to my crown of glory.

Defend me always from my spiritual enemies, particularly in the last moments of my life.

Come then, O Glorious Prince, and succor me in my last struggle, and with your powerful weapon cast far from me into the infernal abyss that prevaricator and proud angel that one day you prostrated in the Celestial Battle.

Amen.

† *Chaplet of St. Michael* †

A sincere Act of Contrition

V. O God, come to my assistance

R. O Lord, make haste to help me.

Glory be to the Father, etc.

1. By the intercession of St. Michael and the celestial Choir of Seraphim, may the Lord make us worthy to burn with the fire of perfect charity. Amen.

1 Our Father, 3 Hail Mary's

2. By the intercession of St. Michael and the celestial Choir of Cherubim, may the Lord vouchsafe to grant us grace to leave the ways of wickedness to run in the paths of Christian perfection. Amen.

1 Our Father, 3 Hail Mary's

3. By the intercession of St. Michael and the celestial Choir of Thrones, may the Lord infuse into our hearts a true and sincere spirit of humility. Amen.

1 Our Father, 3 Hail Mary's

4. By the intercession of St. Michael and the celestial Choir of Dominations, may the Lord give us grace to govern our senses and subdue our unruly passions.

Amen

1 Our Father, 3 Hail Mary's

5. By the intercession of St. Michael and the celestial Choir of Virtues, may the Lord preserve us from evil and suffer us not to fall into temptation.

Amen.

1 Our Father, 3 Hail Mary's

6. By the intercession of St. Michael and the celestial Choir of Powers, may the Lord vouchsafe to protect our souls against the snares and temptations of the devil. Amen.

1 Our Father, 3 Hail Mary's

7. By the intercession of St. Michael and the celestial Choir of Principalities, may God fill our souls with a true spirit of obedience.

1 Our Father, 3 Hail Mary's

8. By the intercession of St. Michael and the celestial Choir of Archangels, may the Lord give us perseverance in faith and in all good works, in order that we gain the glory of Paradise. Amen.

1 Our Father, 3 Hail Mary's

9. By the intercession of St. Michael and the celestial Choir of Guardian Angels, may the Lord grant us to be protected by them in this mortal life and conducted hereafter to eternal glory. Amen.

1 Our Father, 3 Hail Mary's

1 Our Father In honor of St. Michael.

1 Our Father In honor of St. Gabriel.

1 Our Father In honor of St. Raphael.

1 Our Father In honor of our Guardian Angel.

O glorious Prince St. Michael, chief and commander of the heavenly hosts, guardian of souls, vanquisher of rebel spirits, servant in the house of the Divine King, and our admirable conductor, thou who dost shine with excellence and superhuman virtue, vouchsafe to deliver us from all evil, who turn to thee with confidence, and enable us by thy gracious protection to serve God more and more faithfully every day.

V. Pray for us, O glorious St. Michael, Prince of the Church of Jesus Christ

R. That we may be made worthy of His promises.

Almighty and Everlasting God, who by a prodigy of goodness and a merciful desire for the salvation of all men, hast appointed the most glorious Archangel, St. Michael, Prince of Thy Church, make us worthy, we beseech Thee, to be delivered from all our enemies that none of them may harass us at the hour of death, but that we may be conducted by him into the august presence of Thy Divine Majesty. This we beg through the merits of Jesus Christ, our Lord.

Amen.

† *Prayer to the Principality of the United States* †

O glorious Principality of the United States, to whom God has entrusted the care of our beloved country, we honor you and thank you for the care and protection you have given to this great nation from the first moment of its inception.

O powerful Principality, whose watchful glance encompasses this vast land from shore to shore, we know that our sins have grieved our Lord and God and marred the beauty of our heritage. Lead us to a deep conversion, so that we may return to the embrace of His merciful love!

O Holy Angel, obtain for us through the intercession of the Queen of Heaven before the throne of God the graces we need to overcome the forces of evil so rampant in our beloved land. Help us, our God-given protector and friend, to respond wholeheartedly to the urgent pleas of the Mother of God at Fatima. Assist us to offer the prayers and sacrifices necessary to bring peace and goodness to our nation.

We want to make you known and loved throughout our land, so that docile to your inspirations we may know, love and serve our Lord more faithfully and so become once more "one Nation under God"!

Amen.

ꟽARIAN PRAYERS

† *Hail Mary* †

Hail Mary, Full of Grace, The Lord is with thee. Blessed art thou among women, and blessed is the fruit of thy womb, Jesus. Holy Mary, Mother of God, pray for us sinners now, and at the hour of our death.
Amen.

† *Memorare* †

Remember, O most gracious Virgin Mary, that never was it known that anyone who fled to your protection, implored your help, or sought your intercession, was left unaided. Inspired by this confidence, I fly unto thee, O Virgin of virgins, my Mother. To thee do I come, before thee I stand, sinful and sorrowful. O Mother of the Word Incarnate, despise not my petitions, but in your mercy, hear and answer me.
Amen.

† *Hail, Holy Queen* †

Hail, holy Queen, Mother of mercy, our life, our sweetness and our hope. To thee do we cry, poor banished children of Eve: to thee do we send up our sighs, mourning and weeping in this vale of tears. Turn then, O most gracious Advocate, thine eyes of mercy toward us, and after this our exile, show unto us the blessed fruit of thy womb, Jesus, O clement, O loving, O sweet Virgin Mary!
Amen.

† *The Magnificat* †
(Luke 1:46-55)

My soul proclaims the greatness of the Lord,

my spirit rejoices in God my Savior

for He has looked with favor on His lowly servant.

From this day on, all generations shall call me blessed:

for The Almighty has done great things for me,

and holy is His Name.

He has mercy on those who fear Him

in every generation.

He has shown the strength of His arm,

He has scattered the proud in their conceit.

He has cast down the mighty from their thrones,

and has lifted up the lowly.

He has filled the hungry with good things,

and the rich He has sent away empty.

He has come to the help of His servant Israel

for He remembered His promise of mercy,

the promise He made to our fathers,

to Abraham and his children forever.

Glory be to the Father, and to the Son, and to the Holy Spirit,

as it was in the beginning, is now, and ever shall be forever.

Amen, Alleluia.

† *Praying the Holy Rosary* †

1. Begin by making the Sign of the Cross.

2. Holding the Crucifix, pray the Apostles' Creed.

3. On the first bead, pray an Our Father, in honor of St. Joseph.

4. Pray one Hail Mary on each of the next three beads, for the infusion of:

    i. Indomitable Faith

    ii. Holy Hope

    iii. Perfect Charity

5. Pray the Glory Be:

    i. "Glory Be to the Father and to the Son and to the Holy Spirit, as it was in the Beginning, is now, and ever shall be, world without end. Amen."

6. For each of the five decades, announce the Mystery:

(Scripture is to be recalled or recited with each Mystery.)

    i. Joyful Mysteries (Monday & Saturday)

        1st Mystery: The Annunciation of our Lord Jesus

        2nd Mystery: The Visitation

        3rd Mystery: The Nativity of our Lord Jesus

        4th Mystery: The Presentation at the Temple

        5th Mystery: The Finding in the Temple

    ii. Luminous Mysteries (Thursday)

        1st Mystery: The Baptism of Jesus in the Jordan

        2nd Mystery: The Wedding at Cana

        3rd Mystery: The Proclamation of the Kingdom of God

        4th Mystery: The Transfiguration of our Lord Jesus

        5th Mystery: The Institution of the Most Holy Eucharist

iii. Sorrowful Mysteries (Tuesday & Friday)

1st Mystery: The Agony of Jesus in the Garden

2nd Mystery: The Scourging at the Pillar

3rd Mystery: The Crowning of Thorns

4th Mystery: The Carrying of the Cross

5th Mystery: The Crucifixion and Death of Jesus

iv. Glorious Mysteries (Wednesday & Sunday)

1st Mystery: The Resurrection of our Lord Jesus

2nd Mystery: The Ascension of our Lord Jesus

3rd Mystery: The Descent of the Holy Spirit

4th Mystery: The Assumption of Mary into Heaven

5th Mystery: The Coronation of Mary as Queen of Heaven and Earth

7. Begin each decade by praying the Our Father, then while fingering each of the ten beads of the decade, pray ten Hail Marys while meditating on the specific Mystery for that day. Conclude the decade by praying a Glory Be.

8. After finishing each decade, it is custom to recite 3 prayers in Honor of the Holy Family:

i. The first was requested by the Blessed Virgin Mary at Fatima:

"O my Jesus, forgive us our sins, save us from the fires of Hell; lead all souls to Heaven, especially those in most need of Your mercy."

ii. The second Mary gave to St. Catherine Labouré:

"O Mary conceived without sin, pray for us who have recourse to thee."

iii. The third is newly added in Honor St. Joseph and the Holy Family:

"O Joseph, Head of the Holy Family, bestow your blessing and protection upon us."

9. After finishing all five decades, pray the Hail, Holy Queen, followed by this dialogue and prayer:

V. Pray for us, O holy Mother of God.

R. That we may be made worthy of the promises of Christ.

"Let us pray: O God, whose Only Begotten Son, by His life, Death, and Resurrection, has purchased for us the rewards of eternal life, grant, we beseech Thee, that while meditating on these mysteries of the most holy Rosary of the Blessed Virgin Mary, we may imitate what they contain and obtain what they promise, through the same Christ our Lord. Amen."

Made in the USA
Columbia, SC
06 July 2024

cde3a9c5-09e9-40ce-b4b1-4c304e358da9R02